POPULATION AGEI
AND INTERNATION
DEVELOPMENT

D1382085

From generalisation to evidence

Peter Lloyd-Sherlock

This edition published in Great Britain in 2010 by

The Policy Press
University of Bristol
Fourth Floor
Beacon House
Queen's Road
Bristol BS8 1QU
UK

t: +44 (0)117 331 4054
f: +44 (0)117 331 4093
e: tpp-info@bristol.ac.uk
www.policypress.co.uk

North American office:
The Policy Press
c/o International Specialized Books Services
920 NE 58th Avenue, Suite 300
Portland, OR 97213-3786, USA
t: +1 503 287 3093
f: +1 503 280 8832
e: info@isbs.com

British Library Cataloguing in Publication Data
A catalogue record for this book is available from the British Library.

Library of Congress Cataloging-in-Publication Data
A catalog record for this book has been requested.

ISBN 978 1 84742 192 0 paperback
ISBN 978 1 84742 193 7 hardcover

Cover design by Qube Design Associates, Bristol
Front cover: image kindly supplied by www.photodisc.com
Printed and bound in Great Britain by TJ International, Padstow

Contents

List of figures and tables

Figures

Tables

List of abbreviations

ADL   activities of daily living
ANC   African National Congress
DALY   Disability-Adjusted Life Year
EPF   Employee Provident Fund
GDP   Gross Domestic Product
ILO   International Labour Organisation
IMF   International Monetary Fund
IMSS   Instituto Mexicano del Seguro Social
          [Mexican Institute for Social Security]
ISI   import substituting industrialisation
LTC   long-term care
NGO   non-governmental organisation
PAMI   Programa de Atención Médica Integral
PHC   primary healthcare
PPP   purchasing power parity
SSF   Social Security Fund
TFR   total fertility rate
WHO   World Health Organization

Acknowledgements

The research and writing time for this book was mainly funded by a research fellowship from the Leverhulme Trust.

A large number of people made helpful contributions to the book, including Kathrin Forstner, Paramita Muljono, Joel Busher, Milena Arranciaba, Penny Vera-Sanso, Janet Seeley, Marium Moyet, Rajib Biswal, Sharaf Abbas Khan and several anonymous readers commissioned by The Policy Press.

Notes on the author

Peter Lloyd-Sherlock is Professor of Social Policy and International Development at the School of International Development, University of East Anglia. He previously held lectureships at the London School of Hygiene and Tropical Medicine and the University of Glasgow. Peter has led research projects on population ageing and older people in Argentina, Brazil, South Africa and Thailand. His published books include P. Lloyd-Sherlock and P. Johnson (eds) *Ageing and social policy: Global comparisons*, London, STICERD Publications (1996); P. Lloyd-Sherlock *Old age and poverty in the developing world: The shanty towns of Buenos Aires*, London, Macmillan (1997); P. Lloyd-Sherlock, (ed) *Healthcare reform and poverty in Latin America*, Institute of Latin American Studies and Brookings Institution (2000); P. Lloyd-Sherlock (ed) *Living longer: Ageing, development and social protection*, Zed Books/ United Nations Research Institute for Social Development (2004). He was lead author for *Guide to the National Implementation of the Madrid International Plan of Action on Ageing*, United Nations Department of Economic and Social Affairs (2008).

Peter was 43 years old at the time of publication, and is looking forward to an active and fulfilled old age.

Notes on the author

Introduction

The number of people aged 60 and over is projected to increase by one and a quarter billion between 2010 and 2050, reaching 22% of the world's total population. Of these, 81% will be living in Asia, Africa, Latin America or the Caribbean (United Nations Population Division, 2008). What will this mean for the world and what will old age mean for these people?

In April 2009, as part of a larger study, I interviewed two older women living on the same street in Cape Town, South Africa. Both were aged in their early sixties and both received a basic pension from the government. The first woman I interviewed was paralysed and bed-bound, having suffered a series of strokes. She was depressed and gave a confused account of her life and experiences. She had been frequently hospitalised and was dependent on her immediate family to meet her care needs and keep her spirits up. The second woman was in good health and had a positive outlook on life. She helped care for several grandchildren, ran errands for other family members and was a regular church-goer.

These contrasting experiences of later life are not unusual. Instead, they are typical of the huge diversity of situations faced by older people around the world. Despite this, discussions about population ageing and the lives of older people are often framed by a number of stereotypes and generalisations. These include:

- Population ageing is 'problematic' for development.
- The situation faced by older people across developing countries is broadly similar. For example, it is often claimed that the vast majority of older people in these countries experience poverty, vulnerability and withdrawal.

This book contends that:

- Population ageing must be seen as an integral part of development, rather than an external threat to it.
- Processes of development are complex and highly variable, giving rise to diverse patterns of population change.
- At the same time, complex and variable processes of development lead to diverse experiences of later life.
- Population ageing can affect most aspects of development, but these effects will be significantly modified by how later life is experienced.

Put bluntly, if most experiences of old age are similar to the first woman mentioned above, then population ageing will indeed be 'problematic' for development. In this case, extended life expectancy will add little to an individual's lifetime wellbeing. If, on the other hand, most experiences of old age are closer to the second woman's, then the effects of population ageing will be benign and extended life expectancy will represent a significant contribution to individual wellbeing.

• Experiences of later life and the effects of population ageing on development are strongly influenced by policy choices. These include policies specifically directed towards older people (such as pensions and health services). They also include many other areas of policy that affect societies more generally (such as labour market policies or taxation).

Given the complexity and diversity of development experiences, any claims about the effects of population ageing or experiences of later life must be based on firm, specific evidence. For example, it should not be assumed that the situation currently faced by older people in the UK broadly represents the future for people in less developed countries. Similarly, research conducted with older people in one part of a developing country may not always be nationally representative, and studies of one set of older people may not capture the experience of an entire older population. This book draws on the author's personal experience of research with older people in a wide range of settings, including different parts of Latin America, Asia and southern Africa. It also draws on the rapidly growing body of published research on population ageing and older people. In the best traditions of gerontology and development studies, the book takes a multidisciplinary approach, drawing ideas from sociology, economics, demography and other fields. It should be easily understood by students and policy makers with a general grounding in the social sciences. The book recognises that development is a global process and refers to the experiences of a wide range of countries, including those from the so-called 'developed world'. However, it pays particular attention to low- and middle-income countries. These countries have been relatively neglected in research on ageing, despite accounting for the great majority of the world's older population.

Chapters One and Two provide general introductions to the book's main themes: how population ageing may affect international development, and how development affects people's experiences of old age. Chapter One shows that relationships between population ageing and international development are complex and two-way. It starts with a brief discussion of the concept of development itself, emphasising its multifaceted and contested nature. The chapter then explores how processes of economic and social transformation affect population trends. It pays particular attention to fertility rates, as these are usually the most important cause of population ageing. This analysis demonstrates how different patterns of development influence the timing and pace of population ageing. The second part of the chapter explores the other side of this relationship: the potential consequences of accelerated population ageing for future economic performance and other aspects of development. Taking a number of key effects in turn, it shows that the available evidence is not always as robust nor as coherent as is widely thought. The effects of population ageing on development are heavily mediated by a range of other factors, including policy choices and the health and functional status of older populations.

Chapter Two looks at people's experiences of later life. Again, there is a tendency to generalise about these experiences and to make sweeping assertions about how older people are affected by processes of development. An important limitation of many studies is that they use a simplified life-stage approach to exploring these effects, comparing populations aged 60 or over to other age groups at a fixed point in time. This chapter develops a more sophisticated and dynamic analytical framework based on the concepts of lifecourse, cohort and generation. It applies this framework to demonstrate the complex potential effects of long-term economic and social changes on different groups of older people. As part of this, the chapter reveals the diversity of later life experiences in terms of socioeconomic status and wider aspects of wellbeing. Gender differences are one key aspect of this diversity. Even here, however, general claims about the situation of older men and older women are not always supported by the evidence and patterns vary across different settings.

Chapters Three, Four and Five look at three key policy areas relating to older people and development. The first of these is pension policy. Chapter Three provides an overview of different forms of pension provision and charts the global dissemination of pension programmes during the 20th century. The chapter provides a powerful critique of the role of contributory pension programmes in low- and middle-income countries. These are shown to have mainly benefited older people from wealthier economic strata and to have been the vehicles of inequality, exclusion and clientelism. The application of pension reforms since the 1990s has done little to reduce these problems. By contrast, non-contributory 'social' pensions have often been effective in reaching economically vulnerable older people. Nevertheless, the many claims made about the wider, indirect benefits of social pensions are not always based on robust evidence and so should be treated with caution.

Chapter Four turns to the issue of health in later life. It explores relationships between individual ageing and health status, as well as between national development and overall health trends. The chapter then examines epidemiological patterns associated with population ageing. This highlights the growing profile of chronic diseases, such as stroke, heart disease, cancer and diabetes in low- and middle-income countries. Nevertheless, the epidemiological consequences of population ageing are not inevitable, as the risk factors for chronic diseases are strongly affected by other effects such as diet, lifestyle and earlier life experiences. The chapter goes on to present a strong critique of existing health services for older people in developing countries. These tend to focus on relatively costly curative interventions, rather than more affordable interventions geared towards prevention. Also, the health systems of poorer countries remain strongly oriented towards the needs of people of other ages. At the same time, specific groups of older people (such as the poorest, least-educated and women) face substantial barriers in accessing healthcare. As such, the chapter calls for an urgent reorientation of healthcare services.

Chapter Five deals with the issue of social relations in later life, paying particular attention to family dynamics, the effects of migration and the provision of care for those in need. The chapter starts by mapping changing patterns of older people's living arrangements across developing countries. Among other things, this points to a steady rise in the number of older people living alone. The chapter then considers the implications of these changing living arrangements for older people's wellbeing. Reviewing the available evidence, it finds that these are more complex and less predictable than is often claimed. For example, living with younger adults does not necessarily enhance older people's economic and social wellbeing. The chapter goes on to explore the effects of migration on older people's social relations, before turning to the issue of long-term care. This discussion emphasises the failure of most governments both as providers of long-term care and in adopting policies to support and oversee family and private sector provision. It predicts a rapid expansion in demand for long-term care in developing countries and the emergence of a largely unregulated private care industry.

Chapters Six, Seven and Eight contain three country case studies: South Africa, Argentina and India. These cases illustrate the diversity of national trajectories of economic and social development, and how they feed into patterns of population ageing and experiences of later life. Each chapter follows the same structure. They open with a general review of economic and social development, before focusing more directly on patterns of population change and ageing. They then explore a set of issues of particular saliency for the country in question. The chapters close with three detailed life histories of older men and women. These life histories complement the wider analysis and demonstrate how trends at the national level can affect personal experiences.

Chapter Six looks at the case of South Africa and pays particular attention to relationships between later life and race. Twentieth-century South African development was driven by the mining sector, which depended on large supplies of migrant African labour. This gave rise to divided families and complex patterns of social relations, which have persisted to the present day. The Apartheid system formalised discrimination between racial groups and its legacy endures 15 years after it was dismantled. As a result, experiences of later life vary profoundly across different racial groups, although all face increasing fears of crime and violence. The chapter focuses on the impact of the HIV/AIDS epidemic on older people, along with the effects of the country's extensive social pension programme. Overall, the benefits of relative economic security for older people are offset by the vulnerabilities generated by high unemployment among younger age groups, and by HIV/AIDS.

Chapter Seven turns to the case of Argentina. This provides an example of rapid economic growth in the early 20th century, which has been followed by a more disappointing performance. Early economic growth led to falls in fertility rates, which in turn led to the early onset of population ageing. It also provided the basis for an extensive set of state welfare schemes, including pensions and health insurance. The chapter pays particular attention to the economic effects of early population ageing in Argentina. These include impacts on dependency rates, as well as the costs of providing pensions, health services and long-term care. The chapter concludes that the high cost of welfare services has been mainly due to policy failures, rather than a direct consequence of population ageing. As such, Argentina provides a clear warning for countries facing similar patterns of population change.

The final case study, presented in Chapter Eight, looks at the experiences of India, where 'development' has had only limited effects on large parts of the population, who remain trapped in rural poverty. There is little evidence that the recent economic boom will benefit more than a small minority of the population. As a result, fertility rates have remained high and population ageing has been less pronounced than in Argentina or South Africa. Nevertheless, national data mask large regional variations, seen in the contrasting experiences of Kerala and Uttar Pradesh. The chapter explores how experiences of later life in India are shaped by gender relations and charts the rising impact of chronic health conditions such as stroke and dementia. It then assesses the country's various pension schemes, which are shown to provide minimal protection to the vast majority of older people, despite high levels of expenditure. Overall, the chapter concludes that India is poorly placed to meet the challenges of future population ageing.

Taken together, these three case studies illustrate the diversity of experiences of development, population ageing and later life. In each country, there are clear examples of how policies have failed to meet the challenges of population change or to ensure the wellbeing of older people. Contributory pension schemes have been expensive, poorly managed and inequitable; health provision is becoming increasingly privatised, limiting provision for many older people; and health promotion and long-term care continue to be neglected despite the obvious need for concerted state intervention. On a more positive note, in most countries future cohorts of older people are likely to be better educated and healthier than their forebears. This means that there are still opportunities to develop effective interventions, although these will require shifts in deep-seated popular attitudes towards later life and public policy. If policy makers get it right, we may have fewer reasons to worry about population ageing or our own future lives as older people.

ONE

International development and population ageing

> Population ageing is unprecedented, without parallel in
> the history of humanity.... Population ageing is pervasive,
> a global phenomenon affecting every man, woman and
> child.... Population ageing is profound, having major
> consequences and implications for all facets of human life.
> (United Nations Population Division, 2002: xxviii)

Introduction

Population ageing is now recognised as a major issue for international
development; at the same time, processes associated with development
strongly influence how later life is experienced around the world. This
chapter explores relationships between development, demographic
change and population ageing. It begins by briefly outlining what is
meant by 'development', drawing attention to the concept's complexity
and differences in interpretation. The chapter goes onto explore links
between development and population change, identifying different
scenarios with particular implications for population ageing. The second
half of the chapter reviews current knowledge about how population
ageing may feed back into development. This discussion questions the
widely held view that ageing is a threat to economic performance.
It also considers impacts on other aspects of development, including
political change.

What is development?

To assess the effects of population ageing on development, and how
development influences the lives of older people, we first need to have
some understanding of what is meant by 'international development'.
This is not an easy task: the concept can be interpreted in very different
ways and these views have changed radically over time. Without getting
into the detail of these complex and important debates, this section
will map out some key issues and consider their implications for the
central themes of this book.

The most basic (and least helpful) interpretation of 'international development' is a crude shorthand for a particular concern with the so-called 'developing regions'. Focusing exclusively on these regions is, however, highly problematic in a number of ways. First, any distinction between a less-developed region or country and a more developed one is somewhat arbitrary, particularly at the margins. For example, it is unclear whether many formerly socialist countries belong in one camp or the other. Second, it implies a neat, polarised distinction between conditions prevailing in developing and developed countries, and this goes on to imply that it is safe to make generalisations about older people in one set of countries vis-à-vis the other set. In fact, the extent of socioeconomic, epidemiological and demographic variation among developing countries is much greater than the variation between the developed and developing worlds (Table 1.1). Taking per capita gross domestic product (GDP), the most widely used indicator of national wealth, Brazil's is only a third of the UK's, but Ethiopia's is less than a tenth of Brazil's. The majority of deaths in Senegal and Ethiopia are caused by infectious diseases, such as malaria, AIDS and tuberculosis. By contrast, China and Brazil have experienced an epidemiological transformation, with mortality profiles moving quickly towards those of countries like the UK. This diversity suggests that generalisations about later life experiences among developing countries are even less appropriate than they are for the developed world. The case study chapters at the end of this book provide detailed analyses of very different development contexts.

Table 1.1: Socioeconomic and epidemiological indicators, selected countries

	UK	Brazil	China	Ethiopia	Senegal
GDP/capita, US$ ppp*, 2003	27,147	7,790	5,003	711	1,648
% of total mortality due to chronic disease, 2002	87	63	66	32	30
% of population living in urban areas, 2005	89.2	84.2	40.5	16.2	51.0

Note: * Purchasing power parity: this is a weighting for national variations in living costs.
Sources: UNDP (2005); WHO (2007); United Nations Population Division (2008)

Rather than an exclusive geographical focus, it is more helpful to think of international development in terms of processes of change and transformation. Views about these have shifted in important ways over the past half-century. Until the 1970s, conventional views of development and change were quite narrow and prescriptive.

Development was mainly understood in terms of increasing economic output, investing in basic infrastructure and the establishment of institutions modelled on those of the West (Hettne, 2002). This was closely linked to a vision of modernisation and 'progress' as a linear set of processes, which largely entailed replicating and emulating the experiences of the 'developed world'. It was assumed that sustained economic growth would automatically lead to generalised improvements in material wellbeing and the elimination of poverty. By the 1970s, the failure to achieve economic 'take-off' in many countries prompted scepticism and attacks on this view of development from a number of fronts. These included Marxist and 'dependency' critiques, which argued that global capitalist structures actively hindered the development of poorer countries (Frank, 1967). A separate group of 'anti-development' writers argued that development is an inherently western, neocolonial concept, which has been imposed on non-western societies with largely negative effects (Escobar, 1995). More generally, postmodernists have deconstructed a range of meta-narratives associated with development, and challenged the generalisability and linear inevitability of modernisation processes (Brown, 1996). By the 1990s, the growing prominence of globalisation called into question a key component of traditional development thinking: the role of a relatively autonomous nation state as policy maker.

Shifts in approaches to development can be seen in policy as well as in theory. These have included both priorities for development and the means by which they can be achieved. On paper at least, there has been a shift away from focusing exclusively on economic growth towards poverty reduction as the principal goal for all development policies. This has been complemented by the emergence of new development agendas highlighting issues such as the environment, gender relations and human rights (Remenyi, 2004). Table 1.2 provides summaries of current emphases in development thinking and their potential implications for older people. At the same time, there has been a shift away from state-led, planned development in the 1950s and 1960s towards neoliberal approaches, which seek to limit the role of the state and prioritise the market. A diverse range of non-governmental organisations (NGOs), ranging from local grassroots initiatives to influential international agencies, have come to play an increasingly prominent role, both as providers of services and advocates of particular approaches to development (Hulme and Edwards, 1992). Just as economic growth is no longer viewed as the be all and end all of international development, the wellbeing of individual people is no longer seen purely in terms of income and material wealth. Human development agendas emphasise the importance of health, education and freedom to achieve the things in life we value (Sen, 1999). This links into the growing emphasis that gerontologists place on issues such as dignity, personal autonomy and 'successful ageing' (Rowe and Khan, 1998).

Table 1.2: Different approaches to development and their policy implications for older people

Approach	Definition	Potential implications
Economic development	Promoting structural changes that will foster long-run economic growth	Enabling older people to realise their full economic potential, and avoiding policies that promote dependency in later life
Sustainable development	Development that meets the needs of the present without compromising the ability of future generations to meet their own needs (World Commission on Environment and Development, 1987)	Ensuring that current development does not harm the wellbeing of future cohorts of older people
Human development	'Human development is first and foremost about allowing people to lead a life that they value and enabling them to realise their potential as human beings' (United Nations Development Programme, 2006: v)	The inclusion of older people in human development strategies, including education, training and good health
Poverty reduction	Reducing the number of people living on very low incomes is the first of the Millennium Development Goals (MDGs) and the principal objective of international development agencies such as the World Bank	Understanding the causes and consequences of poverty in later life. Including older people into the MDGs

These theoretical challenges and policy shifts have not led to a new consensus about what we should now understand development to mean. Instead, development has come to be seen as a dynamic and increasingly contested concept. Rather than question the relevance of development per se, these processes of contention have added richness to the theory and debate. It means that for any assertion made about development, ageing and older people, we must appreciate which particular interpretation of development is being used.

Most often when population ageing is portrayed as a threat or (perhaps euphemistically) a challenge to development, this refers to economic performance and increased material levels of consumption. The standard argument goes that population ageing increases the ratio of dependants to workers, lowers productivity, depresses savings and puts pressure on public spending for social provision (Petersen, 1999). The evidence for these claims is not as clear as often supposed, and is reviewed later in this chapter. As we will see in a later section, reducing population growth by lowering fertility was a key element of traditional approaches to economic development, and population ageing was the direct consequence. Thus, it becomes meaningless to assert that ageing is an exogenous threat to development, since population change is itself an integral part of these processes. If we use other interpretations of development, such as the promotion of individual opportunities and capabilities to live a long and fulfilled life, the proposition that population ageing is somehow a threat is patently spurious.

Similarly, when making claims about the impact of development on older people, we must keep in mind the gap between stylised models of change and more complex realities. As will be seen in Chapter Two, there has been a tendency to associate modernisation with increased isolation and marginalisation in later life (Cowgill, 1976). At the same time, it is observed that economic growth has led to unprecedented levels of material wellbeing for at least some groups of older people. Yet the nature and consequences of 'development' for older people vary across different settings. Even in the same locale, the consequences may vary among older people, depending on factors such as their lifetime socioeconomic status and gender. As such, any generalisation is very dangerous.

Inevitably, research on older people and development is influenced by current global priorities, such as poverty eradication and AIDS mitigation. These may provide opportunities to attract funding and increase the leverage of organisations concerned with older people. However, this may risk skewing priorities and overlooking other key areas of concern. In particular, it raises the issue as to whether gerontologists working in development should largely ignore older people from middle or upper socioeconomic strata. Since these may account for the majority of older people in some countries, this is a large group to exclude.

Global trends in population ageing

Population ageing (or demographic ageing) is defined by the United Nations as 'the process whereby older individuals become a proportionately larger share of the total population' (United Nations Population Division, 2002: 1).[1] This raises a number of issues. First, it is essential to distinguish between individuals growing older – something that happens to all of us all of the time – and the ageing of an entire population. Because of this, the general term 'ageing' is not very helpful, as it can refer to both. Second, the United Nations' definition leaves open how we identify 'older individuals' and how these can be distinguished from the rest of a population. Generally, economists and demographers refer to individuals aged 60 or 65 years and more. However, this can be misleadingly simplistic, and different definitions can have important implications for research and policy, as is discussed in Chapter Two. Third, it is necessary to delimit a 'population', and how this is done can have a large influence on ageing trends. Typically, we refer to the populations of individual countries. While this might seem the obvious approach to take, we should bear in mind that national populations range from over a billion to just a few thousand, making this a potentially misleading unit for comparison. Also, using national populations may mask important variations at the subnational level, such as between regions and ethnic groups. For example, the US's 2000 National Census found that 14% of the total population were aged 65 and over, but this fell to 10% for African Americans and only 6% for native Americans (US Census Bureau, 2008).

Given increased globalisation and population movement, the best starting point for analysis is population ageing for the world as a whole. Table 1.3 shows that between 1950 and 2000 the trend was noticeable, but not spectacular. It also reveals significant sex disparities, with a higher proportion of women in older age groups than was the case for

Table 1.3: Global ageing trends (% of the total population)

	1950	2000	2025*	2050*
Total 60+	8.2	10.0	15.0	21.1
Total 80+	0.5	1.1	1.9	4.1
Women 60+	9.0	11.1	16.3	22.7
Women 80+	0.7	1.5	2.5	5.0
Men 60+	7.3	8.9	13.6	19.4
Men 80+	0.4	0.8	1.1	3.1

Note: * Projected.
Source: United Nations Population Division (2008)

—

men. The projections for the next 50 years give a very different picture, with population ageing predicted to accelerate rapidly. This raises the questions: how are we able to predict population ageing, and why is it expected to 'take off' in the next few decades?

Focusing on national experiences, Table 1.4 reveals that these trends are not consistent. Predictably, there is a rough relationship between national prosperity and population ageing. Between 1950 and 2000, most developed countries, such as the UK, were already experiencing significant population ageing. In many formerly socialist countries, such as Russia, the trend was even more pronounced. Globally, this effect was cancelled out by the experiences of many developing countries, where there were rapid rises in the proportion of younger age groups.

Table 1.4: Population aged 60 years or more, selected countries (% of the total population)

	1950	2000	2025*	2050*
UK	15.5	20.8	25.8	28.8
Russia	9.2	18.4	24.3	31.7
China	7.5	10.0	19.6	31.1
Brazil	4.9	8.1	16.5	29.3
Ethiopia	4.8	4.7	5.7	9.6

Note: * Projected.
Source: United Nations Population Division (2008)

More interesting is the degree of convergence between the UK and all but the world's poorest countries by 2050. The speed of population ageing in countries such as Brazil and China will mean a doubling of the proportion of their older populations roughly every 25 years. This is much faster than the historical experiences of the developed world. By contrast, the relative size of the older population in Ethiopia will scarcely change over the hundred years between 1950 and 2050. Despite this, rapid total population growth means that, in absolute terms, the number of Ethiopians aged 60 or more is projected to rise from around 900,000 to over 12 million.

The causes of population ageing

Why is the world's population ageing, and why do the above trends vary across different countries? These questions can be answered on a number of different levels, including:

- *direct determinants:* these are the essential demographic determinants of population ageing, and include fertility, life expectancy and migration;
- *indirect determinants:* these include complex sets of socioeconomic and cultural transformations associated with development, and which underlie demographic change.

Direct determinants of population ageing

Changing rates of fertility are by far the most important direct determinant of demographic ageing. At first sight, this might seem surprising: why should the number of children being born influence the ageing of a population? The reason is that population ageing is a product of the overall age distribution of a population – if the relative number of children falls, then the proportion in older age groups will rise. Since 1950, global fertility (usually measured by the total fertility rate or TFR) has almost halved from around 5 to 2.7 children per woman.[2] Table 1.5 shows that, excepting the poorest countries, there was a marked global convergence in TFRs between 1950 and 2000. By 2000, fertility in China had fallen spectacularly to reach the same level as in the UK. At 1.7, this stands well below the 'replacement fertility rate' of 2.1, which is the level of fertility required for a low mortality population to replenish itself. Thus, as well as population ageing, the consequences of low fertility include falls in the total size of the population. By 2000, fertility had fallen below the replacement rate in around 60 countries, containing over half of the world's population. Despite this, high levels of fertility in countries like Ethiopia mean that more people are added to the planet's population each year than ever before.

Comparing the data for China and Brazil in Tables 1.4 and 1.5, we can see that there is a lag between fertility decline and population ageing. This is because the impact of falling numbers of children takes

Table 1.5: Total fertility rates, selected countries

	1950–55	2000–05	2020–25*	2045–50*
UK	2.18	1.70	1.85	1.85
Russia	2.85	1.30	1.58	1.83
China	6.11	1.77	1.85	1.85
Brazil	6.15	2.25	1.52	1.75
Ethiopia	7.17	5.87	3.69	2.19

Note: * Median variant projection.
Source: United Nations Population Division (2008)

its time to work its way through the entire population age structure. Population pyramids are useful for demonstrating this effect. Figure 1.1 shows changes to the age and sex distribution of Brazil's population between 1970 and 2020. Falls in fertility since 1970 lead to a 'bulge', which works its way up the pyramid between 2000 and 2020. As such, the middle-aged baby boomers of 2020 will reach their sixties by 2030 or 2040, thus triggering an acceleration in population ageing.

Through population pyramids and simple models, *past* fertility trends can be a relatively reliable predictor for ageing trends over the following 50 or 60 years. By contrast, whether the *future* fertility rates projected for 2025 and 2050 in Table 1.5 will turn out to be accurate is much less certain. Changes in fertility are notoriously fickle and projections are complex, drawing on a wide range of assumptions (National Research Council, 2000). Table 1.5 provides the middle of a range of projections produced by the United Nations. The official 'low variant' projection for China is 1.35 by 2045-50: this would lead to much higher rates of population ageing in the years beyond 2050.[3]

Increasing life expectancy is another direct determinant of population ageing, but the effect is not as strong or always as direct as sometimes thought. Table 1.6 shows that in Russia, where the share of older people doubled between 1950 and 2000, life expectancy at birth barely changed. The impressive progress made by many developing countries since 1950 was largely achieved through reducing the chances of dying in infancy or early childhood, rather than increased longevity in old age. In China, for example, the number of children who did not survive their first year of life fell from around 20% to only 2% between 1950 and 2000. These declines in infant mortality will have partly offset the effect of fertility reductions on population pyramids, slowing the rate of population ageing.

Table 1.6: Life expectancy at birth, selected countries

	1950–55	2000–05	2020–25*	2045–50*
UK	69.2	78.5	81.3	84.1
Russia	64.5	64.8	70.6	74.9
China	40.8	72.0	75.8	79.3
Brazil	50.9	71.0	75.9	79.9
Ethiopia	34.1	52.5	60.9	68.7

Note: * Median variant projection.
Source: United Nations Population Division (2008)

Figure 1.1: Population pyramids for Brazil

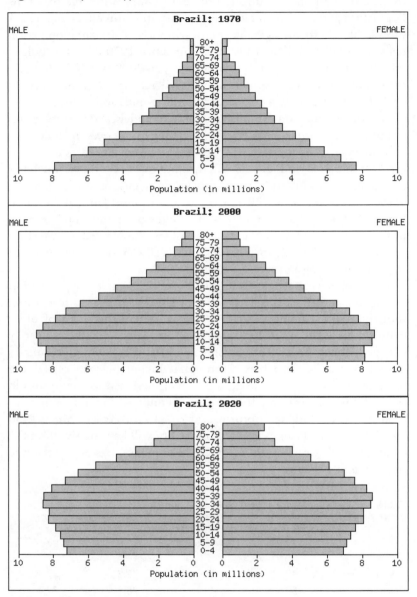

Source: US Census Bureau (2008)

To escape this effect, it is necessary to replace data on life expectancy at birth with life expectancy at older ages. Where these are available, they show that rising life expectancy in old age has influenced population ageing, but less significantly than fertility trends. In developed countries, increases in life expectancy at old age over recent decades have not been as spectacular as sometimes thought. For example, in the UK, between 1950 and 2000, life expectancy for men aged 65 or over only increased by around three years, reaching 15.5 years. In some rapidly ageing countries such as Russia, life expectancy at old age has actually fallen, due to the social and economic fallout of the transition to a market economy.

As with fertility, there is uncertainty about future life expectancy levels. Some scientists predict that rising rates of obesity may lead to significant falls in life expectancy in the US and other developed countries (Olshansky et al, 2005). Others predict that new technologies may lead to historically unprecedented increases in longevity (de Gray, 2007). It is also important to remember that life expectancy can vary widely between different groups in the same country, thus influencing their likelihood of reaching and surviving through old age. Variations in life expectancy between men and women explain the disproportionate number of older people who are female (Table 1.3).[4] More specifically, in 1999 British men with a history of employment in 'professional' activities could expect to live on average 7.4 years longer than those working in activities defined as 'unskilled' (ONS, 2004). Data are less available for developing countries, but it is likely that gaps in life expectancy between the rich and poor will be even larger. This 'survival bias' can have an important impact on the prevalence of poverty in old age (see Chapter Two).

In countries badly affected by the HIV/AIDS pandemic, particularly those in southern and eastern Africa, the past decade has seen a sharp rise in overall levels of mortality. Due to the nature of the epidemic, this has been most pronounced among people aged 15 to 40 years, although infants and older people have also been affected. Where AIDS-related mortality has been age-selective this will have consequences for the overall age composition of a population. However, in terms of population ageing, the effects to date have not been large. For example, in Botswana, whose HIV prevalence rates of around 40% are probably the world's highest, population ageing is still relatively gradual. This is mainly because levels of fertility remain quite high in these countries (Barnett and Whiteside, 2002). The impact of AIDS on population ageing is more likely to be felt in 20 to 30 years' time, when people currently in their forties might have been expected to reach old age. Even so, this effect is hard to predict, as widening access to anti-retroviral drugs may increase survival periods for people with AIDS.

Migration is the third direct determinant of population ageing. This occurs where migration is age-selective, thus influencing the age structures of both the origins and destinations. Despite growing levels of movement across borders, the contribution of migration to population ageing at the national level is far less important than fertility and life expectancy (United Nations Population Division, 2002). This is because the main flow of international migrants is away from poorer countries where population structures still remain relatively youthful. Many richer countries on the receiving end now see the promotion of international migration of young adults as a potential strategy to reduce their own rates of population ageing and to bolster the ratio of workers to pensioners. However, the effect is likely to be marginal and such policies are politically controversial (Demeny, 2002).

The impact of migration is often more apparent at the subnational level. In recent decades, many developing countries have seen unprecedented rates of rural to urban migration. For example, it is estimated that there were over 20 million rural to urban migrants in India during the 1990s. This migration primarily involves young adults, with older people (and often grandchildren) left behind in rural areas. The consequences can be seen in several sub-Saharan African countries, where rates of population ageing in the countryside are more than double those of the cities (Stloukal, 2001). Rural–urban disparities in population ageing can have a range of implications for older people and policy makers, and these are discussed throughout the book.

Indirect determinants of population ageing

The main *direct* determinants of population ageing are fertility rates and, to a lesser extent, adult life expectancy, with migration playing a relatively marginal role. However, it is important to go further and examine the factors that underlie these demographic processes. These can be understood as the *indirect* drivers of population ageing. As will be seen, they are a complex and sometimes disputed set of effects, which are broadly associated with wider experiences of development and social change.

The demographic transition model is a good starting point for understanding fertility and mortality trends (Figure 1.2). This model, based on the experiences of a number of western countries during the 19th and 20th centuries, observes that countries tend to go through a sequence of stages in fertility and mortality trends (Caldwell, 1996). Before the 19th century, both birth and death rates were high across Europe, although mortality was more variable due to the effects of sporadic events such as wars, famines and epidemics. At some point in the 19th century, transition began with a decline in death rates. Initially, this was not accompanied by falls in fertility, leading to substantial increases in population growth. Several decades later, European countries began to see significant and sustained falls in fertility rates, leading to a deceleration of population growth. By the second half of the 20th century, most countries in the region appeared to have come close to a more stable demographic situation, where a rough balance between low birth and death rates gave rise to minimal population growth.

Figure 1.2: Demographic transition and population ageing

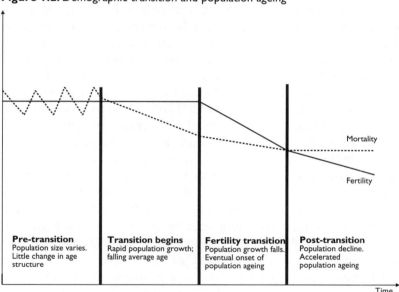

Figure 1.2 also refers to the impact of demographic transition on the age structures of populations. During the pre-transition phase, low life expectancy and high fertility might be expected to restrict the size of older populations. In fact, mortality was highly concentrated in the early years of life and so a significant proportion of people reaching adulthood would go on to survive until their sixties (Johnson, 2004). As transition began, reductions in mortality could in theory promote ageing, but these largely affected people at younger ages, swelling the bottom of the population pyramid. This effect was bolstered by continued high fertility rates. Thus, the initial impact of demographic transition in European countries was a reduction in the average age of national populations.

This only changed when fertility reduction became pronounced. Figure 1.2 provides an additional stage of transition to that provided by the standard model, based on more recent experiences: a stage of continued falls in fertility below the replacement rate. This has led to population decline and higher levels of population ageing than those predicted in the original model.

The demographic transition model is a helpful starting point for exploring trends in fertility and mortality, but suffers from several shortcomings. First and foremost, it is a *model*, not a *theory*. It is derived from historical observations in a number of developed countries and postulates that these may be replicated in other parts of the world. It does not, however, set out to explain why mortality fell when it did or why the decline in fertility tended to come later. Implicitly, the timing of the model suggests that these trends were linked to wider processes of development, such as industrialisation, urbanisation and extended access to education. It follows that similar experiences of development in other countries should therefore lead to similar demographic trends. However, as seen earlier in this chapter, assumptions about development as a simple linear process of modernisation and progress have been increasingly challenged. It is, therefore, not surprising that demographic trends in Asia, Africa and Latin America have not always replicated those of Europe. In a small number of countries with strong Islamic cultures or with extreme levels of poverty there is little if any sign of significant and sustained drops in fertility (Winkvist, and Akhtar, 2000). In those parts of sub-Saharan Africa badly affected by HIV/AIDS, mortality rates have risen dramatically in recent years (McMichael et al, 2004). In many developing countries the 'lag period' between falls in mortality and falls in fertility lasted much longer than it did in Europe, greatly increasing population growth. In many of the same countries, the eventual fall in fertility was much faster than it had been Europe. For example, in India the average number of children a woman would be expected to bear fell from 5.4 in 1970 to 2.7 in 2000. As a result, countries like India are now dealing with the consequences both of the long lag period (a very large total population) and of the halving of fertility in a single generation (rapid changes in its age structure).

The timing and speed of fertility transition exerts a major influence over patterns of population ageing. There is an extensive body of theoretical and empirical research on factors that influence fertility trends. Some key, general lessons that emerge from this are:

• As with population ageing, the list of potential factors includes *direct* determinants such as natural fertility, age of marriage and use of contraception; as well as *indirect* ones, such as female education and employment, and rising income levels.

- Causality is complex and there is normally no single factor that triggers sustained fertility transitions. Instead, there is usually an interplay of socioeconomic conditions (which affect material incentives for raising large or small families) and more subtle cultural factors, such as the status childrearing may confer on women in some societies.
- Population policies such as family planning programmes can play a role, but in most cases have had a limited impact, and are sometimes difficult to disentangle from the wider developmental contexts in which they play out.
- One of the many interconnected factors thought to influence fertility rates is a desire for surviving children to provide support in later life, usually referred to as the 'old-age security motive' (Rendall and Bahchieva, 1998). In cultures where caregiving is mainly provided by daughters-in-law, old-age security may depend on having at least one married son. Studies from countries such as Brazil have argued that the development of formal pension programmes has reduced these concerns, thus contributing to fertility reduction (Martine, 1996). This demonstrates the complexity of relationships between wellbeing in later life, public policy and population growth.

Since every experience of demographic transition is unique, Box 1.1 provides four very different examples and explores some of the consequences for population ageing, older people and social policy.

Box 1.1: Demographic transition in Japan, China, Kenya and Ukraine

Japan: classical demographic transition

Japan experienced a steady rapid fertility decline from the mid-1920s. This was strongly associated with rapid economic growth and urbanisation. Changing cultural values are also thought to have played an important role, including new attitudes to marriage, female education and employment (Retherford et al, 1996). Japan did not adopt high-profile government family planning programmes, as policy remained strongly influenced by conservative social attitudes and an ideology of minimal state intervention (Nogami, 2005). The relatively early onset of fertility transition in Japan meant that it had fallen below the replacement rate by the 1960s and by the 1990s Japan had the most aged population structure in the world. Along with demographic change, the country has experienced rapid rises in material prosperity and complex processes of cultural change (Maeda and Ishikawa, 2000). The needs of older Japanese have led to a revision of the established strategy of minimal state intervention in 'family affairs'. Japan has had a long time to plan for population ageing, and its government began to implement significant initiatives in areas such as pensions and long-term care in the 1960s.

China: forced demographic transition

Between 1950 and 2000, the population of China roughly doubled from 500 million to over a billion. From the 1970s, the government began to implement a series of measures to reduce the birth rate, culminating with the One Child One Family Policy, introduced in 1979 (Hesketh and Xing, 2005). This included a wide range of substantial incentives and penalties, such as prioritised access to education and fines. While the policy has sometimes been criticised for being authoritarian, its apparent impact on fertility rates was dramatic, with the TFR dropping from around six births per woman in the 1960s to 2.5 in the 1980s. As well as a direct policy effect, it is thought that China's sudden economic take-off and associated social changes have also played a role. The predictable consequence has been a sudden acceleration in population ageing, and concerns have been raised about capacity of the 'one-child families' to meet this potential need. Unlike Japan, China is grappling with a large number of challenges associated with the initial stages of rapid economic development, and the country's population continues to grow. Consequently, there has been less time to develop policy responses to population ageing and this issue competes with other priorities. Despite rapid urbanisation, around three quarters of older people still live in rural areas, where pension schemes and other social policies for older people remain very limited (Peng and Zhi-Gang, 2000).

Kenya: delayed demographic transition

During the 1950s, 1960s and 1970s, fertility levels remained stubbornly high, despite a range of family planning programmes. In the mid-1970s, Kenya had one of the highest fertility rates in the world, at over eight births per woman. To a large extent this was blamed on a lack of progress in reducing poverty, along with cultural barriers, such as the low status of women and religious beliefs (Robinson, 1992). Since then, Kenya has seen a rapid fertility transition, with the TFR falling to 4.7 in 1995, and it has been put forward as a model for other countries in sub-Saharan Africa. The main direct factor responsible for this decline is thought to have been a wider use of contraceptives, especially condoms. This, in turn, is thought to have been promoted by improvements to government population programmes, rising levels of female education and access to basic health services. These achievements have occurred despite a patchy economic performance, and the majority of Kenyans, young and old, continue to experience severe poverty.

Since the mid-1990s, fertility rates have levelled off. The reasons for this are not entirely clear, but are thought to be related to changing attitudes to contraception and childrearing in the wake of a rapid rise in AIDS-related mortality (Westoff and Cross, 2006). As a result, the total population is expected to grow by around 50% between 2005 and 2020, reaching 52 million. The share of the population aged 60 or over is expected to remain at around 4 to 5% over the next 20 years. Not surprisingly, the focus of policy remains firmly on other age groups and it is assumed that a good supply of younger people will guarantee adequate support for most older people. Kenya's stalled fertility transition means that old-age experiences will be framed by a wider context of poverty, rapid population growth and limited resources.

Ukraine: demographic meltdown?
As in much of Eastern Europe, Ukraine had already experienced demographic transition by the mid-20th century, with TFRs of less than three births per woman. As a result, demographic ageing was already well advanced, with 11% of the population aged 60 or over in 1950. Consequently, the needs of older people were a prominent policy concern during the 1950s and 1960s, when relatively embracing social policies were established. As with Japan, fertility has since fallen well below the replacement rate. In this case, however, the main driver of change was not continued prosperity, but the social and economic fallout of the country's difficult transition from socialism. Falling standards of living and increased economic insecurity discouraged large families. This combined with high levels of out-migration and rising mortality among adult males (due to factors such as stress, alcoholism and chronic disease) to lead to a sudden decline in the country's total population. Between 1995 and 2005, the total population fell from 51 to 47 million. Thus, the wider demographic and developmental context of population ageing in Ukraine is very different to Japan's. The older population have been particularly vulnerable to the decline in state healthcare, pensions and social services (Bezrukov and Foigt, 2004). Historical low fertility, combined with more recent out-migration, mean that many have limited access to or contact with younger relatives.

The impact of population ageing on economic performance

By the 1980s and early 1990s, it was becoming increasingly apparent that developed countries were entering a new phase of demographic transition, which had not been foreseen in the original version of the model. Rather than a stable population size and age structure, this entailed continued falls in the fertility rate and accelerating population ageing (Chesnais, 1999). At the same time, the more populous developing countries were starting to experience delayed but unexpectedly rapid fertility transition. Thus, although the world's population continued to grow, earlier concerns about a 'population timebomb' gave way to new fears about the consequences of dwindling birth rates and an 'old-age crisis'. Some commentators foresaw the long-run economic consequences of population ageing as potentially calamitous. According to an article in the influential journal *Foreign Affairs*, 'Global ageing could trigger a crisis that engulfs the world economy. This crisis may even threaten democracy itself' (Petersen, 1999: 55). In a similar vein, in 1994 the World Bank published a highly influential report, *Averting the old age crisis*, which states: 'The world is approaching an old age crisis....The proportion of the population that is old is expanding rapidly, swelling the potential economic burden on the young' (World Bank, 1994a: no page number). Likewise, in 2006, Japan's Policy Council for Declining Fertility reported that low fertility and population ageing 'will not only have an impact on economic, industrial and social security issues, but ... is intertwined with the very existence and viability of Japan as a country' (*BBC News Online*, 19 November 2007).

These worrying predictions are underpinned by a range of longstanding assumptions about population ageing and older people. Back in the 1940s, an official enquiry into the consequences of population ageing for the British economy warned:

> Older people excel in experience, patience, in wisdom and breadth of view; the young are noted for energy, enterprise, enthusiasm, the capacity to learn new things, to adapt themselves, to innovate. It thus seems possible that a society in which the proportion of young people is diminishing will become dangerously unprogressive.' (cited in Blaikie, 1999: 39)

More specifically, it is widely held that most if not all older people are economically dependent and unproductive, and that older people have expensive welfare needs they cannot meet personally. The following sections review each of these assumptions in turn.

Population ageing and economic dependency

Dependency ratios are a commonly used tool for assessing the economic consequences of population ageing. These ratios compare the component of a population considered either too old or too young to be 'workers' to those of 'working age' (usually assumed to be between 15 and 64 years old). More specifically, old-age dependency ratios compare the shares of a population aged 65 and over to those aged 15 to 64.

Table 1.7 provides these ratios for a range of countries. In terms of overall dependency, the gradual rises projected for rapidly ageing societies such as the UK and Russia do not appear to justify the alarmist predictions. This is because the impact of population ageing is partly offset by a reduction in the numbers in dependent childhood. In the case of countries where fertility transition has been more recent, such as China and Brazil, the effect is even stronger, so that overall dependency rates have fallen sharply in recent decades and are expected to remain stable for some time to come. Where fertility transition has been slow and limited, as in Ethiopia, the overall level of demographic dependency remains very high and there are few prospects of a reduction. Comparisons between the overall dependency ratio and the old-age ratio demonstrate the importance of analysing population ageing with reference to wider changes in the age structure of a population. How meaningful these comparisons are is difficult to assess. While there may be economic trade-offs, it would be wrong to assume that a dependent

Table 1.7: Demographic dependency ratios (DDRs) and old-age dependency ratios (ODRs), selected countries

		1950	2000	2025*
UK	DDR	49	53	59
	ODR	16	24	35
Russia	DDR	54	44	47
	ODR	10	18	28
China	DDR	61	46	46
	ODR	7	10	19
Brazil	DDR	80	51	48
	ODR	5	8	15
Ethiopia	DDR	89	93	83
	ODR	6	6	6

Notes: DDR: population under 15 and over 65 per 100 people aged 15–64.
ODR: population over 65 per 100 people aged 15–64.
* Median variant projection.
Source: United Nations Population Division (2002)

older person equates to a dependent younger one, or, more crudely, that we can exchange investment in schools for pensions.

Dependency ratios, be they for the population as a whole or specifically for older age groups, are in fact a very limited and potentially misleading tool for assessing the economic consequences of population ageing. There are several reasons for this. First, they are based on highly generalised assumptions about age and economic activity: that all those of working age are active and that the rest of a population are not. Unsurprisingly, there is evidence that rates of economic activity fall progressively through later life in both developed and developing countries.[5] Despite this, it is estimated that globally around 20% of people aged 65 and over continue to work (United Nations Population Division, 2002). Levels of old-age employment are higher in countries with lower per capita incomes, where more than half of those aged 65 and over are estimated to be working. However, in many developed countries, rates of economic activity are likely to increase in future decades, due to changes to minimum retirement ages. At the same time, there are dangers in assuming that all those aged 15 to 64 are economically active. Growing numbers of people aged over 15 remain in or return to full-time education, which must be added to the effects of adult unemployment. Also, a simple division between workers and non-workers ignores the complexity of work status, which needs to take into account part-time work (which has become increasingly prevalent in many countries) and under-employment, informal employment and seasonal employment (which are widespread phenomena in poorer countries).

A further problem with dependency ratios is that they suggest that being dependent or being depended upon is entirely down to salaried employment. In fact, significant economic contributions can be made in a number of other ways, most notably through unpaid domestic work and childcare. The important contributions of some older people as carers of grandchildren, particularly in the context of extensive migration and high AIDS prevalence, are well documented and are discussed in detail in Chapter Five. In many countries, retired older people can play a substantial role in charity work and the voluntary sector more generally. Some older people also make important contributions to public revenue, particularly through taxes such as inheritance tax. A recent study of older people in the UK estimated that people aged between 60 and 79 contributed £5.5 billion each year in tax, £4.2 billion in voluntary work and over £50 billion worth of unpaid family care (HSBC, 2007). This does not include the transfer of capital to younger generations to help establish them in the country's increasingly expensive housing market.

Yet another problem with dependency ratios is that they contribute to oversimplistic notions of what dependency is. First, they imply that individuals are either dependent or providers. This flies in the face of most research on material exchange between older people and younger relatives, which reveals complex patterns of *inter*dependency (Aboderin, 2004; Schröder-Butterfill, 2004). Second, they focus on a single point in time, ignoring past contributions that dependent older people may have made to those who are currently 'of working age'. These may have included past investments in the human capital of children whose earning capacities were consequently increased. Since ageing is associated with lower fertility, this may have increased the amount of such investment in each individual child, thus boosting their capacity to pay something back in the future. Beyond this, it is important to avoid confusing economic dependency with other forms of dependency, such as those related to physical and emotional needs (Baltes, 1996).

Not all dependency ratios focus on the relative numbers of workers and non-workers. Parent support ratios analyse the expected care needs of frail older people, by comparing the share of a population aged 85 years and over, to those aged between 50 and 64. This is based on the assumption that all of those aged over 85 will require substantial amounts of care and that this will mainly come from their children. Table 1.8 shows a very rapid increase for countries like the UK, due to larger numbers of people surviving to extreme old age. By contrast, the parent support ratio for countries like Ethiopia is set to remain very low. Although this sort of calculation is an interesting exercise, the assumptions it is based on are highly questionable. For example, for many people frailty and care needs may become significant well before they are 85 years old, particularly in poorer countries.

Table 1.8: Parent support ratios, selected countries (population aged 85+ per 100 people aged 50–64)

	1950	2000	2025*
UK	3.6	11.4	13.6
Russia	3.5	6.1	8.6
China	0.7	2.5	3.9
Brazil	1.2	2.4	3.8
Ethiopia	0.7	1.1	2.5

Note: * Median variant projection.
Source: United Nations Population Division (2002)

Population ageing and economic productivity

Given their many problems and limitations, it is likely that dependency ratios provide a distorted and over-pessimistic view of the economic consequences of population ageing. A separate issue is whether ageing workforces are inherently less productive than those mainly containing younger workers. The standard argument goes that biological ageing is essentially degenerative, involving inevitable reductions in physical strength and, to a lesser extent, mental capacities. It is also observed that older people are more likely to experience episodes of ill-health, thus reducing their reliability as workers. In some countries, there is a widespread view that older people tend to be more conservative and less adaptable as workers than younger age groups (McGregor and Gray, 2002). Linked to this, there are concerns that the skill sets of older people tend to be less appropriate to the needs of rapidly changing workplaces. Finally, it is noted that older workers tend to be more expensive, as salaries increase with seniority or years on the job, regardless of the contribution made. Not all the standard wisdoms about individual ageing and productivity are negative, however, and some studies stress the value of experience and lifelong learning, which may compensate for any effects of biological decline (Barth et al, 1993).

The degree of truth in these different generalisations is highly variable. There is clear evidence that strength and stamina do decline significantly in later life, although this process can vary greatly between individuals (Ilmarinen, 2001). However, the relationship between intellectual capacity, memory and age is much less apparent. Although mental functioning can decline in very old age, research shows that most older people have the potential to perform intellectually on a comparable level to other age groups (Jackson, 1998). Claims about flexibility, worker attitudes and skills tend to be anecdotal and there appear to be examples where the opposite is the case (Robinson et al, 1985). There may be more basis for concerns about skill sets, at least in some settings. In many developing countries, levels of illiteracy are much higher for older people than for other age groups. This is not an inevitable consequence of age, but reflects the limited supply of education 50 or more years ago, when these people experienced childhood. Subsequent extensions of the education system mean that future generations of older people will have higher levels of formal schooling. Indeed, investing in the human capital of both current and future generations of older people has been identified as a key strategy for boosting both economic activity and productivity in later life (Lutz et al, 2004).

Taking all of this together, the overall impact of age on productivity is variable and depends on the nature of economic activity. Studies on a range of activities in the UK show that most older people are capable of being as productive as the young (Disney, 1996). In the case of hard manual labour, which predominates in rural zones of developing countries, it may be expected that there will be a significant negative effect.[6] In more sedentary, cerebral activities, where job experience matters, old age may well be an asset. The proportion of jobs in this second category tends to rise with economic development. At the same time, there has been a tendency for individual employment histories to become more complex, with frequent changes of employer and activity. As jobs for life have increasingly become a thing of the past, the impact of seniority on wage levels is becoming less obvious. The evidence also indicates that specific education and employment policies can do much to boost older people's rates of activity and productivity.

Population ageing, welfare provision and public spending

Beyond economic activity and productivity, a further area of concern relates to the costs of providing for needs that are specifically associated with later life: income support (through pensions and other transfers), healthcare and social services (Dang et al, 2001). Chapters Three, Four and Five deal with each of these issues more broadly and in some detail. This chapter will restrict its analysis to the potential of a 'cost explosion' in healthcare, before making some more general observations.

Referring to developing countries, Bicknell and Parks (1989: 59) argue that population ageing will lead to a 'morbidity burden [that] can quickly overwhelm fragile and often underfinanced health infrastructures already unable to meet fully the prevention and treatment needs of a younger population'. These concerns echo debates in developed countries, which, in their more extreme form, make apocalyptic predictions about collapsing healthcare systems (Petersen, 1999). At first sight, there would appear to be a strong, logical basis for these concerns. Health spending in developed countries is significantly higher for older people than for other age groups, and the same might be expected in developing countries (McGrail et al, 2000). For example, a survey in Mexico reported that ageing was associated with extended periods of morbidity, and that diagnoses were being made earlier, which further extended the overall period of treatment (Castro et al, 1998). It would therefore seem logical that population ageing will inevitably lead to an increased financial burden on health services.

Nevertheless, claims that population ageing will *inevitably* lead to a healthcare cost explosion, either in developed or developing countries, would appear to be exaggerated for a number of reasons. First, the data simply do not support this claim. Table 1.9 shows levels of health spending, national wealth and population ageing for a selection of countries. It shows that the US spends more than double the UK, despite containing a lower proportion of older people. Likewise, levels of spending in India are less than a 10th of Mexico's, despite similar levels of population ageing. The table also shows the extent of national variations, with expenditure falling to as little as US$5 per person per year in countries such as Ethiopia.

Table 1.9: Health expenditure, national wealth and population ageing, selected countries

	Health expenditure per capita, US$, 1997–2000	Gross national income (ppp), US$, 2002	Population aged 65 or over (%) 2000
US	4,499	35,060	12.4
UK	1,747	25,870	15.9
Mexico	311	8,540	5.2
India	23	2,570	4.3
Ethiopia	5	720	2.9

Sources: World Bank (2004); United Nations Population Division (2008)

Population ageing may potentially influence health spending, but any effect will be strongly mediated by a range of other factors. Comparisons across developed countries have found that patterns of technological change (such as the discovery of new drugs) and national wealth have been particularly significant (van der Gaag and Precker, 1997). A more specific explanation for the difference in expenditure between the UK and US relates to inefficiencies in the US private health insurance market, compared with the relative cheapness of the UK National Health Service. To some extent, differences between Mexico and India relate to varying political priorities. Research from developed countries suggests that concentration of expenditure on older age groups may give a misleading view of population ageing effects. Spending is heavily concentrated in the last years of an individual's life, regardless of their age at death, and so is more influenced by overall levels of mortality than by the average age of the population (Fuchs, 1984). Indeed, the costs of dying may be lower for older people than for younger ones, if they receive less treatment as a result of ageist bias (McGrail et al, 2000).

Thus, even when population ageing is associated with a global increase in the incidence of certain forms of chronic disease (see Chapter Four), its impact on health services may not be as direct as is widely predicted. Rather than driving up health spending, the main impact of ageing may be a shifting of priorities. Any society is faced with a higher demand for health services than it can meet, and therefore some form of rationing is always present. The gap between demand and provision is especially wide in lower-income countries such as Ethiopia, highlighted by failures such as the lack of access of most AIDS sufferers to effective drug therapies. The likelihood that changing demographics will lead to a healthcare cost explosion in these contexts is remote.

A considered analysis of the health expenditure effects of population ageing reveals a number of key issues that are relevant to wider discussions about the 'costs' of older people. The first is that any ageing effects will be mediated by a range of intervening factors. Some of these may be determined by political decisions (such as how to organise healthcare financing or where to set the retirement age); others may be less obviously controllable (such as the discovery of expensive new therapies or the performance of pension fund investments). Linked to this, levels of public spending are likely to respond more directly to political processes and reflect wider societal priorities than to demographic trends. Concerns about the affordability and sustainability of spending on older people (as well as anyone else) must be located in a wider context of economic development. In resource-scarce countries like Ethiopia, cost explosion concerns are as offensive as they are absurd. In richer countries, long-run economic growth and increases in productivity should mean that the resources for meeting the needs of older people will be available, and spending will largely depend on wider priorities. Finally, as population ageing usually coincides with falling numbers of young children, these particular potential costs will be offset by potential savings in areas such as education, maternal healthcare and social services concerned with children.

Taken together, these findings mean that the links between ageing and public spending are not as direct or as predictable as sometimes claimed, and that policy makers have considerable influence on how they occur. The most sophisticated analysis currently available for countries in the European Commission predicts that the impact of demographic change on public spending over the next 50 years will vary sharply between countries (European Commission, 2006). For developing countries, limited data and an absence of robust analysis mean that the consequences are even harder to gauge. As is argued in later chapters, these consequences will largely depend on the ability of such countries to implement policies that are suitable to their particular contexts and not overly influenced by developed world approaches.

Extensive discussion about the 'costs' of maintaining older people is not matched by a parallel discussion about the costs of raising young children. A recent study from the UK estimated that the cost of parenting a single child through into adulthood is around £180,000 (Bennett, 2006). This does not include costs met by the state, such as the provision of free education and healthcare. In economic terms, spending on children might be viewed as investing in long-term human capital, leading to future economic dividends. Nevertheless, the contrast between societies' apparent willingness to meet these childcare costs and public alarm about the 'economic burden' of older people suggests a fundamental bias in priorities towards the needs and rights of different age groups.

Other economic effects of population ageing

Population ageing may influence economic performance in a range of other ways, such as through changes to patterns of savings and consumption. Traditional views suggested that population ageing would reduce savings rates, due to lifecourse effects. This assumes that people save during their working years in order to draw on these funds in later life. In this case, a growing older population will reduce the ratio of savers to non-savers and thus reduce the overall level of savings in an economy. This will restrict the supply of funds available for investment in productive activities and therefore hinder economic growth (OECD, 1998). There are, however, a number of problems with this claim. It is based on assumptions about age and savings that may be just as questionable as those made by dependency ratios about age and economic activity. Some micro-economic research has challenged this finding, observing that older people continue to save, albeit at a lower rate than previously (Disney, 1996). One incentive for later life saving may be to sustain the size of future bequests, so that younger family members have a greater incentive to provide support and keep in contact. On a more altruistic note, older people may place a high value on ensuring that they have wealth to pass on to younger relatives. The overall impact of population ageing on savings rates also depends on how the prospect of surviving to a long old age affects decisions to save earlier in life. Some studies have suggested that this prospect may boost overall savings and asset accumulation, particularly if people do not expect to receive economic support from families or from government transfers when they reach old age (Mason and Lee, 2006).[7] In many developing countries, saving rates are low, partly due to the weaknesses of banking systems and capital markets, and so the likelihood that population ageing will have a large, independent impact on national savings is questionable. The effects of other factors, such as appropriate macro-economic policies and institutional stability, are potentially more significant than population change.

Population ageing will influence patterns and, possibly, overall levels of consumption and this may also be important for economic performance. For example, between 2003 and 2005 a consumption boom among older people in Japan was a key factor in mitigating that country's economic recession. This boom was partly driven by the introduction of substantial inheritance taxes, which reduced the incentive to save for bequests after death. Current cohorts of older people in Japan have been able to accumulate substantial wealth through their lives, thanks to the country's exceptional economic boom of the 1950s to 1990s. In countries without a long period of economic growth, the spending power of current and future cohorts of older people will be less obvious. For countries suffering from an indifferent economic performance and widespread poverty, the prospects of any old-age consumption dividend are remote. The impact of population ageing on patterns of consumption is a different matter. This should be seen as a major economic opportunity for those countries and businesses that are most successful at adapting to this market shift. Even poor developing countries may benefit from this: the growing demand for workers in social care is largely being filled by international migrants.

Population ageing, politics and development

As we saw at the start of this chapter, development encompasses a complex, multifaceted set of processes and should not just be reduced to economic performance. Population ageing will have a much wider range of social, political and even cultural impacts, and these will vary across and within countries. The available evidence on likely effects is negligible, however. All countries, especially those in the developing world, are experiencing accelerating and highly complex processes of social and cultural change, associated with globalisation and other aspects of development. It would be very difficult to identify a specific set of ageing effects from this wider context of transformation. For example, declining average household sizes may partly result from growing numbers of widowed older people. Yet they are also a reflection of fertility transition, rising divorce rates, shifting social preferences and many other effects. As such, it is very hard to predict quite how population ageing will contribute to this complex mix of changes.

As older people account for a larger proportion of populations, it is to be expected that they will wield greater political influence over time. This may, in turn, have important economic and social effects. For example, it may increase political pressure for investing public resources in areas of particular benefit for older people, such as pensions or care services. Some authors have predicted that population ageing may therefore promote intergenerational resource conflict and competition for resources and public goods (Binstock and Day, 1995). In countries where ageing is already advanced, there are claims that this has already occurred: 'In Japan, the needs of older voters are given priority over the needs of younger voters. As a partial consequence of this, the financial burden on Japan's young people is the heaviest in the world' (Dugger, 2003: no page number).

Table 1.10 provides a rough indication of the proportion of potential voters made up by older people in a range of countries. Since children are not entitled to vote, older people inevitably account for a higher share of potential voters than of the total population. In developed countries such as the UK and Japan, those over the age of 60 already account for a quarter or more of the potential electorate, and their importance as voters has not been lost on politicians. In low–income countries there is often a large discrepancy between older people's share of total population and of potential voters. This is because large proportions of these countries' populations are still in age groups that are too young to vote. Consequently, in countries like Nigeria and Ghana, people over the age of 60 already account for more than 10% of potential voters. The significance of older voters in such countries is not widely recognised and, in a context of democratic deepening, could have important implications for the political acceptability of development policies there.

It might be expected that poor health and disability would reduce voting rates among older groups. However, research from developed countries shows that older people were consistently more interested in politics and more likely to vote than younger ones (Naegele, 1999; Binstock, 1997). Comparative research across Western Europe found that around 93% of people aged 60 to 96 used their votes in general elections, compared with 87% of the population as a whole (International IDEA, 2002). It is unclear whether this is due to a cohort effect (that is, current older people are part of a generation who tend to vote) or a lifecourse effect (that is, all people become more likely to vote as they grow older). Whichever is the case, new technologies, such as postal voting, will increase the propensity of older people to vote. Data on voting patterns by age are not widely available for most developing countries. One key issue here is that older people often experience higher levels of illiteracy than other age groups, which may impede their political participation.[8]

Table 1.10: Population aged 60 or over as a percentage of the potential voting population, selected countries, 2000 and 2020

	% of total population aged 60+ in 2000	% of voting population aged 60+ in 2000**	% of total population aged 60+ in 2020***	% of voting population aged 60+ in 2020**
Brazil	7.8	12.8	13.1	19.0
China*	10.1	15.0	16.7	22.3
Ghana	5.1	10.8	6.7	12.0
Japan	23.2	29.2	33.7	40.8
India	7.6	13.5	11.0	16.5
Indonesia	7.6	12.9	11.2	16.4
Nigeria	4.8	10.9	5.4	10.9
Russian Federation	18.5	25.0	23.6	28.9
UK	20.6	27.5	26.7	33.5
US	16.1	22.6	22.8	30.3

Notes: * Excluding Hong Kong and Macao.
** Calculated as population aged 60+ as a % of total population aged 20+.
*** Medium variant projection.
Source: United Nations Population Division (2001)

High rates of voting among older people have been contrasted with relative low turnout among younger age groups, especially youth. In some cases, this has raised fears that older voters' interests will be given preferential treatment. During Korea's 2004 presidential election, a leading politician was forced to resign for suggesting that older people might prefer to stay at home on election day, so that younger age groups would be encouraged to come forward (*BBC News Online*, 12 April 2004). Where the politics of ageing are framed in terms of a zero-sum intergenerational conflict, such concerns are more likely to emerge.

Do older people vote in a self-interested way and do they act as a unified political force? The evidence for this is limited and inconclusive. Research from Ukraine found that older people were more likely to vote for pro-communist parties and were more likely to be in a favour of a return to socialism (Bezrukov and Foigt, 2004). Presumably, this was because past regimes were associated with more generous pensions and other social policies of benefit to older people. By contrast, during France's 2007 presidential election, older voters were much more likely to support a right-wing welfare-reforming candidate, while the pro-welfare socialist party was strongly favoured by youth. This suggests that the behaviour of older voters is not entirely predictable and it is essential to examine varying patterns within the older population. Research from the US shows that, in terms of political attitudes and behaviour, there tends to be more difference within age groups than between them (Binstock and Day, 1995).

It should not be assumed that voting directly translates into political influence, especially when institutional governance and democratic structures are weak. There is widespread evidence that the priority of older people's concerns has risen for most political parties in most developed countries. The impact in developing countries has not been systematically researched, but it is not inevitable that it will mirror the West. To take just one example, where pension coverage is less complete, there are likely to be major divisions of interest between old-age pensioners (who are primarily concerned with improving benefit values) and other older people (who will have little interest in pensions).

Beyond voting, older people can exert political influence through the activities of pressure groups and other civil society organisations. Most developed countries contain a wide range of groups with a specific focus on older people. For example, in the US the American Association of Retired People (AARP) had 36 million members by 2003. Given its size and resources, the AARP has become a formidable political actor. Similar organisations have begun to emerge in some middle-income developing countries, albeit on a much more limited scale.[9] Pensioner protest groups have become increasingly vocal and organised, especially in Latin America and formerly socialist countries (Mesa-Lago and Muller, 2002). Separately, a number of grassroots initiatives, often sponsored by organisations affiliated to HelpAge International, have focused on the situation of poor older people, regardless of their pension status. These include a network of Older Citizen's Monitoring initiatives in which older people are trained and encouraged to hold local service providers to account. These activities can have an important impact on policy makers, but the great majority of older people in low-income countries are not yet involved in them. As such, their influence is often smaller than that of relatively affluent pensioner pressure groups, whose membership tends to be literate and have lifelong experiences of political activism.

Conclusions

The first part of this chapter located population ageing within a wider context of demographic change, and, to some extent, linked demographic change to experiences of development. Globally, population ageing was quite slow before the end of the 20th century, but there will be a sharp acceleration over the next few decades. National experiences have been diverse: for some countries population ageing is well established; for others, there is little prospect of it occurring in the foreseeable future. However, high levels of total population growth in countries like Ethiopia and Kenya mean that, in absolute terms, they will see large increases in their older populations. The main direct driver of population ageing is a decline in fertility rates. These, in turn, are influenced by a large range of factors, linked to countries' wider experiences of development. Complex causality means that fertility trends are not easily predicted, and not all countries have followed the patterns predicted by the demographic transition model. Comparing the demographic experiences of countries such as Japan, China, Kenya and Ukraine provides essential background for understanding the nature and potential consequences of population ageing in each country.

The second part of the chapter explored some of the potential ways in which population ageing may influence a country's economic performance. These include changing patterns of workforce participation, relationships between age and productivity and pressures on expenditure specifically related to later life. In each of these areas, we have seen that the evidence is not always as clear as is sometimes claimed, and that effects are complex and influenced by a wide range of other factors. Two key issues are policy choices for organising welfare services for older people and the extent to which older people are able to enjoy continued active and healthy lifestyles. The next three chapters will look at these issues in greater detail. The present chapter also considered the wider developmental consequences of population ageing, such as changing political dynamics. Again, we found that the evidence for any effects is quite limited and inconclusive.

Taken as a whole, this chapter shows that although population ageing is an inevitable global phenomenon, its consequences are not. Gradually, initial alarm has given way to more considered analysis and some developed countries have come to recognise that population ageing is not an impending crisis. Instead, it creates manageable challenges and even potential economic opportunities for exploiting new markets associated with later life. A recent official review from the United Kingdom concludes that: 'The extent of potential interaction between demographic structure and the economy is vast....We conclude that population ageing does not pose a threat to the continued prosperity of the United Kingdom economy' (UK House of Lords Select Committee on Economic Affairs, 2003: 14-15).

If we look beyond developed countries or at aspects of development that lie outside economic performance, then all we can safely conclude is that population ageing will have significant impacts on many aspects of development, but they are difficult to predict and cannot be considered in isolation from many other processes of change and uncertainty. These are issues that urgently need more research.

Notes

[1] A separate, albeit seldom-used, definition is that population ageing involves an increase in the median age of a population.

[2] The precise definition of the TFR is the average number of children a hypothetical cohort of women would have at the end of their reproductive period if they were subject during their whole lives to the fertility rates of a given period and if they were not subject to mortality. It is expressed as children per woman (United Nations Population Division, 2008).

[3] In some countries, fears about the potential impacts of population ageing have led to calls for more pro-natalist policies to boost fertility rates (see Longman, 2004). Where implemented, such policies have rarely had a sustainable impact on long-run fertility trends. For example, since 2006, the Russian government has introduced substantial child benefit programmes, but these are thought to be having little effect. Some commentators suggest that countries may fall into a low fertility trap, whereby the shrinking proportion of women having children raises the opportunity costs (such as lost career opportunities) for those women who do (Lutz et al, 2006).

[4] In some developing countries, this effect has partly been offset by higher levels of infant mortality among girls, as well as maternal mortality, so that older populations are not disproportionately female.

[5] Economic activity is usually understood as participation in salaried work, excluding unsalaried labour such as housework.

[6] In rural areas where AIDS mortality is high, the limited physical capacity of surviving age groups may lead to a collapse in farming systems and the risk of 'new variant famine' (Barnett and Whiteside, 2002).

[7] The direct policy implication might therefore be to discourage family and government transfers to older people, so that younger age groups realise that they need to save for their future welfare. The wider consequences of such policies would be highly undesirable, especially in the short run.

[8] The limited available data can be accessed at www.idea.int/vt/by-age.cfm

[9] A good database on political activity by older people in developing countries can be found at Global Action on Aging (www.globalaging.org/index. htm).

TWO

Experiencing later life in contexts of development

Introduction

Chapter One looked at population ageing as an intrinsic part of development and considered how it will influence future development experiences. This chapter examines how changes associated with development affect the lives of older people. These relationships are complex and diverse, since patterns of development are variable and older people are a heterogeneous group. Chapter One showed that countries do not all follow the same pathways of development and modernisation. For example, patterns of fertility transition have been highly variable. At the same time, people will not all be affected by the same changes in the same ways. For example, the benefits of economic growth are not evenly distributed, so that people from different socioeconomic strata fare quite differently. Similarly, if women remain excluded from paid employment, they may see fewer benefits from economic development through their lives. This means that it is dangerous to generalise about the impacts of development on older people and any claims must be based on firm evidence.

This chapter begins by reviewing general assertions about the effects of development on older people. These claims pay particular attention to harmful consequences and say less about the potential benefits that development may bring. The rest of the chapter is devoted to reviewing the evidence for these claims, which begins by establishing clear terms of reference for the analysis, by reviewing the concepts of old age and later life. As part of this, the chapter contrasts simple life-stage models of old age with more sophisticated approaches based on lifecourse, cohort and generation. It then focuses on two key sets of issues. First, it explores the effects of development on poverty and wellbeing in later life; then, it focuses on how later life is experienced differently by men and women.

Throughout the chapter particular attention is paid to whether development encourages positive and active experiences of old age, or whether it promotes deprivation and dependency. This has a major bearing on the consequences of population ageing for development. If a large proportion of an older population is able to lead relatively healthy, active and independent lives, then the challenges created by population ageing should be manageable. In this scenario, older people are more likely to have a good quality of life, which should be an important end in itself, regardless of the wider development implications.

Development, modernisation and experiences of later life

Most discussion about the effects of development on older people is heavily generalised and tends towards a negative and gloomy set of predictions. For example, some historians argue that older people had privileged levels of power and status in past centuries and in less modern societies, but that this has since been undermined (Fischer, 1977). Back in the early 1950s, one anthropological study of rural Mexico observed that: 'It appears to be the consensus that less and less respect for older people is being shown ... there are more sources of conflict between older and younger generations because of recent social and economic changes' (Lewis, 1951: 411–12).

As well as social and economic changes, some commentators have suggested that the globalisation of western culture (with its supposed emphasis on youth and individualism) has weakened traditional cultural values of respect for older people. In marking Nigeria's International Day of Senior Citizens in 2007, the President of the National Union of Pensioners stated: 'Western urbanization and modernization have led to the breakdown of traditional social order, and even undermined the traditional mechanism in support and protection of the elderly. Monetization of the society has also made the elderly lose their former enviable position' (*Daily Trust*, 2007).

These general views about the harmful effects of development on older people are linked to more specific sets of claims made by Donald Cowgill (1976) in his seminal work on older people and modernisation. His study identifies a number of ways in which modernisation can lead to disadvantage in later life:

- First, increased technological sophistication and changeability of labour processes reduce the relevance of older people's skill sets.
- Second, the separation of workplace from home, resulting from urbanisation and industrialisation, increases older people's social isolation.

- Third, as the relative size of older populations grows, there will be intensified competition for resources between them and other age groups.

Despite being over 30 years old, Cowgill's generalisations remain the point of departure for many studies on development and experiences of later life (El Ghannan, 2001; Aboderin, 2004). More recent studies have added a further dimension to this negative scenario, with reference to the vulnerability of older people due to increases in violence, crime and insecurity (Daichman, 2005).

The evidence to support these generalised, negative claims is not always strong, however. For example, considered historical research rejects the view that the past was a 'Golden Age' for older people (Kertzer and Laslett, 1995; Johnson, 2004). Instead, they provide a more complex and nuanced picture, revealing that for many people, old age was brief and unpleasant. For example, there is evidence that older people (especially women) were sometimes exposed to social violence, mistreatment and abuse (Brogden and Nijhar, 2000). Despite this, claims that younger generations now pay older people less respect than in the past are strongly supported by the testimonies of older people across a wide range of countries (Jamuna, 2003; van der Geest, 2004a). While the weight of this evidence cannot be dismissed, personal testimonies are highly subjective, and there is evidence that older people have been making similar observations for centuries (Johnson, 2004). In some countries, such as Thailand, respect for elders appears to have endured, despite rapid development (Knodel et al, 2007). As such, it would be dangerous to assume that development *inevitably* harms older people's social standing.

Considerably less is said about the potential *benefits* of development for older people, although they can be very significant. For example, in most countries development has been associated with the establishment of extensive welfare systems and these pay particular attention to the needs of groups such as older people. Without economic growth, large-scale pension programmes would not be affordable and nor would a range of healthcare services that boost the quality and quantity of life in old age. While the operation of these welfare programmes leaves a lot to be desired, and the needs of many older people remain neglected (see Chapters Three and Four), large numbers are now much richer, better educated and healthier than in the past. These tangible material benefits should go some way to compensate for any negative social and cultural impacts of modernisation. By contrast, for poorer groups (who often have less access to welfare programmes) and in poorer countries (where these services are less developed), older people may be exposed to both social and economic upheaval, as well as continued material deprivation. In these cases, the quality of later life may be little better, or even worse, than in the past.

Both positive and negative generalisations about the consequences of development for different groups of people are fraught with danger. Since there is tremendous diversity within older populations, any changes associated with development create both winners and losers: from the freedom, privileges and second adolescence of Third Age 'silver-surfers', to the continued life of toil faced by some older people in poor countries, to more marginal, isolated and dependent lifestyles. To go beyond generalisations, to review the available evidence and to map out the complexity of development impacts, we need a clear understanding of old age as a concept. We also need to identify helpful indicators of quality of life and wellbeing, for making comparisons over time and between places.

Later life as a simple life stage? Problems with the '60 plus' approach

The simplest and arguably least helpful approach to understanding old age is as a separate life stage, which follows on from childhood and adulthood. This approach is based on a number of assumptions:

• that all people in this life stage share common characteristics and experiences;
• that these characteristics and experiences are clearly differentiated from other life stages;
• that it is possible to identify clear thresholds between later life and the stages that precede it.

All of these assumptions are highly questionable, contributing to misunderstandings about old age and potentially encouraging inappropriate policies. In particular, identifying clear thresholds between mid-life and old age is extremely problematic. Most academics recognise that the concept of old age is subjective and complex, and so it eludes simple and universally valid definitions (Degnen, 2006). Despite this, policy makers and analysts usually apply simple age-based markers of old age (most commonly people aged 60 or 65 and over). Within older populations, distinctions are sometimes made between the 'young old' (those aged in their sixties) and the 'very old' (those aged 80 or over). Nevertheless, it is often assumed that later life can be taken as a single, simple life-stage category for the purposes of analysis and policy. Dependency ratios (see Chapter One) are a clear example of this, assuming that all 60-year-olds are dependent, while all those aged 59 are economically productive. Similarly, most reports and documents on older people produced by the United Nations and other international agencies restrict their analyses to populations aged 60 and over. For example, the United Nations Population Division's (2005) report *Living arrangements of older persons around the world* (UN Population Division, 2005) makes a number of important statements about the situation of 'older people'. People aged 59 years and 11 months are entirely excluded from its analysis, with 60 years used as an absolute global marker of later life, be it for Burkina Faso or Belgium.

This simple life-stage approach is seen in most aspects of public policy for older people, with entitlements linked to particular age categories. It is especially apparent in pension policies; other common examples include entitlements to free government health services or cheap public transport. In some developed countries, these entitlements and perceptions of old age have become so interlinked that the term 'pensioner' is popularly seen as synonymous for 'older person'. Several countries are now considering increases in standard retirement ages due to rising longevity and pressures on pension funds. This begs the interesting question as to whether 'old age' lasts longer than it did in the past, or whether it starts at a later age. In most low- and middle-income countries, significant numbers of older people do not receive pensions and so the link between pensioner status and later life is less apparent. In these cases, identifying meaningful thresholds between mid-life and old age is particularly difficult.

The use of a single age-based definition of later life across diverse settings is highly problematic. Table 2.1 provides data for Japan, Brazil and Senegal – three countries facing different developmental, demographic and epidemiological scenarios. It shows that 'older women' account for over a quarter of Japan's population; substantially more than in Brazil and Senegal. Yet being aged 60 or over means

Table 2.1: Indicators of ageing of the female population, selected countries

	Japan	Brazil	Senegal
Women aged 60+ (% total female population) (2000)	25.7	8.6	4.6
Female life expectancy at age 60 (years) (2002)	27.0	19.8	14.4
Estimated female healthy life expectancy at age 60 (years) (2002)	21.7	13.7	10.7

Source: Calculated from United Nations Population Division (2002) and WHO (2004a)

different things in different countries. Women aged 60 in Japan can expect to live for more than twice as long as their counterparts in Senegal and to enjoy more than twice as many years in good health. This suggests that it may be more helpful to define old age in terms of expected remaining life expectancy, rather than the number of years a person has already lived.[1] If this were set at 25 years, Brazilian women would be categorised as 'old' when they are 56, compared with 63 in Japan. If we take 15 years of life expectancy, Brazilian women would be 'old' at the age of 70, compared with 75 in Japan.[2] The differences between Japan and poorer countries like Senegal (where life-table data are unavailable) would be much larger. Variations may also occur within countries. For example, data for the state of Arizona in the US showed that the average age of death for American Indians was 20 years younger than for white non-Hispanics (Arizona Department of Health Services, 2001). Where pension entitlements and other social policies are linked to age, these variations in survival rates can lead to further discrimination against already disadvantaged groups.

Clinical research also questions the validity of simple life-stage models of old age. It is accepted that biological ageing, involving progressive declines of all the body's physiological functions, usually sets in around the age of 30 (Woodrow, 2002a; Eyetsemitan and Gire, 2003). The links between the rate of physiological decline and chronological age are not straightforward, and there is no evidence that reaching a certain age marker (say 60 years old) is followed by an abrupt acceleration of decline. The rate of many aspects of decline is influenced by a wide range of factors dissociated with age, such as diet, smoking and lifestyle. Thus, even though a person aged 60 will have experienced physiological decline for around five years longer than a person aged 55, it does not necessarily follow that their general condition will be proportionately worse.

Similarly, sociological and anthropological research challenges assumptions about simple links between chronological age and social roles or status. For example, a study from the UK found that around a third of grandparents were aged under 60 and that the majority of these were still working (Clarke and Roberts, 2004). My own research with older women in a deprived neighbourhood of Buenos Aires found that most had already become grandparents in their mid-forties and that this was not directly associated with local definitions of old age. Research from rural Ghana found that key markers of later life were not age related. Instead, they reflected a person's ability to continue working and their household or community status (Ahenkora, 1999). Anthropologists have demonstrated the complexity of understandings of old age and how they vary across and between societies and cultures (Cohen, 1998; Degnen, 2006). For example, old age may be defined and understood very differently by different age groups, with children emphasising aspects of physical appearance and older people themselves paying more attention to ability to perform daily tasks (Kelley, 2005). At the same time, notions of old age can interact with other identities such as ethnicity or gender (Armstrong, 2003). Overall, these studies emphasise the multidimensionality of transitions into what is understood (often in different ways by members of the same societies) as later life. As such, there is little scope for replacing age-based thresholds of later life with some other simple indicator based on perceptions, social role or status.

Another weakness of the life-stage approach is its assumption that all experiences of old age have key things in common. Instead, it is important to recognise the diversity of later life, and that these variations operate in a number of ways. First, they occur through the life of a single person as they grow older. 'Old age' may span 40 or more years of a person's life and so individual circumstances are likely to change significantly between the start of a person's later life and their eventual death. Second, experiences of old age intersect with a range of other identities and statuses, including wealth, gender and ethnicity. For example, a woman aged 65 may have more in common with a 55-year-old woman than with a 65-year-old man. This diversity in later life and the lack of clear distinctions between old age and previous life stages may mean that old age is sometimes an unhelpful or even misleading policy category (we return to this issue with reference to India in Chapter Eight).

At the same time, there are grounds for arguing that old age is in some ways a socially constructed phenomenon, rather than one based on inherent personal attributes (Katz, 1996). For example, obliging someone to retire and take up an old-age pension on their 60th birthday is essentially a socially sanctioned, bureaucratic decision. It is unlikely that this person's capacity to work will have significantly altered overnight to match their new identity and economic status. Nevertheless, fixed compulsory retirement ages may profoundly shape a person's own self-image, making them feel distinctly older from one day to the next. They also may entrench social attitudes that associate old age with dependency and economic withdrawal (Walker, 1990). The adoption of 60 years as a benchmark for later life by the United Nations and other development agencies justifies and reinforces these artificial and arbitrary distinctions.

There is clear evidence, then, that none of the three assumptions underlying simple life-stage models of old age are valid or helpful. Despite this, these models are still widely applied in academic research and policy making, and they continue to shape popular perceptions of later life. There are several reasons for this. First, the life-stage model is attractively simple: it presents a neat, linear view of ageing that is similar to simple, linear (and equally misleading) views of development. Second, the model facilitates analysis and data collection, and simplifies policy making. In fact, much of the analysis and data presented in this book are by necessity based on a simple '60 plus' definition of old age. When doing this, it is important to be aware of the potential distortions and misconceptions that may result. Where possible, research on later life should take a more flexible approach, recognising the blurring of age boundaries and leaving some room for local interpretations and perceptions. There is also scope for applying more complex analytical frameworks, which are outlined in the next section.

More sophisticated approaches: lifecourse, cohort and generation

Lifecourse frameworks represent an important alternative to simple life-stage models of old age. Rather than viewing later life as a distinct phase that is separate from previous life stages, these frameworks look at lives more holistically. This provides a number of helpful insights. First, it reveals how events and experiences in early life can have lasting effects that often continue through into old age. One obvious case is access to education during childhood, which influences employment opportunities during adulthood, which in turn influence economic wellbeing in later life. A growing body of quantitative and qualitative studies shows the many and complex ways in which these lifecourse effects can occur (Gunnarsson, 2002; Smith and Joshi, 2002; Hagestad, 2003). In particular, clinical research has demonstrated significant links between early life experiences and health risks in old age (see Chapter Four). As part of this, lifecourse frameworks see individual ageing as an ongoing lifelong process, including periods of relative stability and specific moments of critical change. These points of change are not always predictable and vary across individual lives, rather than at age 18 or 60 as implied in life-stage models.

Lifecourse frameworks offer valuable insights into how social and economic development can influence older people's lives (Elder Jr, 1998; Heinz and Krüger, 2001). These include four guiding principles:

- Individual lifecourses are embedded in the historical times and places people experience over their lifetimes (context).
- The impact of a succession of life transitions or events depends on when they occur in an individual's life (timing).
- Lives are lived interdependently, with historical and social influences expressed through networks of shared relationships (linked lives).
- Individuals construct their own lifecourses through the choices and actions they take within the opportunities and constraints of history and social circumstances (agency).[3]

We will now explore the meaning of these principles with reference to a single country case study. Table 2.2 provides some data relating to the lifecourse experiences of two sets of birth cohorts (people born in the same year) for Chile: people born in 1940 and people born in 1960. The data provide some indications about the different opportunities faced by each cohort. For the 1940 cohort, the chances of surviving infancy were significantly lower than for the 1960 cohort. Although most of the 1940 cohort could expect to attend primary school, only around a quarter could expect to spend significant time in secondary education. The chances of attending secondary school were much higher for the 1960 cohort. By the time people in the 1940 cohort reached an age where they might begin to have children (assumed here

Table 2.2: Factors influencing lifecourse experiences of two birth cohorts in Chile

	Born 1940		Born 1960	
Infant mortality rate per 1,000 live births (annual average)	1940–41	193	1960–61	120
Primary school enrolment rate (% of children aged 5–10)	1945–50	95	1965–70	98
Secondary school enrolment (% of children aged 11–16)	1950–60	23	1970–80	60
Total fertility rate at start of reproductive period (age 15–20)	1955–60	5.5	1975–80	2.7
Female labour market participation rate at start of working life (age 20)	1960	21	1980	27
Age at time of 1982 economic crisis	1982	42	1982	22
People aged 60-64 with a pension (%)	2000	59	2020	No data

Sources: United Nations Population Division (2001); Montenegro and Pagés (2003); Olivarria-Gambi (2003); Rofman and Lucchetti (2006)

to be 15 to 20 years old), TFRs were 5.5 births per woman, compared with only 2.7 for the 1960 cohort. This meant that men and women in the 1940 cohort were likely to have significantly larger numbers of children through their lives than those in the 1960 cohort.

Taken together, these comparisons indicate that people born in 1960 enjoyed many advantages compared with those born 20 years previously, and were better placed to have materially successful lives. However, labour market trends reveal a more mixed picture. A gradual increase in female participation in paid labour meant that women in the 1960 cohort were more likely to be in work, which may have benefited them through their lives. Nevertheless, men and women in this cohort had fewer job opportunities early in their lives, including a major recession in 1982, when unemployment reached 23%. This may have prevented them from obtaining stable work, despite their good education. For those in the 1940 cohort, the early working years saw relatively low unemployment, with rates of only 8% in 1960. Instead, the 1982 economic crisis would have hit this older cohort when they were already middle-aged. Finally, Table 2.2 provides data on old-age pension coverage, although the younger group has yet to reach this age. This analysis provides a simplistic and stylised comparison of life chances between groups born at two different times. First, it draws on aggregate data, which do not reflect variations across the same birth cohorts. For example, people born into poor, rural families in the 1960 cohort may have had less access to education than members of the 1940 cohort who were born to rich, urban families. Second, it only identifies a few of the many potential factors that may have affected the life opportunities of each birth cohort. Despite these limits, the cohort comparison reveals some important insights for thinking about development and older people. First, it shows how early life experiences such as education or fertility may affect later life. For example, infant mortality rates are closely linked to nutrition and general health status in early life, and these may influence individual health all the way through to old age (Harper and Marcus, 2003). As such, general improvements in health and education in Chile during the 1940s and 1950s will have important implications for current generations of older people. This demonstrates the first key lifecourse principle: *individual lifecourses are embedded in the historical times and places people experience over their lifetimes* (**context**).

Table 2.2 also reveals that the impact of important events depends on when they occur in an individual life trajectory. The example given here is Chile's sharp economic recession of 1982. The effects of this crisis on people in mid-life with established careers and families were likely to have been different compared with people who had recently left school. This illustrates the second key lifecourse principle: *the impact of a succession of life transitions or events depends on when they occur in an individual's life* **(timing)**. Key events do not just refer to economic phenomena, but might include natural disasters or sudden political change. Life transitions may also refer to a wide range of experiences such as parenthood, grandparenthood, the onset of chronic illness or unemployment. For example, becoming a grandmother at age 40 will probably have different consequences than at age 70.

Declining fertility rates between 1955 and 2000 meant that Chileans in the 1960 birth cohort had on average fewer children than those in the 1940 cohort. The implications of this change for each group are complex and illustrate the third key lifecourse principle: *lives are lived interdependently, with historical and social influences expressed through networks of shared relationships* **(linked lives)**. Traditionally, it was assumed that having large numbers of children would initially represent a net drain on a parent's opportunities (due to the costs of raising and educating them), but would go on to create net benefits in later life (as children support their older parents) (Clay and van den Haar, 1993). This shows that it is important not to analyse lifecourses of isolated individuals, but to consider how their life trajectories are affected by the lives of other people around them. In more 'developed' societies the drawbacks of fewer children in later life may theoretically be reduced through the creation of embracing old-age pension schemes. At the same time, women may benefit if lower lifetime fertility leads to increased employment opportunities, enabling them to strengthen their economic position in later life. The assumptions underlying these generalised views about lifecourse dynamics are revisited in Chapter Five, which looks at social relations in later life.

In our simple cohort comparison, some of the 1960 birth cohort will have parents from the 1940 cohort. In some cases, they may still live together in the same household at the time of the 1982 crisis and may function as a single economic unit (pooling their income and consumption). In these cases, the impacts of the crisis will be shared across both generations living in the same household. How individual household members are affected will depend on how intergenerational relations play out in the household. For example, if the older generation attaches a greater value on the wellbeing of their children than these children do on them, then the 1960 cohort may be allocated a larger share of household wealth. In this case, they will be less affected by the crisis than their parents are. This scenario demonstrates how factors such as timing, linked lives and intergenerational dynamics can interact in complex ways to influence wellbeing outcomes.

Of course, it is not possible to predict the lifecourses of individuals from the information given in Table 2.2. As already pointed out, these data are too simple and limited to capture the diversity of circumstances facing different groups within the same birth cohort. Another reason is that people usually have at least some element of control over the directions their lives take, despite wider 'structural' factors. For example, a woman born in 1940, with little education and having large numbers of children, may still have been able to earn and save during her adult life and reach old age in a strong economic condition. Rather than assume that individual lives are entirely governed by the wider structures they inhabit, we must not lose sight of people's capacity to act independently. This relates to the final key lifecourse principle: *individuals construct their own lifecourses through the choices and actions they take within the opportunities and constraints of history and social circumstances* **(agency)**. The relationships between personal agency and wider structural or environmental factors are especially important for understanding later life. There is a tendency to assume that most older people exert little if any personal agency, but rather play a passive, dependent role in their own lives as well as in those of others. These negative views of later life have increasingly been challenged by NGOs and other organisations, which seek to project a more positive view of 'active ageing' (HelpAge International, 1999; WHO, 2002a).

Every country's experience of development is unique in terms of timing and specific aspects of change. Nevertheless, the Chilean experience described here shares some common features with many other countries. These include:

- *A gradual extension of formal education.* The consequences of this change for older people depend on the timing of this extension. If it occurred before the 1950s, then older people will have benefited directly. If it occurred later, older people may have been too old to benefit personally, but may still benefit indirectly through their children's improved education. This second scenario assumes that children share some of their own 'educational dividend' with their parents, although this may not be the case. The benefits of education also depend on the extent to which increased schooling can be converted into improved access to employment and other life chances. In many developing countries, older people may have children who are better educated than they are but who have less access to paid employment than previous cohorts did.
- *A decline in fertility rates.* As discussed above, this will have different effects at different points in the lifecourse. Whether declining

fertility is disadvantageous in later life will largely depend on intergenerational relations. Large numbers of surviving children are not in themselves a guarantee of income security and general care in old age (see Chapter Five).

• *Economic ups and downs – but long-term material progress.* All economies experience variations in growth rates, punctuated by crises and recessions. How the timing of these events intersects with individual life trajectories (and those of other family members) will have large effects on life chances that may continue into later life. At the same time, most countries have seen general long-run improvements in material welfare, even though these improvements may not have been evenly distributed. Among other things, this may provide the resources for extended pension provision.

Other common experiences of development and change include urbanisation, changing patterns of employment, the diffusion of new technologies (including health interventions) and more subtle shifts in attitudes and cultural values. Taking all of these together, the task of predicting their impact on different cohorts of older people is very challenging indeed.

To summarise, lifecourse frameworks offer a more sophisticated alternative for understanding old age, and provide valuable insights into how experiences of development may affect the lives of different cohorts of older people. They reveal how experiences in earlier life can have lasting effects through into old age, and how personal life trajectories intersect with wider events and processes of change. Using lifecourse frameworks also throws some light on linked lives and intergenerational relationships. As such, it is essential to locate individual ageing experiences within household and family dynamics. For example, the serious illness or loss of job for a child may have as much economic impact on an older person as their personal access to a pension. At the same time, personal agency reduces the predictability of life trajectories, as individuals seek their own pathways through the opportunities and constraints presented to them. Finally, lifecourse analysis reveals that experiences of old age do not just vary through individual lives and across specific groupings (such as by gender or socioeconomic status): they also vary between different birth cohorts. This means that the situation of current cohorts of older people will be markedly different from those in the future.

Economic performance and income in later life

The previous sections have demonstrated the dangers of making broad generalisations about development and older people, and the need for analysis to go beyond simplistic concepts. The remainder of the chapter seeks to set out a more systematic and nuanced assessment. We begin by focusing on how development affects economic status in later life, before turning to other aspects of wellbeing.

The capacity for development to improve the economic status of older people depends on overall rates of economic growth and the distribution of wealth across populations. There is strong evidence that the world as a whole has seen substantial long-run increases in material prosperity, with estimates that global wealth grew by over 2% annually between 1820 and 1998 (Maddison, 2001). To some extent, these gains were cancelled out by large increases in global population (see Chapter One). Also, there was considerable instability in economic performance over time and this has continued through to the present day. For example, between 1987 and 2002, global per capita wealth was roughly stable, but the following six years saw it grow by almost 60%. It is currently predicted that the world economy will contract by between 7 and 8% in 2009, as a result of the global crisis. The timing of these economic variations may have large effects on the life chances of different birth cohorts, as we have already seen with reference to Chile's 1982 recession.

At the same time, there have been sharp regional variations in economic performance and national wealth. Table 2.3 provides data for four countries chosen to represent this international diversity. The population of the UK was nearly twice as rich in 2000 as it was in 1980. Chile sees accelerating growth over time, as does China. Yet despite China's steep growth trajectory, it remains a long way behind Chile and the UK in terms of absolute wealth. Uganda presents a less positive scenario, with little change in per capita wealth, as continued population growth offsets any economic progress.

Table 2.3: Per capita GDP, selected countries, 1960 to 2000 (1990 US$)

	Chile	China	UK	Uganda
1960	4,300	500	8,600	700
1980	5,700	800	12,900	600
2000	10,300	2,600	20,400	800

Source: Groningen Growth and Development Centre (2009)

Each of these national scenarios will have varied implications for different age groups, birth cohorts and generations, and these effects are difficult to unravel. Data on income poverty are available for most countries and these are sometimes broken down for different age groups and time periods, which can give us some insights into older people's economic status.

Table 2.4 shows income poverty data for different age groups in Chile in 1990 and 2006 and indicates a positive experience for older people. In both years, older people experienced significantly lower rates of poverty than younger age groups. Also, there was a sharp fall in old-age poverty over time, so that more recent birth cohorts less likely to be poor than earlier cohorts. This may have been because people who reached old age in 1990 and 2006 had access to better lifetime economic opportunities than younger cohorts. It may also reflect Chile's welfare programmes for older people, which are relatively embracing and were upgraded between 1990 and 2006.

Table 2.4: Incidence of income poverty for different age groups in Chile, 1990 and 2006 (%)

	1990	2006
Under 18	51	21
18–29	36	11
30–44	38	14
45–59	27	9
60 and over	21	8

Source: MIDEPLAN (2006)

Table 2.4 suggests that older people in Chile have clearly benefited from development in terms of income levels. Nevertheless, this claim needs treating with caution, due to the limits of the available data. Most obviously, income poverty data tell us nothing about the non-poor or about how income is distributed across cohorts and age groups. As we have seen, older people are a highly diverse group and experience varied economic circumstances. Table 2.5 provides income distribution data for Chilean households whose average age was 60 or more, compared with those with an average age of 25 to 59. It compares the poorest 10% (decile one) with the richest 10% (decile ten) for each category. The figures reveal large variations in income distribution, which affect all age groups. For older households, the richest decile reported incomes of 75 times the poorest decile. General data on income distribution show that Chile is by no means an exceptional case, with significantly higher levels of inequality in countries like Brazil and South Africa.

Table 2.5: Per capita monthly income (pesos) by average age of household, Chile, 1996

	Average age 25 to 59	Average age 60 or more
Decile one	12,180	7,798
Decile ten	554,455	598,891

Source: Schatan (1998)

A second set of problems relates to how we interpret income poverty data. When comparing poverty in later life to other ages, it is difficult to separate out two effects:

- *Survival bias.* The relative prevalence of poverty in later life is influenced by variations in adult life expectancy between richer and poorer people. If richer people are more likely to reach and survive through old age, then poverty will be less widespread among the older population than for other age groups. Research from India, Indonesia and Vietnam has demonstrated this effect (Banerjee and Duflo, 2007). Where this is the case, it could be argued that equitable development policies should target groups currently less likely to reach old age, rather than older people themselves (Pal and Palacios, 2006).
- *Lifecourse effects.* People's experiences of wealth and poverty may vary through their lives. People who spend most of their lives out of poverty may fall into it when they become old, due to the loss of work earnings, the economic impact of health problems and other effects. Research across several developed countries has found that wealth declines as people move through old age (Disney and Whitehouse, 2003). Where these effects are strong (and not mitigated by interventions such as pensions and health insurance), we may expect higher levels of poverty among older people. In this case, there are strong arguments for promoting policies that target key forms of economic vulnerability associated with later life.

The problem is that all countries are influenced by both these effects, to a greater or lesser extent. Both are likely to be especially marked in poorer countries where large segments of the population may never reach old age and where pension schemes are limited. In such countries, among those who reach old age, some people are likely to have led economically privileged lives. Others may have experienced more difficult circumstances and their accumulated lifecourse disadvantages will leave them vulnerable to age-related impoverishment. Even if they only account for a small minority of the older population, this second group faces high levels of deprivation and requires particular attention from policy makers.

A further problem with income data is that living costs vary sharply over time and space, which can hinder comparisons. In a study of old age and poverty in Thailand, I found that average household incomes in selected villages were less than a quarter of those in selected urban slums. However, this disparity exaggerated the overall gap in deprivation, since the costs of food, housing and other key requirements were much higher in the city than in the countryside (Lloyd-Sherlock, 2006). Income data are usually provided for households, rather than individuals, but we should not assume that a household's wealth is always evenly distributed across its members. Many studies have shown that, even if older people live with other family members, they do not always share income (Palloni, 2001). For example, research from India has shown that older widows are systematically discriminated against in the allocation of household resources (Alter Chen, 1998). Studies from around the world show that women, young and old, tend to lose out in terms of household income (Chant, 2007). It is often claimed that older people share their pension income with other household members, only retaining a small part for their personal use (see Chapter Three). As such, income data must be interpreted with reference to a wider context of linked lives and intergenerational relationships.

Along with these general problems, there are a number of specific ways in which income data may systematically under-represent deprivation in old age. In particular, they assume that older people's basic consumption needs are identical to those of other age groups. This may be true for areas such as daily calorific requirements, but there is strong evidence that the opposite occurs in other areas, particularly health.[4] Older people are more likely to experience health problems than other age groups and are more likely to require medication. In many developing countries drugs are not provided for free, and so paying for life-saving medicine can be a major drain on financial resources. In these cases, there is a strong justification for assuming that basic consumption needs are higher for older people, and this could then be factored into age-specific income poverty measurements.[5]

Taken together, these various problems with income poverty data considerably limit their usefulness for assessing the actual economic status of older people. As such, the data for Chile presented in Table 2.4 should be interpreted with caution. Also, it should not be assumed that Chile's experience is representative of wider international trends. A comparative analysis of 30 developing countries found 18 cases where income poverty was less widespread among older people than for other age groups, and five cases where it was more common (Barrientos et al, 2003a). Predictably, a key factor behind these national variations was the extent and generosity of old-age pension programmes. In Mexico, where pensions are less well developed, older people experience significantly higher rates of poverty than other age groups (Scott, 2008). A relatively sophisticated study from India suggested that households containing older people were no more likely to be poor than households in general (Pal and Palacios, 2006).[6] Even here, there were significant variations between individual states, with some registering a positive correlation between old age and poverty. Taken together, these studies indicate that economic status in old age depends on a range of factors including:

- overall levels of national wealth and growth rates;
- the extent of welfare programmes, such as pension schemes;
- cohort variations in lifetime economic opportunities.

Development and wellbeing in later life

The previous section focused on income and poverty in later life. These are important indicators of wellbeing and have considerable influence over policy agendas. However, they exclude a number of other factors that can significantly influence wellbeing and quality of life, such as health status and social relationships. Table 2.1 shows that a 60-year-old woman in Japan can expect to have twice as many remaining years of good health as her equivalent in Senegal. At the same time, older women in Japan are significantly more likely to be living alone than is the case in Senegal. Chapters Four and Five provide more detailed analysis of how development can affect health and social relations in later life. A key issue is that these different factors should not be treated in isolation, since they interact to shape individual wellbeing.

Several years ago when I was researching older people living in Buenos Aires shanty towns, I befriended an older man who lived in a middle-class district of town. He received the basic state pension, so that his income was just above the official poverty line, yet this said little about his actual quality of life. He was very unwell, with limited mobility, had no contact with relatives and was largely a prisoner in his rented apartment, since the building's lift was out of service. I compared his condition to some of the 'poor' older people I met in the shanty towns, many of whom were in relatively good health, had active lives and enjoyed extensive contact with family and friends. Clearly income matters, but, perhaps especially at old age, it provides a very limited and potentially misleading perspective on what constitutes a 'good life'.

Beyond income data, there is a range of other methods for analysing and measuring wellbeing. Some take a holistic, subjective approach, drawing on participatory surveys, where the personal opinions of research subjects are taken into account (Chambers, 1995). A related theoretical development has been to conceptualise wellbeing in terms of 'capabilities', which refer to a person's freedom to do or be the things they value (Sen, 1999; Lloyd-Sherlock, 2002a). These can provide rich insights into different dimensions of wellbeing and how they are affected by wider changes or individual ageing. However, they cannot produce easily quantifiable, comparative data for systematic analysis. An overview of participatory surveys in developing countries found that older people associated poverty with (among other things) a lack of family and social support, an inability to fulfil economic and social roles, and poor health (Barrientos et al, 2003a).

Quality-of-life indicators provide another approach for analysing experiences of old age. These are usually based on composite scores taken from a range of questions older people are asked about their lives. Typically, questions are grouped into different areas (or domains) – economic wellbeing, health status, social relations, mental wellbeing and so forth (Bowling, 2005; Gough et al, 2006). This can provide a relatively complete view of older people's lives, as they see them themselves. Surveys of wellbeing and quality of life have been more widely applied in the developed world than in poorer countries. A recent study from the UK found that quality of life in old age was strongly influenced by a person's expectations, their sense of optimism about life, health status, social networks, community resources and sense of security. It added that: 'These factors contributed far more to perceived quality of life than indicators of material circumstances, such as actual level of income, education, home ownership or social class' (ESRC, 2007). This suggests that indicators focusing on income and poverty tell us very little about what makes older people contented or unhappy about their lives. It also indicates that remaining active and keeping a sense of personal autonomy in old age is essential for a good quality of life (Rowe and Kahn, 1998). In other words, enhancing personal agency is good for older people, as well as for society at large.

To what extent do these findings apply outside the UK, particularly in poorer countries? As ever, comparative data are largely absent, since no developing countries have conducted wellbeing research on a large scale. There may be good grounds for assuming that, in contexts of extreme, chronic poverty, income and access to basic services become much more important determinants of wellbeing. However, participatory surveys of older people in poor countries conclude that money is just one of many concerns, and that the capacity to live an active and dignified life is just as important as it is for richer parts of the world (Barrientos et al, 2003a).

To sum up, current knowledge about the relationship between poverty, wellbeing and later life in developing countries remains very sketchy. To the extent that development leads to the disruption of social networks, the weakening of community infrastructure and a decrease in trust and security, it is likely to reduce older people's quality of life. To the extent that development improves older people's health status, creates new opportunities and promotes their freedom to live as they choose, it will boost their quality of life.[7] The relative importance of these effects will vary geographically and across groups of older people, and our information about this is minimal. Data combining age and wellbeing are limited and do not permit the separation of survival bias from lifecourse effects. Most data refer to income poverty, an approach that has a number of flaws, and which may systematically understate real levels of hardship among older people. As with all aspects of later life, it is highly dangerous to generalise about patterns of poverty. The older populations of all developing countries will include a number of extremely wealthy and privileged individuals. They will also include a number who live in extreme poverty, either because they have been poor all their lives or because of age-related impoverishment. Rather than make generalisations, the key challenge is to identify those subgroups of the older population who suffer greatest deprivation. More sophisticated approaches exploring wellbeing and quality of life offer a better opportunity for understanding how development affects older people. However, these approaches are more complex and resource-intensive than income measurements, and this has greatly limited their application in developing countries.

Gender, diversity and later life

Already in this chapter we have seen that experiences of later life vary substantially within older populations. Old age cross-cuts with a range of personal attributes and identities, including race, class and religion. Particular attention has been paid to how old age is experienced differently by men and women, and this sometimes leads to a range of generalised claims (Ewing, 1999; UN-DESA, 2002):

- that older women outnumber older men;
- that older women are more likely to live alone;
- that older women are consistently economically disadvantaged, due to a lifetime of limited opportunities;
- that older widows are especially vulnerable to economic and social exclusion.

The evidence for the first of these two claims is fairly consistent across countries (see Chapters One and Five), although the predominance of older women is now falling in most developed countries. The main explanation for this imbalance is that women usually enjoy longer life expectancies than men, especially at older ages. Between 2000 and 2005, average female life expectancy at age 60 was 20.4 years, compared with only 17.0 for men (United Nations Population Division, 2002). Gaps of between two and four years are found across all world regions. Since most married women outlive their partners, they are more likely to live alone.

What about the claim that older women consistently face more disadvantage than older men? Table 2.6 provides comparisons across a range of indicators for Thailand in 2007. It reveals a number of important differences. First, older men were more than twice as likely as older women to have completed secondary education. Limited education and gender discrimination in the labour market appear to have restricted women's lifetime employment opportunities, and this had carried through into later life. As a result, older men were nearly twice as likely to receive work income. Pension entitlements are often linked to lifetime employment, which explains why older men were three times as likely to receive pensions as women were. This analysis demonstrates how disadvantages experienced through the lifecourse are

Table 2.6: Comparisons of older women and older men in Thailand, 2007

	Men aged 60 and over	Women aged 60 and over
Completed secondary education (%)	13.6	6.2
Live alone (%)	6.0	8.9
Receive income from work (%)	51.0	27.2
Receive income from pension (%)	8.5	2.9
Receive economic support from children (%)	79.5	85.3
Care for co-resident minor-aged grandchild whose parents have died (%)	3.2	8.5
Annual income below 1000 baht	13.9	19.1

Source: Adapted from Knodel and Chayovan (2008)

important in shaping circumstances in old age. Research in developed countries has found similar lifecourse effects, such as a tendency to work in part-time and low-paid jobs, which feed into economic disadvantage later in life, particularly for single older women (Gunnarsson, 2002; Disney and Whitehouse, 2003).

Quite how these lifecourse effects play out will depend on wider socioeconomic and developmental contexts and they will change over time. For example, gender gaps in education are especially marked in parts of Asia and Africa, but are less substantial in much of Latin America and developed countries. Overall, most countries have seen falls in gender gaps for school enrolment and so this effect will be less important for future cohorts of older people. Similarly, restrictions on female economic activity and discrimination in the labour market vary between countries and, in some cases at least, may be easing (Standing, 1999). In the case of Thailand, gender differences in later life are shaped by a number of specific factors. For example, pension coverage is limited for all people, regardless of sex, leaving the vast majority of older men as well as women reliant on other forms of income. In countries with more extensive pension systems, differential entitlements to benefits will have a larger impact on the situation of older people (we return to this issue in Chapter Three).

Another example of Thailand's particular context is that attitudes towards widowed older women are relatively liberal. This contrasts with some other developing countries, such as Nigeria and India, where the condition of widowhood is highly stigmatised, leading to wide-ranging discrimination (Table 2.7). In some countries, widows are barred from inheriting their husband's property, and are strongly discouraged from working or socialising (Alter Chen, 1998; Ewelukwa, 2002). Chapter Eight explores the effects of widowhood in some detail, with reference to India. It finds that, although widowhood can have substantial effects on women's lives, these are not as straightforward as is sometimes

Table 2.7: Reported attitudes towards widows, selected countries, 2008

	% of respondents reporting that widows are treated 'a great deal worse' than other women	% of respondents reporting that widows are treated 'somewhat worse' than other women
Thailand	7	22
France	6	11
India	18	24
Nigeria	25	33
Mexico	21	26

Source: WorldPublicOpinion.org (2009)

claimed. Similarly, patterns of gender relations within households and societies in general are complex and diverse. While there is a broad tendency for women to face disadvantages in these relations, the extent of patriarchal dominance varies and there is growing evidence that power relations are deeply ambivalent (Whitehead and Kabeer, 2001).

It is sometimes claimed that transitions from mid-life to old age can have different effects on men and women. Since men are more likely to be in established paid work, these transitions are more likely to be associated with retirement. This may represent either a moment of liberation or a threat to socioeconomic status and personal identity (Kim and Moen, 2002). In most developing countries the limited value of pension benefits means that the latter is more likely. For older women who have had less access to paid employment, transitions to old age may be less abrupt. For many of these women, later life may not see a significant change to daily routines, which continue to be shaped by domestic duties (UN-DESA, 2002). For example, childcare may give way to care for parents, grandchildren and ailing spouses. In the case of Thailand, the orphaning of grandchildren due to HIV/AIDS has added another dimension to these caring duties (Table 2.6). Some studies report that older women may feel burdened by continuing demands for care and support from other household members (Sagner and Mtati, 1999). While a lifetime of caring can disadvantage older women, studies from Africa and Latin America claim that it may enable older women to enjoy better relations with children than older men do (Aboderin, 2004; Gomes da Conceição and Montes de Oca Zavala, 2004). However, the evidence for these important claims is very limited, and other studies have found patterns of relationships with children to be considerably more complex (Varley and Blasco, 2003; Lloyd-Sherlock and Locke, 2008). We revisit these issues in Chapter Five, with reference to social relations in later life.

In sum, old age is a profoundly gendered experience for both men and women. Rather than compare the experiences of older men and older women, it is often more useful to consider broader interactions between gender relations and later life. The precise nature of these effects is more complex and sometimes more subtle than is frequently claimed. They are highly dependent on local contexts and are subject to change over time.

Conclusions

Taken as a whole, this chapter shows that processes of development have important implications for how later life is experienced, but that these implications are complex, variable and unpredictable. Instead of recognising this complexity, many commentators make stylised and generalised statements. It is claimed that the material benefits of economic growth are often offset by social changes that marginalise older people. In developing countries, older people are often characterised as universally impoverished, with older women facing particular disadvantage. These general claims are not always completely wrong, but they simplify what is meant by development, what is meant by old age and how one affects the other.

This chapter started by examining the limitations of widely used life-stage models of old age. These are based on a number of problematic assumptions, and encourage simplistic and generalised understandings. They were contrasted with the more sophisticated analytical insights that can be obtained by applying the concepts of lifecourse, cohort and generation. Using data from Chile, we explored how national patterns of development shape lifecourses and, ultimately, experiences of old age. This reveals a number of important effects. For example, the timing of national events (such as the extension of education or a sudden economic crisis) in relation to personal life trajectories (whether they occur in childhood, youth, middle age and so on) has a large effect on the life chances of different cohorts. At the same time, lifetime opportunities and wellbeing in later life are strongly influenced by intergenerational relationships and linked lives. This means that assessing or predicting the impacts of development on older people is both complex and challenging.

These difficulties become more evident when we try to assess the effects of development on older people's economic status. This analysis is hindered by the lack of useful data, the limitations of what the data tell us and problems of interpretation. Nevertheless, it is possible to draw some broad conclusions. In many countries, development has led to massive increases in national wealth, and it is likely that many older people will have benefited from this, even if they have done less well than other age groups. Despite this, there is considerable economic diversity across older populations: while some older people may experience abject poverty, others experience a lifetime of relative wealth. Similarly, women's lifetime disadvantages may lead to heightened vulnerability in old age, but these patterns are highly variable and older men may also face specific forms of deprivation.

Overall, the evidence in this chapter challenges Cowgill's (1976) gloomy predictions about development and older people. Through the 20th century, most countries enjoyed dramatic and unprecedented improvements in material living standards. As well as rising incomes, this included improved access to education, health and a wide range of infrastructure and new technologies. Even though the benefits of this transformation have not been distributed evenly, it is evident that the majority of older people now have a higher standard of living than their parents or grandparents did. Nevertheless, there are important exceptions to this positive global story – countries that continue to contain generalised poverty, or particular groups who have been excluded for one reason or another. Rapid social change and shifting cultural norms do leave some older people isolated and vulnerable, although firm evidence for these effects is hard to pin down. Also, as we will see in the next chapters, the potential benefits of extended healthcare and pension provision have often been watered down by inappropriate policies. Whether rapid improvements in living standards will be sustained in the current century is a matter for debate. Future populations of old and young may face heightened economic volatility, increased exposure to environmental hazards and unforeseen epidemiological crises.

Notes

[1] Arguably, it would be more appropriate to use remaining years of *healthy* life expectancy. Comparative estimates are provided in Table 2.1, but a lack of age-specific epidemiological data in many developing countries means that these figures are very unreliable (Mathers et al, 2004).

[2] These calculations are taken from year-specific life tables published by Ministry of Health, Labour and Welfare, Japan (2004) and IBGE (2004). Both were obtained via the Human Life-Table Database at www.lifetable.de

[3] These four principles were first set out in Elder Jr (1998).

[4] In fact, many income poverty surveys assume that older people consume *less* than people in mid-life. For example, Argentina's state statistical agency assumes that people aged 60 or over require 20% less food. Since poverty lines are based entirely on food consumption, this leads to the systematic underestimation of old-age poverty.

⁵ See Barrientos (2002) for a detailed, technical discussion of other ways in which standard income poverty measures may specifically discriminate against older people.

⁶ On the basis of this finding, they conclude that 'This would seem to weaken the case for categorical targeting of the elderly in anti-poverty programs' (Pal and Palacios, 2006: 10). Since Roberto Palacios is a senior member of the World Bank pensions team, this conclusion may have a major policy impact in India. It demonstrates the importance of poverty data for setting policy agendas.

⁷ For a more detailed theoretical treatment of these issues, see Lloyd-Sherlock (2002a).

THREE

Older people, pensions and development

Introduction

Judging by the outputs of academics, policy makers and NGOs, pensions are by far the most important issue affecting the lives of older people in the developing world. For example, between 1984 and 2004, the World Bank issued over 200 loans and 350 papers on pension policy, but provided no loans or papers for other projects explicitly concerned with older people (Bretton Woods Project, 2006). This focus on pensions has dwarfed the amount of attention paid to issues such as health policy or the care economy. Much of the discussion about pension schemes is complex, full of jargon and deeply theoretical, making it challenging for readers who lack specialised technical knowledge of pension economics. This chapter provides a simplified analysis of two key issues, and it should be easily understood by non-economists. These two issues link into two widespread assumptions about pensions, development and older people. The first is that pension schemes have a large and obvious impact on the wellbeing of older people. The second is that one of the main ways in which population ageing affects development is through the associated costs of pension provision.

At first sight, it would seem obvious that there is a direct and simple link between pension benefits and the wellbeing of older people. In developed countries this is broadly true, since the great majority of older people receive pensions. As such, variations in the value of benefits and how they are calculated can have a large impact on older people's lives and are a high-profile political issue. Even so, pensions represent just one form of income and support for older people, and it is important to see the bigger picture. Also, becoming a pensioner is often linked with compulsory retirement from paid employment, and this may potentially limit older people's incomes, as well as their social networks.

In many developing countries, the link between pension policy and older people's wellbeing is much less direct. First, the majority of older people in developing countries do not receive a pension. For example, in Cameroon, which is quite typical of low-income countries, only around 10% of older people, mainly retired soldiers and civil servants, receive pensions (Fonchingong Che, 2008). Even in richer countries, such as India, China and Indonesia, pension schemes do not reach the majority of older people. Second, for many who do receive a pension, the values of benefits fall well short of their basic living needs. There is growing evidence that pensions tend to be shared across entire households, especially among poorer social groups. This may dilute the economic benefit for older people, but may also boost their family standing and encourage relatives to treat them with respect. In the most negative scenario, pension cash may be violently misappropriated by other family members, leaving the pensioner vulnerable and penniless. The key point is that we cannot assume how pension benefits are spent and how they affect older people without a good understanding of households and intergenerational dynamics. We will return to these complex issues later in the chapter.

In Chapter Two, we saw that the link between population ageing and healthcare costs was neither simple nor direct, and that other factors could exert a larger influence. The same can be said about pension costs. Table 3.1 shows that public spending on pensions in Turkey is several times higher than in Korea, yet both countries have roughly similar age structures. If the ratio of pension spending to older people in Poland were equivalent to Korea's, it would fall to just 2% of GDP. There are several potential reasons for these variations. For example, some Turkish pension benefits have been criticised for being overgenerous, and widespread early retirement means that over half of pensioners are aged under 60 (Morgan Stanley Global Economic Forum, 2005). Poland offers state pensions for all older people, whereas in Korea only around a third of people aged 65 and over receive state benefits (Choi, 2000).

Table 3.1: Public spending on old-age pensions and population ageing, selected OECD countries, 2001

	Public spending on old-age pensions (% GDP)	Population aged 65+ (% total population)
Korea	1.1	10.4
Poland	8.5	17.8
Turkey	5.1	8.8

Source: Whiteford and Whitehouse (2006)

In this chapter we will see that the cost of pension schemes depends on factors such as how they are financed and administered, the value of benefits and rules of entitlement. On the surface, these often appear to be technical issues. However, we will see that decisions about pension policy are mainly driven by political processes and these processes are embedded in wider experiences of development. In recent decades, growing concerns about the financial sustainability of pension schemes have been framed in terms of an 'old-age crisis' (World Bank, 1994a). This chapter will argue that population ageing is rarely the main cause of financial problems: in other words, it is more accurate to portray these problems as a 'pension crisis' rather than one of old age.

Spending on pension programmes should not be seen simply as a drain on public resources and hence economic development. Most pension systems involve an element of saving for the future. Usually, these savings will be invested over the course of a person's working years, in order to generate an adequate pot of money for later life. As all economists know, savings are one of the driving forces of economic growth and in many developing countries, savings are very scarce. Pension savings may be used to stimulate capital and financial markets in developing countries, providing much-needed funding for development projects. In a few cases, such as Singapore, pension savings have been invested in activities that generated high rates of return for pensioners and were also of value to the country's general development (Huff, 1995). More often, pension savings have been poorly invested, due to problems of weak institutions and poor governance. As well as promoting savings, pensions affect consumption, another key driver of development. In developed countries, pensioners have become an important market, providing a range of new business opportunities. Overall, then, the links between pension programmes and development are complex and should not be viewed purely in negative terms.

Before discussing these issues in more detail, we will briefly review the main forms that pension programmes can take, since many of these technical details can have major effects on pension finances, as well as on older people's lives. We will then examine the origins, evolution and international diffusion of old-age pension schemes, identifying key factors that shaped these developments. This leads on to a more detailed analysis of the most recent period of global pension history, a time characterised by mounting concerns about pension sustainability and a new wave of reforms. We then return to the two main themes of this chapter: links between population ageing and pension finance, and the effects of pensions on older people themselves. Given the complexity of these issues and the breadth of international experience, the chapter closes with case studies from Mexico, Thailand, Poland and Ghana.

How are pension schemes financed and organised?

Traditionally, the financing and organisation of pension programmes have been mainly in the hands of the public sector, as part of a wider set of social security systems. The International Labour Office (ILO) defines social security as:

> The adoption of public measures to ensure basic income security to all in need of protection, in order to relieve want and prevent destitution by restoring up to a certain level income which is lost or reduced by reason of inability to work or to obtain remunerative work due to the occurrence of various contingencies: sickness, unemployment, old age, employment injury, family responsibilities, maternity, invalidity or the death of the breadwinner. (ILO, 2008: 3)

Social security can be divided into two distinct components: social insurance and social assistance. Social insurance schemes usually target particular groups of workers. Theoretically, they are funded by these workers, their employers and, in some cases, government. This usually takes the form of a monthly quota levied on the worker's gross salary. Workers in selected occupational categories are legally required to participate in these social insurance schemes. In return, they (and sometimes their families) are legally entitled to various benefits when they retire or when other contingencies (see above definition) arise. People who do not contribute to these schemes are not entitled to any benefits. Pension funds organised on the basis of social insurance are usually referred to as **contributory schemes**. Provident funds can be understood as a variant of this mechanism, and pay out a single lump-sum rather than a monthly pension. Contributory pensions and provident funds account for the majority of pension schemes in developing countries.

Social assistance is usually funded by the state, through general taxation or support from overseas aid agencies. It does not target particular groups of workers. Schemes can include services provided to an entire population (universal services): often, basic health and education provision is managed in this way. They can also involve more targeted approaches, which seek to benefit specific population groups. This might involve means-testing (assessing income and assets to identify those in greatest need) or some other form of targeting, such as community prioritisation (see Thailand case study later in this chapter). Pension schemes organised on the basis of social assistance are usually referred to as non-contributory schemes or **social pensions**. Although not as widespread as contributory funds, this form of financing has gained popularity in recent years, especially in poorer countries.

The financing and entitlements offered by contributory pension schemes can vary in a number of important ways. One key distinction is between **capitalised** (sometimes referred to as fully funded) and **pay-as-you-go** mechanisms. In the former, each contributor's savings are invested over time and their retirement benefit will be derived from the amount saved plus returns on investment. In the second approach, the contributions of active workers are pooled together for a given year and this money is used to pay for the pension benefits of people who have already retired. To be financially sustainable, a pay-as-you-go system needs to maintain a balance between the money paid in during a given year and the value of benefits paid out. This is not an easy balance to strike. For example, a sudden rise in unemployment would reduce the number of contributing workers, but the number of pensioners would be unchanged. In this case, it would be necessary to cut individual benefits, which is likely to be politically difficult. Another option might be to raise contribution rates, but this would probably increase labour costs, thus reducing international competitiveness and leading to further rises in unemployment (as firms relocate in search of cheaper workers). As we will see later in the chapter, many developing countries originally organised their pension systems on a pay-as-you-go basis. This was fine during the early years of these pension schemes, since few workers had yet reached retirement age and so much more money was being paid in than out. Once growing numbers of workers started to retire, however, financial equilibrium ended and this led to massive financial deficits. Since then, many countries have sought to move towards a capitalised funding system.

Another important distinction for contributory programmes is between **defined benefit** (also known as final salary) schemes and **defined contribution** ones. In the former, pension benefits are guaranteed, usually as a fixed percentage of a worker's final salary. These schemes are normally funded on a pay-as-you-go basis and, at least in theory, contribution rates will vary from one year to the next, depending on the total costs of the benefits. Some developing countries, such as Turkey, have very generous defined benefit rules for influential groups of workers. For example, civil servants are entitled to 106% of their final salaries (Morgan Stanley Global Economic Forum, 2005). Unless worker contributions are correspondingly high, this will increase financial pressure on the pension system. In defined contribution schemes, the value of final benefits is not guaranteed.

Instead, the contributions paid by workers, employers and the state remain fixed and the pension varies accordingly. To maintain financial equilibrium, a pension fund cannot be run on principles of both defined contributions and defined benefits, yet this has often been the case in developing countries.

Another key consideration is the coverage of contributory schemes. This can refer to either the proportion of workers enrolled in pension schemes (who will be entitled to a contributory pension when they retire) or the proportion of older people who currently receive contributory benefits. Since contributory social insurance schemes are provided to selected occupational groups, the coverage of workers depends on the proportion employed in these protected groups. In developed countries, the vast majority of workers are employed in the organised sector of the economy, in activities governed by labour legislation. In most developing countries this is not the case. Many people, especially the poor, work in less organised economic activities where labour legislation does not exist or is not enforced. These include rural workers, people working on a casual basis and the self-employed. In most cases, governments have failed to extend social insurance to workers in this informal sector of the labour market, and so contributory pension schemes mainly provide for relatively privileged workers employed in the civil service or in large (often foreign-owned) firms.

Table 3.2 provides data on social insurance coverage in Mexico for 2002. It reveals the limited extent of social insurance schemes, such that less than a fifth of older people were receiving a pension. It also shows that coverage has favoured particular sectors of the population who were more likely to work in organised economic activities. This has led to large gaps in protection between the rural and urban

Table 3.2: Social insurance coverage in Mexico, 2002

	Coverage of economically active population (%)	Coverage of people aged 65+ (%)
Total	34	19
Men	34	26
Women	34	12
Quintile 1	7	3
Quintile 2	56	30
Rural	12	8
Urban	41	23

Source: Rofman and Lucchetti (2006)

population, as well as between the richest 20% of Mexicans (quintile 5) and the poorest 20% (quintile 1). In other words, social insurance pensions schemes in Mexico fail to reach those most in need and tend to redistribute large amounts of wealth towards the rich. This would seem to contradict the main purpose of social security, as stated by the ILO. Worryingly, the Mexican case is not exceptional: indeed, it is quite representative of the limited coverage and inequality of social insurance in many developing countries. Social insurance systems also tend to discriminate against women, since they are often under-represented in protected occupations. The Mexican data in Table 3.2 suggest that this is not the case, since coverage of the economically active population is identical. However, economic activity is defined here in terms of salaried work, and overall levels of economic participation for women are about half men's. This explains why there is a substantial gender gap in access to pensions in old age.

So far, the discussion has focused on contributory pension schemes. Most of these issues do not apply to non-contributory social pensions, since these are financed out of the general state budget on a year-by-year basis. The main determinants of social pension financing are the value of benefits and entitlements to receive them. In 2004, Lesotho introduced a universal social pension for all people aged 70 and over. Since the value of the pension is relatively modest (US$22 a month) and since only 2.5% of the total population are in this age category, the total cost of the programme is expected to be manageable. If the age of entitlement were reduced to 60 years and over, the costs of the scheme would roughly treble. Social pension schemes need to avoid setting an entitlement age that is so high and benefit levels so low that the overall impact for older people is negligible. Another key issue is whether entitlements are legally enshrined rights (that is, backed up by a constitutional guarantee) or an act of state charity. In the latter case, governments are free to change the rules of entitlement or even disband the entire scheme if they no longer wish to finance it.

Private pension funds have grown rapidly in recent years, both globally and in developing countries. To some extent, these have sought to fill the gaps left by incomplete social security coverage, especially for more affluent population groups. In some countries, pension reforms have enabled private schemes to become integral parts of the main social security system. The consequences of this 'pension privatisation' have been very controversial and we return to this issue later in the chapter. Even in relatively poor countries, private pensions can be large and manage substantial amounts of finance. For example, in Kenya, voluntary private pensions cover around 15% of the workforce and hold assets worth around US$3 billion (18% of Kenya's GDP) (US Social Security Administration, 2008). Private pensions may be provided on a voluntary or a compulsory basis and are financed on a fully funded, defined contribution basis. In developing countries, a key challenge is the capacity of states to provide effective regulation, to ensure financial fair play and to protect the interests of customers. Experiences from developed countries like the UK indicate how difficult regulation can be. Problems have included notorious cases of corruption, such as the abuse of Mirror Group pension assets by Robert Maxwell and revelations that many customers were misinformed about their private pension plans (*BBC News*, 1999; *BBC News*, 2002). In 2008, the main UK financial regulator reported that nearly half of pension companies did not comply with its rules (*BBC News*, 2008). Worryingly, data and research about the regulation of private pension funds in most developing countries simply do not exist.

The origin of pension programmes: from Bismarck to Beveridge

The first ever national pension scheme was established in Germany in 1889 by the government of Count Otto von Bismarck. This was a compulsory social insurance fund, based on contributions from workers, employers and (indirectly) the state. The age of retirement was set at 70 years of age. The pension was linked into separate programmes of accident and health insurance, to provide a general programme of social insurance for people working in the formal sector of the economy. It mainly targeted factory workers, as a separate scheme for civil servants had been established back in 1825.

Bismarck himself did not fit the usual profile of a social reformer. He was a staunch conservative and his regime violently repressed left-wing political movements, including social democrats (Lerman, 2004). He was strongly opposed to labour legislation, including any restrictions on the working hours of women and young children. So why, then, did he pioneer this new form of welfare policy? In fact, the main purpose of the new scheme was to obtain the political support of Germany's growing and increasingly militant working classes. Bismarck was unsuccessful: factory unrest increased and employers were strongly opposed to compulsory contributions (Abrams, 2006). In 1890, as his political support crumbled, Bismarck was forced to resign office, just a year after the pension had been introduced. Despite his resignation, the social insurance system was left in place, although its impact on workers' welfare was initially quite limited. Around half the workforce was employed in agriculture or other activities that were not included in the scheme. Only around 20% of factory workers could expect to survive to age 70 and benefits were worth little (Williamson and Pampel, 1993). Dependants and survivors (widows and widowers) received no financial support. This limited impact contrasted with the much more generous benefits and entitlements of the older civil service pension fund. Despite these shortcomings, Bismarck's reforms were hailed as a success by other European countries and the German system came to be seen as a template for social insurance in both the developed and developing worlds. For example, Britain established a similar social insurance pension in 1908 and many countries in Latin America set up schemes for specific groups of workers before the First World War.

Germany's early experience with social insurance reveals a number of important issues that have framed the development of contributory pension funds around the world ever since. Pension legislation was not motivated by concerns about population ageing or fears for the welfare of older people. Instead, it was driven by a complex set of political factors and it offered different groups of workers (civil servants, factory workers and excluded groups) widely varying benefits and entitlements. As part of this, a 'golden rule' of pension policy is that schemes for civil servants will be set up first and will usually provide more generous protection. Also, Bismarck's initiative shows that policies that seem substantial on paper do not always translate into substantial welfare gains in the real world.

In the decades after Bismarck, the German pension system was substantially upgraded. In 1911, benefits were extended to widows and dependants. In the same year, a new fund was established for high-income white-collar workers, providing larger pensions in return for higher contributions. The preference for separate funds, rather than a unified system, enabled governments to promote tensions between different labour unions as part of a strategy of divide and rule. During the early 20th century, the share of workers employed in agriculture fell, so that the overall coverage of the social insurance system grew. New schemes were later set up for farm workers and even (in 1972) for housewives. From 1957, legislation led to substantial increases in the value of pensions, with benefits linked to average earnings. What had started life as a limited system, providing selective benefits to different groups of workers, had evolved into a universal and generous system of old-age income support.

Britain offered an alternative approach for moving from selective social insurance to a more embracing system. This was through adopting a universal flat-rate pension, payable to all men aged over 64 and women aged over 59 (Thane, 2000). The universal pension was a key part of Beveridge's new 'cradle to the grave' welfare state, which Britain adopted after the Second World War. Despite the international acclaim for the Beveridge Report, its direct influence on most developing countries was rather limited. Instead, selective, Bismarckian occupation-specific social insurance remained the policy of preference for most of the 20th century.

The globalisation of pension programmes: three pathways

By the 1980s, virtually every country in the world, including most low-income countries, had set up national pension schemes for at least some groups of workers. The global diffusion of pension programmes was driven by a number of forces. First, it can be understood as part of a wider development paradigm whereby policies implemented in industrialised countries were often transferred with little modification to the developing world. As with schools, hospitals and large industrial projects, pension schemes were seen as helpful for the formation of a modern, developmental state. International organisations, especially the ILO, played a key role, advising and encouraging many countries. Fundamental to this was a belief that developing countries could follow the example set by Germany, so that programmes for selected groups of workers could later be extended across the population at large (Strang and Chang, 1993). Yet, just as in Germany, the main motivation for establishing social insurance schemes was often the political opportunities they provided for controlling and rewarding different sections of the labour force (Mesa-Lago, 1978: Malloy, 1979; Midgley, 1984).

While the experiences of developing countries were quite diverse, it is possible to identify three general pathways of social insurance and pension policy during the 20th century. *The first pathway* included countries that took a limited approach, mainly restricting protection to civil servants and the military. This included many low-income countries, where schemes were set up around the time of independence. For example, Nigeria established a generous defined benefit pension fund for civil servants in 1946, with contributions paid entirely by the state. In 1961, a separate National Provident Fund was created for private sector workers, but it only covered 8% of the workforce by the mid-1980s and the values of lump-sum payments were quite small (Williamson and Pampel, 1993). This category also included several

Asian countries. For example, Indonesia set up a generous, state-funded defined benefit scheme for civil servants in 1969, and a very limited provident fund for the private sector in 1977 (Schröder-Butterfill and Lloyd-Sherlock, 2008). Similarly, India's private sector provident fund only covered 7% of the total workforce by the mid-1980s, but its civil servants had a defined benefit scheme financed entirely by the state (Gillingham and Kanda, 2001).

The second pathway included countries that set up a more ambitious range of schemes with a view to providing substantial pensions to all people who worked in the formal sector of the economy, be it in the civil service or for private firms. In some cases, efforts were also made to extend social insurance to groups of informal sector workers, although these usually met with little success. Most countries in Latin America fell into this category, conforming closely to the Bismarckian model, with separate funds for separate occupations. Different groups of workers pressured governments into providing them with their own pension funds (Mesa-Lago, 1978). These were almost always defined benefit schemes and financed on a pay-as-you-go basis. Pensions were generally generous, although values and entitlements varied, with the more powerful unions obtaining more favourable terms. Despite this, success in moving towards universal coverage was quite limited, as seen in the Mexican case (Table 3.2).

The third pathway included countries whose systems of governance were structured according to socialist ideologies. In the Soviet Union and most of Eastern Europe, Bismarckian schemes were quickly unified and financing was transferred to general state budgets. By the 1970s, all had achieved universal workforce coverage, with relatively generous pensions. Schemes were run on a pay-as-you-go basis and links between contributions and benefit values were vague. National state pension schemes were seen as a major achievement of the socialist system and contributed to the political legitimacy of authoritarian regimes (Müller, 2003). Outside Europe, other socialist regimes provided less embracing protection. For example, in China a clear distinction was made between rural and urban workers. For the former, the family and community were expected to provide old-age support and so direct state involvement was minimal. In the cities, state-owned enterprises were required to provide their workers with a range of welfare services, including pensions after retirement (Ahmad and Hussain, 1991).

Whichever pathway a country took, most pension schemes were usually organised on a contributory basis. In the case of many civil service funds, these contributions were somewhat notional, since they were paid entirely by government. In many ways, civil service pensions represented social assistance schemes that targeted powerful and well-paid groups of workers. There were few examples of social assistance pensions targeting the poor. Rare cases included limited, means-tested pensions in parts of the Caribbean and the Indian state of Kerala (Midgley, 1984). More substantial programmes were established in southern Africa and, later, in Brazil: we return to these cases later in the chapter.

In the first two pathways, pension schemes were largely modelled on those of the West, on either a limited or a more extensive basis. However, national contexts were often very different from those of developed countries. Two key aspects of difference were the nature of labour markets and the strength of local institutions. In most developing countries, only a minority of the workforce were employed in the formal sector of the economy. Predictions that development would lead to an increasingly formalised economy, as had happened in Germany, largely failed to materialise. This meant that the German route to universal social insurance coverage was unfeasible and programmes remained focused on relatively privileged groups of workers.

In many developing countries, most government agencies were not as strong, independent nor as well resourced as those in the West. For example, there was a general shortage of staff trained in pension management who would be able to establish effective financial systems (Strang and Chang, 1993). Often, state agencies struggled to collect tax and social insurance contributions from firms and individuals. This led to high rates of evasion, which undermined pension fund finances (Mesa-Lago, 1978; Charlton and McKinnon, 2001). With some notable exceptions such as Singapore, most state agencies lacked skills to invest pension surpluses in order to generate high rates of return. Also, local opportunities for investment were usually limited, encouraging many governments to plough pension money into questionable state-led development ventures (Iglesias and Palacios, 2000). Poor systems of control and accounting meant that large sums of money were sometimes lost to corruption (Ribeiro, 1990). In many countries, government agencies were exposed to constant interference from politicians, encouraging short-term decision making rather than a more sustainable approach.

This combination of limited coverage and weak government controls gave rise to a very inequitable welfare system, in which wealth was transferred away from poorer social groups to richer ones. Government funding for civil service pensions was often considerably greater than the resources devoted to social policies reaching out to the poor. In most of Latin America, high rates of evasion and generous benefits quickly led to large pension deficits and these were mainly covered by general tax revenues. Again, this depleted public finances that could have been devoted to less privileged social groups. Although many countries devoted large amounts of government spending to contributory pension systems, the great majority of older people still lacked access to pensions. By contrast, many civil servants were allowed to retire in their fifties or even younger.

By the 1980s, many contributory pension schemes and provident funds had started to generate large financial deficits, due to the growing numbers of scheme members who were qualifying for retirement. The problem was exacerbated by failures to invest past surpluses effectively and continuing high rates of evasion. In some countries, pension benefits were radically reduced, although rarely for senior civil servants or the military. This was not enough to prevent spiralling deficits, which in some cases reached billions of dollars. The collapse of contributory pension funds and mounting state debt added to the economic crises experienced by many developing countries during the 1980s (Mesa-Lago, 1989). As a separate development, political transition and economic collapse in Russia and much of Eastern Europe in the 1990s led to growing questions about the affordability of socialist welfare programmes, including pensions (Müller, 2003).

The crisis of pension funds in developing countries coincided with growing concerns about the onset of an 'old-age crisis' in the developed world (World Bank, 1994a). In this case, there were more grounds for linking pension problems with population ageing, although financial mismanagement had also played an important role (Disney, 2000). The deficits of contributory pensions in developing countries, the collapse of the socialist welfare model and concerns about long-term pension liabilities in the West all combined to inspire a radical global pension reform agenda.

Pension reform

During the 1980s, Thatcher's Britain and Pinochet's Chile pioneered a shift away from state-centred development towards neoliberal strategies, setting a course later followed by many developing countries. As part of this, they implemented a series of social security reforms that created a new template for global pension policy. In 1978, the UK permitted people to partly opt out of the state contributory pension scheme, contracting out their pension provision to private firms (Disney et al, 2003). From 1986, considerable inducements for contracting out were introduced, state benefit entitlements were cut and government provided a large top-up to private pension contributions. By the mid-1990s, around three quarters of the workforce had contracted out their pension provision, and there had been an explosive growth of firms offering personal pension plans. Chile introduced similar reforms in 1980. New entrants into the workforce were required to take out pension plans with private fund managers rather than with the state pension scheme. As in the UK, existing workers were offered large inducements to shift from the state scheme into private funds (Barrientos, 2004a).

The British and Chilean reforms marked a new era in global pension policy, in which privatisation came to be seen as a panacea for the many problems faced by contributory social insurance. Recognising the shortcomings of state pension management in many developing countries, it was argued that the private sector offered a more efficient, transparent and equitable alternative (World Bank, 1994a). Theoretically, this reflected the inherent efficiency of the private sector, and its freedom from political interference and corruption. The new private funds were to be organised on a fully capitalised, defined contribution basis, breaking with the financial imbalances of the old state-run schemes.

The British and Chilean reforms were initially viewed as successful, with pension investments generating high rates of return (Vittas and Iglesias, 1992). Within a few years, they had inspired a new model of pension governance championed by the World Bank, the International Monetary Fund (IMF) and a range of other influential development agencies (Charlton and McKinnon, 2001). This came to be known as the **Three Pillar Model** and versions of this model have since been rolled out in a large number of low- and middle-income countries. According to this model, pension provision should be organised through three mechanisms, operating in tandem (World Bank, 1994a).

- Pillar one consists of a compulsory privately managed system, operating on a fully capitalised basis.
- Pillar two consists of a state-run social assistance safety net, funded out of general taxation.
- Pillar three consists of voluntary private funds, whereby people may choose to boost their personal saving for retirement.

Between 1984 and 2004, the World Bank provided over 200 separate loans, worth around US$34 billion, to developing countries seeking to implement all or part of the Three Pillar Model (Holzmann and Hinz, 2005). Particular emphasis was placed on the role of the first and third, privately managed pillars, as it was argued that large social assistance schemes would be expensive and would reduce people's incentives to participate in the contributory pillars.

Overall, pension privatisation and the Three Pillar Model have yielded disappointing results and have attracted much criticism (Müller, 2003; D'Haeseleer and Berghman, 2004). First, it quickly became clear that an effective private pension market requires strong state regulation. The miss-selling of private pensions and other abuses in the UK demonstrate the challenges of regulation for developed states, let alone for low- and middle-income countries. There is evidence from a range of developing countries that many private funds charged exorbitant management fees, as well as channelling large amounts of finance into marketing and advertising their products (Dobronogov and Murthi, 2005; Riesco, 2005). Also, cases have been reported of firms misinforming customers about their future pension entitlements (*BBC News*, 2003). Second, in many countries, rates of return for private pension investments have been erratic, falling short of reformers' optimistic predictions. In recent years, even the World Bank has accepted that the instability of financial markets both globally and especially in developing countries, threatens the long-term reliability of returns through a worker's contributory lifespan (Orszag and Stiglitz, 2001). Third, the loss of younger workers to new private pension funds left state pension schemes with members who were close to retirement or already receiving pensions. Governments were required to directly make up for the lost contributions of younger workers, which meant that public spending on pensions actually rose rather than fell. In Chile, for example, these costs are estimated to have been equivalent to 7% of GDP (Arza, 2005). Fourth, claims that greater public faith in the transparency of private management would lead to increased participation have not borne fruit. In many countries, shrinking formal sector employment has led to falls, rather than rises, in pension coverage (Barrientos, 2004b). Finally, strong political resistance to pension privatisation, especially among the civil service, limited the prospects for reform in many countries.

By the start of the 21st century, the credibility of the Three Pillar Model had diminished and the global wave of contributory pension reform had started to lose momentum. Many developed countries, Germany included, chose not to follow the example set by the UK. Rather than promote a wholesale shift to private pension management, these countries have looked to raise retirement ages and strengthen defined contribution mechanisms within their existing social insurance schemes (Busemeyer, 2005).

At the same time, a new reform agenda began to emerge. This highlighted the potential of non-contributory social assistance schemes for providing income security for the poorest old people. In a handful of countries, such as South Africa and Brazil, unusual political and socioeconomic circumstances had led to the establishment of quite large social assistance pension schemes.[1] Studies of these schemes claimed that they not only reduced poverty among older people, but also were shared across entire households, and could contribute towards family solidarity and improved health and education outcomes (Duflo, 2000; Schwartzer and Querino, 2002). This encouraged organisations such as HelpAge International to robustly promote social pension schemes as the main tool for addressing old-age vulnerability in low-income countries (HelpAge International, 2006). Following on from this, international development agencies, including the World Bank and the UK's Department for International Development, have increasingly come to see social pensions as an important option in their wider portfolios of anti-poverty strategies (DFID, 2006). This has prompted several countries, including Bolivia, Mexico, Bangladesh, Lesotho and Zambia, to set up new social pension programmes.

The shift in emphasis away from contributory schemes to social assistance represents a major change in global pension policy and has rightly attracted a lot of attention. Nevertheless, some of the enthusiasm with which social pensions have been promoted needs to be tempered. Whether social pensions promote all the wider benefits that is sometimes claimed should not be taken for granted: we return to this issue with reference to South Africa in Chapter Six. Also, it remains to be seen whether newly established schemes will be equally effective and sustainable. Shifting the spotlight to social pensions may deflect attention from the continued failings of large contributory schemes, which still account for the great majority of pension finance in developing countries.

Population ageing and pension schemes

The previous sections have made almost no reference at all to population ageing and very little to older people. Instead, they have revealed how the extension of pension programmes was largely driven by complex political factors and was closely linked to wider processes of development, including 20th-century modernisation projects and a later shift to neoliberalism. This explains the wide discrepancies between population ageing and pension spending shown in Table 3.1. As with many Asian countries, Korea took the path of more limited pension development, with protection restricted to civil servants until recently. By contrast, Turkey conformed to the more ambitious contributory model, with generous provision for protected workers. Poland represents the third, socialist path of pension development, offering universal coverage, but relatively low pension values.

The financial crises of contributory pension schemes have often been blamed on population ageing and, at first sight, this link seems obvious and straightforward. A growing proportion of older people increases the ratio of pensioners to contributors. Likewise, as pensioners survive until older ages, they will be entitled to receive benefits for longer. In the case of most developing countries, however, the situation was more complex. High levels of evasion, poor returns on investment and unfunded benefit entitlements had larger effects on pension finances than changes in the ratio of pensioners to contributors. Also, limited coverage meant that pension finances depended on ageing trends within the protected groups, rather than the population as a whole.

Table 3.3 provides information about Argentina's national pension programme at a critical juncture in its development – when it moved from overall surplus into overall deficit. There had been a major extension of scheme coverage during the 1940s, but workers in these new schemes were not entitled to pensions until they had worked for 30 years. By the 1960s, many workers were starting to reach retirement age and had made contributions for the required period. This caused the number of pensioners to leap by 86% between 1960 and 1970, even though the national ageing rate was only 26%. As in much of Latin America, the pension scheme was financed on a pay-as-you-go basis and attempted to offer defined benefits as well as defined contributions: a recipe for financial problems. Extending the scheme

Table 3.3: Argentina's national contributory pension scheme: from surplus to deficit

	Contributors (1,000)	Pensioners (1,000)	Pension fund surplus/ deficit (1960 pesos)	Worker coverage (% of total workforce)	Population aged 60 and over (% of total population)
1960	4,011	745	28,880 surplus	44	7.0
1970	5,781	1,389	7,676 deficit	55	8.8
% change 1960– 70	44%	86%		25%	26%

Sources: Mesa-Lago (1978); Feldman et al (1988)

in the 1940s had initially generated large surpluses and if these had been invested effectively, there should have been enough money in the system to cover the costs of these new pensioners. But in a pay-as-you-go system, money is spent from year to year, so past surpluses were no longer available.

There were various options to maintain the Argentine pension scheme's finances. First, the number of contributors could have been increased. This was achieved to some extent, but the pace of growth (44%) was slower than the growing number of pensioners (86%). Many workers were employed in informal sector activities and remained beyond the reach of the social insurance system. Other options were to raise contribution rates, increase the retirement age or reduce pension values. None of these was done, leaving the system to sink into deficit. During the 1970s and 1980s, the overall level of deficit spiralled, leading government to bale the system out with massive transfers. By the early 1990s, these transfers were roughly equivalent to the combined national education and health budgets (Lloyd-Sherlock, 1997a). This was a substantial drain on government resources and contributed to the country's general economic crisis.

One key lesson to take from this story is that Argentina's pension crisis was not driven by population ageing, but was the result of a combination of policy decisions that gave rise to an unsustainable set of arrangements. The capacity of pension systems to provide for growing numbers of older people depends on the political will to develop more balanced funding mechanisms. It also depends on long-term economic performance and the willingness of societies to allocate this wealth to pensioners. Among other things, this may reflect the potency of older people as a political force.

Pensions and older people

The previous sections show that the links between pensions and older people's economic situation are not always straightforward. In most developed and developing countries, pension systems were initially established to provide special privileges to particular occupations. Instead of a concern with old-age welfare, they were mainly driven by political considerations. In Germany and other developed countries, these schemes later evolved into more embracing welfare programmes, but in many developing countries this did not happen. Consequently, many older people do not receive pensions and those who do tend to be from richer social groups. In most developing countries, the values of pension benefits have varied over time and between different social groups. In many cases, the deterioration of pension scheme finances has led to substantial falls in the values of the basic state pensions. Typically, retired military and civil servants (especially those who held senior positions) still receive benefits that are many times higher than those provided to other pensioners. In many countries, retirement ages vary widely between different occupations. It is not unusual for some categories of civil servant to retire in their early fifties, while other workers more usually retire at 60 or 65. Where social pensions have been introduced, the age of entitlement may be as high as 70. In poorer countries where pensions have been limited to the civil service, this may lead to more 'old-age' pensioners aged under 65 than over 65.

Generally, pension programmes provide less protection for older women than for older men. As we saw with reference to Mexico, women are less likely to have been in paid employment and are less likely to have worked in occupations included in contributory programmes (Bertranou, 2004). Also, women are more likely to experience career interruptions, which will reduce the years they contribute and potentially disqualify them. Women with a surviving husband are rarely offered a pension in their own name. It is assumed that any pension benefit will be shared equally between husband and wife, yet research often shows that this is an idealised view of household gender relations (Lloyd-Sherlock, 1997b). Excluding women from pension provision may, therefore, represent a continuation of restricted economic opportunities and further embed paternalistic household dynamics.

Almost all contributory pension schemes offer benefits for spouses and young children if the pensioner dies, although these are usually worth rather less than a standard old-age pension. In some countries, male widowers are not permitted a survivor's pension, reflecting an ethos that a man should be the main household breadwinner and should not be economically dependent on his wife (Rofman and Grushka, 2003). Although widows' pensions do much to reduce the vulnerability of some older women, only those who were married to a contributory pensioner are entitled to receive them. Women usually lose these entitlements if they are divorced, or if they cannot establish that they were legally married. This is a particular problem in regions like Latin America, where the divorce rate has been rising, or sub-Saharan Africa, where marriage practices are sometimes complex and informal. Gender discrimination is less likely to occur in non-contributory social pension programmes, so long as women have an independent entitlement. In Brazil the provision of independent social pension rights to women eliminated the gender poverty gap in old age (Camarano, 2004).

It should not be assumed that pension benefits purely contribute to the income of a single older individual. The great majority of older people in developing countries do not live alone (see Chapter Five), and it is claimed that pensions are often pooled across entire households to support all members, old and young. If a pensioner lives with other people who have their own sources of income, it is more useful to consider their benefit as part of a wider portfolio of goods consumed by the household as a whole. In other words, pensions may be spent on other household members, and pensioners may equally benefit from relatives' money and other forms of support. This means that the link between pension benefits and the economic status of older people is complex and heavily mediated by household and family dynamics. As part of this, a key issue is whether pensions 'crowd out' family support for older people, since younger relatives no longer feel required to provide assistance (Reil-Held, 2006). If this effect is large, older people may make no net gain from inclusion in a pension scheme. An alternative hypothesis is that pensions may 'crowd in' family support, by providing older people income to exchange for other forms of assistance. In this scenario, older people will benefit both financially and through other forms of family support. Even in developed countries, the evidence for either hypothesis is very limited, and this remains a matter of debate.

In developing countries, several studies of social pensions have made impressive claims about 'crowding in' and their wider benefits for poor older people and their households (HelpAge International, 2006). Some studies have shown that pension money may be associated with improved health and education outcomes for young children and is sometimes invested in small family businesses (De Carvalho Filho, 2000; Duflo, 2000). As part of this, it is claimed that pensions can boost the power and status of older people within their households, which may improve the level of general care and support they receive (Schwartzer and Querino, 2002). These arguments can provide a persuasive case for the extension of social pension schemes, as a tool of development and poverty reduction for all (not just older people). In some cases, the evidence for these claims is quite strong; in others, it is less compelling. To some extent, they are based on idealised assumptions about household dynamics: that older people (including men) freely contribute their monthly benefit to the wellbeing of the family as a whole and that this is repaid by care and support from younger relatives. As we will see in Chapter Five, household dynamics are complex and have been affected by processes of rapid social, economic and cultural change. This means that it is dangerous to generalise about what goes on inside households or about the effects of pensions. For example, research from Brazil found that the experiences of families within the same neighbourhoods were very varied. Although most older people claimed to share their pensions, few expected reciprocal support from other household members (Lloyd-Sherlock, 2007). Chapter Six includes a detailed analysis of these issues in South Africa.

In developed countries, older people have traditionally been expected to retire from paid work before they are allowed to receive a pension. In many cases, retirement was compulsory, although recent years have seen efforts to introduce more flexible arrangements. Some critics argue that forced retirement reinforces later life dependency, and increases the social and economic exclusion of older people (Graebner, 1980; Walker, 1990). Where pension values are small, retirement can lead to a substantial fall in income. Older men may face particular difficulties in adapting to life after retirement, as employment is often an important source of social networks and self-esteem. Despite this, research from the US has shown that men tend to experience better psychological wellbeing after retirement than women do (Kim and Moen, 2002). There is almost no research on the impact of retirement in developing countries, although it is likely that the effects will be very variable. For women receiving a social pension, retirement may be the first time in their lives that they receive a regular, independent source of income. For people receiving senior civil service pensions, retirement probably equates to a well-paid holiday. For those receiving smaller amounts, there will be pressure to supplement the pension with other forms of income. Since labour markets in most developing countries tend not to be closely regulated, many older people may continue to work, even if they are not strictly entitled to do so. Often, this will be in the informal sector in relatively low-paid, casual activities (Barrientos, 2003). In these cases, retirement will be postponed until the older person is physically or mentally unable to continue working.

Mexico: pensions and inequality

Mexico can be taken as an example of developing countries that established Bismarckian funds on a large scale and sought to include sections of the private workforce. Pensions for senior civil servants date back as far as 1824, and protection of the entire civil service was established in 1925 (Mesa-Lago, 1978). This was followed by the creation of schemes for strategically important occupations, including oil workers (1935), railway employees (1936) and the electricity industry (1941). In 1944, funds for private sector workers were put under the control of a single agency – the Instituto Mexicano del Seguro Social (IMSS) [Mexican Institute for Social Security] – and efforts were made to extend protection to the entire formal sector workforce. Expansion was slow, however, with the share of protected workers reaching 25% by 1970. Several key groups remained outside the IMSS system, including civil servants, oil workers and the military. These separate schemes provided substantially more generous pensions with few, if any, contributions. For example, in 1969, average public sector pensions were worth six times those paid out by the IMSS (Mesa-Lago, 1978). Although federal civil servants were required to contribute to their pension funds, the amount paid by the government was three times higher.

All the main pension schemes were organised on a pay-as-you-go, defined benefit basis. As in countries like Argentina, the IMSS initially generated large surpluses. In the case of Mexico, these were largely used to finance a health insurance programme, which was also run by IMSS. Mexico's pension funds were notorious for corruption and inefficiency, leading to further drains on their reserves (Rodríguez, 1999). As the IMSS's finances deteriorated, contributions were increased and pensions cut. By 1995, around 90% of IMSS benefits were equivalent to the minimum wage – an amount that did not cover an older person's basic living needs.

The worsening financial position of the IMSS prompted the state to introduce a series of pension reforms in 1992 and 1997. These sought to replace the IMSS fund with a fully funded, defined contribution scheme managed by private firms. As in the UK, the state tops up these private pension contributions as an incentive for workers to affiliate. Since the reform, the private funds have generated good rates of return on their pension investments. However, concerns have been raised about malpractice and high administration costs (Valdés-Prieto, 2007). Most funds deduct these fees from future pension values, so that many clients are unaware that they are being charged. The pension funds for civil servants and other special categories (including IMSS employees) have not been affected by the reform. Civil servants are still entitled to retire regardless of their age after 30 years of employment for men and 28 for women. The schemes for electricity and oil workers are equally generous (Castañeda Sabido, 2006). Not surprisingly, efforts to incorporate the civil servants' fund into the new private system have been strongly resisted (Palacios and Whitehouse, 2006).

Currently, over five million Mexicans aged 65 or over do not receive a contributory pension. Until recently, social assistance pensions were non-existent, but a number of new schemes have been set up since

2001. These began with an initiative in Mexico City, which offered pensions of US$70 a month to anyone aged 70 or over who did not already have a benefit. The scheme proved politically popular and several other Mexican states established similar programmes (Willmore, 2007). In 2007, a rural means-tested pension was rolled out as part of a wider anti-poverty initiative. By the end of 2007, this new scheme was providing benefits worth US$50 a month to around a million people (SEDESOL, 2008). Taken together, these initiatives have substantially increased pension coverage, although around half of the population aged 65 and over still remain excluded. This largely explains why levels of income poverty among older people are around 70% higher than for the population as a whole (Scott, 2008).

Overall, the Mexican pension system has done much to promote inequality among its older population and for the country in general. Spending on social pensions represents a small fraction of the generous state funds ploughed into private pension top-ups and contributions for the civil servants and other protected groups. This leads to a general redistribution of wealth from poorer groups to richer ones. Within the protected population there is huge inequality: the average value of the top 10% of pensions is 287 times higher than the bottom 10% (Scott, 2008).

Thailand: extending the pension system

Historically, Thailand could be taken as an example of the first, minimal pathway of pension development. Until the 1990s, pension provision was largely restricted to a fund for civil servants. As with most developing countries, this civil service scheme was organised on a pay-as-you-go basis, with generous benefits funded entirely out of the government budget (Knodel et al, 2000). The state had encouraged large private employers to set up provident funds for their workers, but refused to provide them with funding or administrative support. A 1986 survey found that only 5% of older men and 1% of older women reported pensions as their main source of income (Hugo, 1988).

During the 1990s, there were several important developments in pension policy. First, concerns about the mounting costs of public sector pensions led to a reform of the civil service fund. The established programme is being replaced by a fully funded, defined contribution scheme, financed by a 3% wage levy and a matching payment from government. It is likely that pensions provided by the new scheme will be worth rather less than the old one, depending on the performance of pension investments. Second, growing popular demands for a more embracing pension system led to the creation of a new, compulsory scheme for non-state workers, known as the Social Security Fund (SSF) (Schramm, 2001). This is a contributory system that guarantees that pensions will be worth at least 15% of average wages over the last five years of employment after 15 years of contributions, with a further 1% for every additional year. By 1997, before the Asian Crisis struck, this new scheme had been extended to 6.1 million workers. Third, the government has developed a programme of targeted 'emergency' social pensions for older people living in rural areas.

Thailand's new pension system appears to offer a comprehensive package of protection that will reach the great majority of older people. There are, however, grounds for concern about the impacts and sustainability of the new schemes, especially the SSF. Taken together, the SSF and civil service programmes cover around a quarter of the workforce, leaving the majority of older people to rely on the emergency scheme. This scheme has been gradually extended over time, but still falls a long way short of a comprehensive safety net for vulnerable older people (Lloyd-Sherlock, 2001a). Currently, around 300,000 benefits are provided, representing only 6% of the population aged 60 or over. Pensions are worth less than US$10 a month, which does not meet the basic living needs of older people. A fixed quota of benefits is allocated to each village, and village heads are required to apply for the support on behalf of needy older people. The fixed quota means that only a minority of needy older people in the poorest communities are able to obtain support and this often depends on the quality of their personal relationships with village heads. As a result, the majority of older people in Thailand lack pensions and this is likely to continue. Older Thais remain heavily dependent on family members for income transfers and other forms of support (Ofstedal et al, 2004).

Given the lead-in time for contributions, no pensions will be paid out by the SSF for at least another 10 years, and it is currently in surplus. The World Bank calculates that a total contribution rate of 13% would be needed to meet future pension promises, but the current rate is only 7% (World Bank, 2000). Investments have concentrated on low-risk, low-return portfolios, further reducing their capacity to meet future liabilities. Evasion of contributions is widespread: estimated at between 25 and 40% (World Bank, 2000). The World Bank and others have expressed concern about the competence of SSF staff to manage such a large programme, which was set up so quickly (World Bank, 2000). These problems echo those that emerged in much of Latin America in the 1970s and 1980s and suggest that the SSF will struggle to provide its members with adequate pensions.

Poland: pensions and transition

Poland represents the third, socialist pathway of pension development. In 1954, the state took over the pre-existing Bismarckian funds and assumed full responsibility for universal pension provision (Leven, 1998). Despite its socialist ideology, the government organised pensions into three separate funds with different benefits and contributions: one for farmers, one for 'strategic sectors' (such as the police and military) and one for other workers. This led to large variations in pension values and in the income of pensioner-headed households. In 1989, 11% of retirement pensions were worth over 70 zloty, whereas 14% were worth 35 or less, and the richest 10% of pensioner households reported average incomes 4.5 times that of the poorest 10% (World Bank, 1993a). Clearly, Poland's socialist pension system had not led to economic equality for its older population.

Poland's socialist regime was toppled in 1990. Faced with an economy in freefall, the new democratic government adopted a hard-line neoliberal package of shock therapy, which included economic opening and widespread privatisation. Despite efforts to restrict the welfare system, government spending on pensions increased sharply during the transition period: between 1991 and 1996, financing for the farmers' and workers' funds rose from 15.7 to 25.5% of GDP (Leven, 1998). The main reason for this increase was that the government used the pension system as a 'safety valve' for softening the impact of massive reductions in state employment. This involved a generous policy of early retirement and a reduction in the gap between pension benefits and state salaries. Between 1990 and 1995, the number of old-age pensioners increased by 37%, while the population aged 65 and over grew by only 10%. The spiralling cost of pensions led to increased worker and employer contribution rates, adding significantly to labour costs.

In 1999, Poland implemented a substantial pension reform. This was strongly influenced by the Chilean model and was supported through advice and loans from the World Bank (Müller, 1999). Political resistance to a three-pillar system led to a compromise two-pillar model. Pillar one is a mandatory, state-managed pay-as-you-go fund; pillar two operates on a fully funded, privately managed basis. The impacts of this reform on future generations of older people are unclear, as pension values will partly depend on the rates of return generated by the second pillar. The impacts of the reform on Poland's stock exchange have been much more evident. By 2005, the five private pension fund managers had accumulated assets worth around £10 billion and were generating large profits (Greenhalgh, 2005). In 2004, the country moved closer to the three-pillar model, by introducing a new pillar of voluntary personal pension plans.

Ghana: pension provision in a low-income country

In 1946, the British colonial government introduced a generous non-contributory pension scheme known as 'CAP 30' for senior civil servants (Rickayzen, 2003). In 1960, the newly independent government set up a separate provident fund known as the SSNIT for all firms employing five or more people. However, its impact on workers and older people was minimal. Less than 10% of the labour force was included, and a combination of low rates of return on investments and high inflation led to 'meaningless' benefits (Dei, 2001). In 1972, new groups of civil servants were brought within the SSNIT and in 1991 it was converted from a provident fund into a scheme offering monthly pensions.

Currently, SSNIT is funded by contributions worth 5% of salaries for workers and 12.5% for employers. Affiliates are permitted to retire when they are aged 60 (men) or 55 (women). Self-employed workers are allowed to join the scheme on a voluntary basis, but are required to pay the entire 17.5% contribution themselves, which is likely to be unaffordable for most. As such, coverage of the labour force has remained at around 10%. SSNIT is a defined benefit scheme, offering pensions worth at least 50% of an affiliate's final salary, depending on the number of years of contributions. Theoretically, it operates on a fully funded basis, although the links between contributions and benefits are not clear. The ratio of SSNIT contributors to beneficiaries is currently quite high and so the fund has continued to generate surpluses. There are indications that much of this money is being invested inappropriately and ineffectively, including a loan scheme for university students (Rickayzen, 2003). As in Mexico, money has also been channelled into a separate health insurance fund. SSNIT suffers from high rates of evasion and its administrative costs are extremely high (accounting for over 30% of its income in 1991). In 2001, the scheme paid out 50,000 old-age and widows' pensions: representing less than 5% of Ghana's population aged 60 and over. Failures to index benefits with high rates of inflation mean that most pensioners receive very little: in 2001, the minimum pension was only worth about £1.50 a month (Rickayzen, 2003). Despite high administration costs, SSNIT pension claims typically take eight months to process.

Most CAP 30 benefits are considerably more generous than those offered by SSNIT and its affiliates may retire as young as 45. The majority of its members make no contributions, and CAP 30 has been generating very large deficits (equivalent to 1.3% of GDP in 2004). This is both a major source of inequality and a drain on public resources, which might otherwise be devoted to poorer groups.

In 2008, the government approved a Bill to radically transform Ghana's pension system. SSNIT and CAP 30 are to be replaced by a new system that closely follows the World Bank's Three Pillar Model. As part of the reform, contribution rates will be increased from 17.5 to 18.5%, of which 13.5% will be devoted to SSNIT (to cover ongoing pension costs) and 5% will be managed by private firms as part of a fully funded pillar. Proponents of the Bill claim that the new system will generate substantially higher pension benefits (*Daily Graphic*, 2008). It is difficult to see how the new system will boost pension coverage: indeed, the higher contribution rates may well serve as a disincentive to participate. To date, the government has made no commitments to develop a separate programme of pensions for impoverished older people. Despite high levels of public spending on pensions and an ambitious reform, the great majority of older people in Ghana do not receive a benefit and this state of affairs is likely to continue.

Conclusions

This chapter has shown that contributory pension schemes have had major impacts on the development experiences of most countries in the world and that, for low- and middle-income countries, most of these impacts have been negative. First and most obviously, most countries have devoted a sizeable amount of public resources to contributory pensions, especially for civil servants. Had these resources been allocated differently and channelled towards poorer social groups, economic and human development outcomes might have been greatly enhanced. Second, pension schemes had a large effect on the politics of development. Contributory pensions enabled governments to allocate the benefits of economic growth across different social groups in order to meet political objectives. Providing special privileges for public sector workers was often seen as useful for ensuring a loyal civil service, and hence an effective, modernising state. In some countries, a high proportion of civil servants were political appointees, with public employment used as a means to reward political allies. In these cases, generous civil service pensions were part of a wider system of political patronage and clientelism. Overall, the selective social insurance model has been socially divisive, leading to the development of entrenched interest groups and promoting inequality. Often, the language of welfare and the entitlements of older age were used to defend pension schemes that mainly benefited richer people aged in their fifties. The exclusion of the poor was often justified on the basis that they made no pension contributions, yet this overlooked the large amounts of government funding that was often ploughed into supposedly contributory schemes. Problems of governance and poor financial reporting systems led to an almost complete absence of accountability in pension management, creating opportunities for the political plundering of surplus funds. Contributory pensions can be thought of as an example of inappropriate technology transfer from richer countries to poorer ones, where labour market conditions and institutional structures were quite different. It is doubtful whether the repackaging of contributory programmes as privatised three pillar systems will lead to more favourable results.

If contributory pensions have been largely 'bad' for development, population ageing should not be held to blame. This chapter has shown that population ageing was a secondary, sometimes minimal, consideration in the establishment of most pension schemes. Pension fund unsustainability was the direct consequence of policy failure rather than demography. In many developing countries, if the resources currently devoted to all pension schemes were pooled into a single programme targeting poor older people, it would be possible to guarantee income security for all in later life. The barriers to achieving this are political rather than demographic.

By contrast, non-contributory social assistance pensions are essentially a welfare mechanism, rather than a resource for political management and financial opportunism. In this case, population ageing has been an important factor, as governments realise that older people account for a growing share of their populations. The spread of social pensions across developing countries is likely to benefit many older people, although some of the wider claims about their positive impacts should be treated with caution.

Given the amounts of money often involved, the attention given to pension funds is understandable. To some extent, however, this has distorted the discussion about older people and population ageing in developing countries, deflecting attention away from other issues that are equally important. This can also be seen in terms of policy. While focusing on pension provision, many developing countries devote minimal resources to health policies and social services for older people (Lloyd-Sherlock, 2002b). For pensions to effectively promote wellbeing in later life, they must be combined with a wider set of policies addressing health and care needs. In some cases, these involve policies that are cheaper and less hazardous than the management of large financial schemes. Perhaps it is time for policy makers to think less about pensions and more about older people.

Afterword: the impacts of the current global economic crisis on pension schemes

Funded pension schemes should successfully invest workers' contributions over their entire working lives – a period of perhaps 40 years. The probability of at least one severe economic shock occurring during such a long period is very high, especially in developing countries. As such, the current economic crisis provides an important test for the long-run performance of pension schemes. The crisis has already led to dramatically reduced returns on pension fund investment. A survey of pension funds in 10 countries across Latin America and Eastern Europe reported that losses on investments ranged from 8 to 50% during 2008 (World Bank, 2009). At the same time, the crisis has led to a weakening of key financial institutions, and increased public sector intervention in financial markets. This may include the re-nationalisation of privatised pension schemes. More broadly, the crisis is leading to a reappraisal of the respective roles of states and the private sector in a range of financial activities, pension management included, and calls for tighter regulatory controls (ISSA, 2009). This may lead to a move away from the World Bank's Three Pillar orthodoxy. The consequences of the crisis for state pay-as-you-go schemes and non-contributory pensions are equally severe. Contracting formal sector employment reduces tax revenue and pension fund income. Fiscal tightening and rising demands on public expenditure may reduce governments' political willingness to maintain social pensions, regardless of their welfare effects. Overall, it is likely that both current and future cohorts of pensioners will see significantly reduced benefits as a result of the crisis. This will combine with other effects, such as reduced returns on savings and the unemployment of other family members, to increase economic vulnerability in later life.

Note

[1] In the case of Brazil, these mainly targeted rural workers, since most of the urban population had access to contributory funds. Among other reasons, the rural pension was initially aimed at reducing political unrest, driven by high levels of rural poverty and landlessness (Brumer, 2002). South Africa's social pension was linked to the apartheid state and to controlling African residency in urban areas (see Chapter Six).

FOUR

Population ageing and health

Introduction

Experiences of health and illness are central to older people's wellbeing and influence how population ageing affects development. Good health may enable older people to continue in employment, facilitate their social networks and enhance their economic and emotional resilience. An old age characterised by high rates of disease and illness increases the potential economic and social 'burden' of older people and reduces their quality of life. While the risk of some diseases increases with old age, overall patterns of health vary markedly across older populations. For example, a 60-year-old woman in Japan can expect on average another 22 years of healthy life, compared with only 10 for her counterpart in Senegal (WHO, 2004a). This means that the relationship between later life and health status should not be viewed as inevitable. To some extent, national differences in healthy life expectancy are largely a consequence of general gaps in prosperity and development. However, this chapter argues that it is possible to significantly improve the health of older people even in contexts of relative poverty. It draws attention to the importance of affordable interventions based on promoting lifelong good health. Currently, most healthcare systems give little attention to such interventions, preferring to focus on advanced, hospital-based health services. As such, this chapter argues that population ageing requires a wholesale reorientation of health policy in developing countries, and that this would be of benefit to young and old.

This chapter begins with a discussion of individual experiences of biological ageing and functioning. It then explores general patterns of development and population health, before focusing more narrowly on patterns of health and disease among older people. This is followed by an account of the evolution of modern healthcare systems in developed and developing countries, including the provision of services that are of specific relevance to older people. This discussion also considers the extent to which older people are able to access health services and patterns of inequality among older people. The chapter closes with two individual case studies of older people's experiences of health and illness.

Individual ageing, health and functioning

Any discussion of health and later life runs the risk of projecting a gloomy and negative view of old age. As we saw in Chapter Two, it is important to strike a balance between overly negative views of population ageing and unrealistic notions of a 'golden third age'. It is also important to remember that later life experiences are very diverse, with variation both between individuals and across lives. Globally, rapid advances in technology and the development of health services mean that many older people enjoy a better health status and a longer life expectancy than at any time in the past. It should, however, not be assumed that these advances have been passed on to all countries and social groups in equal measure.

Strictly speaking, physical ageing begins the day we are born. However, this process is usually divided into two stages: 'adult development' up to the age of 30, and 'biological ageing' thereafter (Eyetsemitan and Gire, 2003). Biological ageing involves progressive declines of all the body's physiological functions (Woodrow, 2002a). There is still debate and uncertainty about what drives this process, although most explanations relate to cell function, including a slowdown in cell reproduction and increased rates of cell damage. A key area of scientific controversy is whether this process is genetically 'programmed' or is simply driven by the wear and tear of being alive. The rate of physical decline varies widely between different individuals and population groups, reflecting the effects of a wide range of factors (Woodrow (2002a). These include:

- genetic inheritance
- poverty
- nutrition
- social status
- smoking and alcohol consumption
- availability of health services
- lifestyle, exercise and stress
- illness through the lifecourse.

Other than genetic inheritance, the relative importance of the factors listed above will vary between richer and poorer settings. In less developed countries, poverty, malnutrition, limited health services and lifelong illness may lead to accelerated biological ageing. In more developed countries, lifestyle, social status, smoking and diet are often key determinants of variations in ageing between individuals. With the exception of genetic inheritance, all these factors operate through the entire life of an individual, and so it is essential to take a lifecourse approach to biological ageing. This has important policy implications. Rather than view illness in later life as largely inevitable, more emphasis should be placed on promoting lifelong good health. For example, policies to reduce smoking among adolescents or to improve nutrition among young children can significantly improve health in later periods of life, including old age (Eyetsemitan and Gire, 2003).

Individual health is a complex and highly subjective phenomenon that is not always easy to pin down or measure.[1] Some studies tease out different dimensions (or 'domains') of health, including physical, mental, emotional and even spiritual ones (Sadana et al, 2001). Rather than operating in isolation, these domains overlap and interact in many ways, as well as linking into other aspects of wellbeing and quality of life. Notions of good health are culturally embedded and reflect individuals' expectations. This is particularly important for older people, whose expectations of good health may be very limited (Cockerham et al, 1983). For example, one older woman I interviewed in Brazil mentioned a range of conditions that affected her daughter and granddaughter, but none that affected her personally. She described her own health in general as 'average'. On closer questioning, however, she revealed that she had several serious conditions including cataracts, angina, a skin disease and dizzy spells. This tendency for older people to overstate their general health status is very problematic when surveys are based on individuals' own assessments, which is often the case in developing countries.

Analysing patterns of health among older people is also complicated by a blurring between conditions that are usually considered health problems and other conditions better understood in terms of disability and frailty.[2] For example, arthritis, which is particularly prevalent among older people, might be understood as both a disease and a disability. Taken together, illness and disability can reduce the capacity of older people to function in particular ways, increasing their dependence on others. Activities of Daily Living (ADLs) are a commonly used indicator of functioning in later life. Table 4.1 shows that the proportion of older people in Thailand with restricted ADLs increased sharply through later life, and varied between men and women. Data for other countries show similar patterns of reduced functioning with age, although the rate of decline varies.[3] In contexts of poverty, where older people need to remain engaged in physically rigorous work in order to survive, it might be justifiable to define ADLs differently. Also, perceptions of what are 'essential' daily activities are culturally determined. For example, a study of women in Saudi Arabia found that an inability to perform prayers standing had a major impact on their perceptions of self-health (Jarallah and Al-Shammari, 1999). The overlaps between ill-health, disability and reduced functioning mean that divisions between health services and the provision of care are often blurred.

Table 4.1: Older people reporting difficulties in performing selected activities of daily living, Thailand, 1995 (%)

Activity	Age group	Men	Women
Walking	65–69	8.4	12.8
	70–74	17.3	17.8
	75+	27.4	33.4
Eating	65–69	1.1	2.2
	70–74	4.2	1.0
	75+	8.1	11.7
Bathing or toileting	65–69	3.0	3.3
	70–74	6.2	4.9
	75+	12.1	17.1
Dressing	65–60	0.7	1.2
	70–74	4.5	1.0
	75+	7.4	10.2

Source: Adapted from Zimmer et al (2003)

Development and population health

Before focusing on the health of older people, it is helpful to review wider relationships between development and population health. Chapter One explored links between development and population change, including reduced mortality and fertility and population ageing. Richer countries have experienced similar changes in population health, which are also associated with increased prosperity and development. These have seen the main causes of death and illness shift from infectious diseases, under-nutrition and inadequate hygiene to a post-transition phase, where 'diseases of wealth' (including chronic diseases, road accidents and stress) are more prominent (Caldwell, 1993; Omran, 2005). This process is known as the 'epidemiological transition'. In Britain, for example, the prevalence of deadly infectious diseases like cholera and tuberculosis declined sharply from the late 19th century. Rather than improved hospital services and new drugs, this progress was mainly driven by increased living standards among the poor. Key factors included improved nutrition, sanitation, clean water and education (particularly of women) (Riley, 2001). By the early 20th century, chronic diseases such as cancers, heart disease and stroke had become the leading causes of mortality in Britain. The growing prominence of these conditions was partly just the consequence of the decline of the old 'diseases of poverty', as well as changing lifestyles and behaviour, such as increased smoking and consumption of fats. Population ageing also contributed to these new patterns, since individuals become increasingly vulnerable to some health conditions as they age.

For most high-income countries, health trends have been broadly similar to the British experience. Also, a number of developing countries, such as Mexico, appear to have followed a similar transition (Table 4.2). Despite this, patterns of population health in developing countries are often more variable and complex than the epidemiological transition model would suggest. Many countries saw rapid improvements in health and declines in mortality in the mid-20th century due to the diffusion of new drugs and technologies from the West (Abel-Smith, 1994). Sustaining these improvements has often proved to be difficult, however, due to limited progress in improving the living standards of poorer groups (Parker and Wilson, 2000). As in Britain, clean water, sanitation and basic education are key building blocks for improved population health, but many countries fail to deliver these to large sections of their populations, old and young. In some cases, this has led to what has been termed an 'incomplete transition' or 'epidemiological polarisation' (Frenk et al, 1991). On the one hand, easily preventable diseases and poverty-related problems still account for a high share of mortality and morbidity. On the other, development and modernisation have meant that the 'diseases of wealth' have also increased. Often, distinct epidemiological scenarios can be identified between different geographical zones (rural/urban regions; rich/poor regions) and between different socioeconomic groups. As such, many developing countries face a double health challenge. In parts of the developing world, such as southern Africa, epidemics of HIV/AIDS and tuberculosis create a further burden of ill-health.

Table 4.2: Five leading causes of mortality in Mexico (% of all deaths)

	1922		1995
Pneumonia and influenza	11.2	Heart disease	14.8
Diarrhoeal diseases	7.1	Cancer	11.2
Malaria and fever	6.9	Violence and accidents	8.3
Whooping cough	3.9	Diabetes	7.7
Smallpox	3.3	Stroke	5.4

Source: Martínez and Leal (2003)

Population ageing and health trends

Given these varied epidemiological settings, it is hard to predict the health needs of older populations in poorer countries, and it should not be assumed that their health profiles will match those in richer ones. Table 4.3 summarises estimated mortality data provided by the World Health Organization (WHO). These data reveal important variations in the health profiles of different developing regions. For example, AIDS is the leading cause of mortality in sub-Saharan Africa, while in South Asia the leading cause is heart disease. In Latin America, cancers account for double the share of deaths compared with South Asia. Predictably, for older age groups, chronic conditions like heart disease, stroke and cancer account for a substantially higher proportion of deaths. Even in sub-Saharan Africa, these three diseases make up nearly a half of deaths for people aged 70 and over. WHO projections for 2030 show that these three diseases will become increasingly prominent, accounting for over 20% of all deaths in sub-Saharan Africa and 48% in Latin America.

These regional estimates show that infectious diseases such as AIDS, tuberculosis and malaria have a relatively small impact on older people's health in most developing countries, and will become even less significant over the next decades. Despite this, diseases like AIDS may still have important indirect effects on older people, including the burden of care for sick and dying children (see Chapter Six). By contrast, cancer and cardiovascular diseases (heart conditions and stroke) account for a large and growing share of ill-health and mortality. Older people are particularly susceptible to cardiovascular disease: in Britain, rates for those aged 65 or over are more than double the rates for those aged between 45 and 64 (Power et al, 2008). The relationship between age and the risk of cancer varies depending on the form of the disease. For example, in some developing countries, lung cancer is more concentrated in younger age groups, as rates of smoking are lower among older people. By contrast, the rate of prostate cancer for those aged over 70 is typically twice that of the general population. Patterns of respiratory disease across age groups are also quite variable. Older people and young children are both highly susceptible to respiratory infections, such as influenza and pneumonia. Chronic respiratory conditions, such as bronchitis, tend to be mainly concentrated in later life.

The data in Table 4.3 provide a helpful snapshot of the epidemiological diversity across developing regions and for different age groups. However, their accuracy is open to question, particularly for poorer regions. In India, for example, only around 14% of deaths were medically certified in the mid-1990s, so cause of death data are very unreliable. This has

Table 4.3: Leading causes of death in selected world regions, 2002

	Total population (% of deaths)	60- to 69-year-olds (% of deaths)	70 and over (% of deaths)
Sub-Saharan Africa			
AIDS	20	6	0
Respiratory infections	11	5	5
Chronic respiratory conditions	2	8	9
Tuberculosis	3	4	2
Cancer	4	14	13
Heart disease	4	16	19
Stroke	4	12	15
South Asia			
Diarrhoeal diseases	5	0	0
Respiratory infections	11	9	11
Chronic respiratory conditions	6	9	8
Tuberculosis	4	4	1
Cancer	7	14	10
Heart disease	15	29	28
Stroke	7	13	15
Latin America and the Caribbean			
AIDS	3	0	0
Respiratory infections	5	3	6
Chronic respiratory conditions	9	9	11
Diabetes	5	9	6
Cancer	15	23	16
Heart disease	15	21	21
Stroke	8	10	12

Source: Calculated from Mathers and Loncar (2006)

led to major discrepancies in estimates of the impact of diseases such as stroke (see Chapter Eight). Data on the cause of deaths for older people may be particularly unreliable, due to a tendency to attribute mortality to old age. For example, almost a quarter of all recorded deaths in India in 1990 were diagnosed as due to 'senility' (Visaria, 2005a). As a result, the impact of specific diseases on older people may be understated. UNAIDS, the United Nations agency responsible for compiling data on AIDS, does not routinely provide data for people aged 50 and over, since it assumes that the disease is rare among older people. In fact, levels of HIV/AIDS prevalence among older people in southern Africa may be as high as 4% (see Chapter Six).

A second limitation of these regional estimates is that they are highly aggregated and do not show variations between countries, let alone within them. A recent study found that the proportion of deaths for people aged 45 and over caused by chronic diseases ranged from 27% in Kenya to 64% in South Africa (World Bank, 2006a). It is likely that there are large differences in the health profiles of different groups of older people living in the same country. For relatively poor groups living in rural areas, the 'diseases of poverty' are likely to remain significant. For example, in the poor, largely rural Mexican state of Oaxaca, intestinal infections were the second most important cause of death for older people in 1990, but only occupied 12th place in the richer, more urban state of Baja California (Ham-Chande, 1996).

Also, cause of death data do not give a complete view of older people's health status. First, they do not tell us how long and how severely people were affected by these diseases before dying. Second, they overlook a range of other health conditions that may not always contribute to mortality, such as arthritis and mental disorders. There is general evidence that older people in poorer countries experience a higher burden of illness than in richer countries (see Table 2.1 in Chapter Two). Table 4.4 provides estimates of the combined effects of different diseases in terms of both mortality and illness. While chronic and respiratory diseases remain significant, a number of other conditions, notably blindness, are shown to have an important impact.

Table 4.4: Global burden of disease for people aged 60 and over, 2002 (% of DALYs[*])

	Latin America and Caribbean	Sub-Saharan Africa	South Asia
Heart disease	15	14	23
Cancer	14	10	9
Stroke	9	11	13
Respiratory infections	3	4	7
Blindness and vision disorders	8	8	6
Diabetes	6	2	2
Alzheimer's disease	4	1	2
Arthritis	3	2	1
Depression	2	1	2

Note: [*] Disability-Adjusted Life Years: the standard unit for combining mortality and illness. For a detailed discussion, see World Bank (1993b).
Source: Calculated from Mathers and Loncar (2006)

Blindness is particularly prevalent among older people: it is estimated that 88% of cases in developing countries were aged 60 and over in 1990 (Thylefors et al, 1995). The majority of cases are caused by cataracts, for which cheap and effective treatment is available. Table 4.4 may understate the true impact of mental illness on older people, as diagnosis is particularly difficult. Individual country studies show that a high proportion of older people suffer from depression, loneliness and anxiety, and that this can have a large effect on their quality of life. For example, surveys of people aged 60 and over in Thailand found that 12% reported that they were very lonely and between a fifth and a third presented depressive symptoms (Chayovan and Knodel, 1997; Jitapunkul and Bunnag, 1998). Despite this, little attention has been paid to mental health in developing countries, either for older people or for the population in general (Desjarlais et al, 1995). Alzheimer's disease is the most common form of dementia, a complex condition that leads to the impairment of higher mental functions, including memory, the performance of learned skills and control of emotions. The prevalence of dementia among older people varies significantly between countries, with some developing countries reporting considerably lower rates than in the West (Kalaria et al, 2008).[4] Despite this geographical variation, most surveys show a clear relationship between age and dementia, with the prevalence roughly doubling for every five-year increase from 60 years of age (Gorelick, 2004).

Population ageing has already contributed to important shifts in health patterns in developed countries and is now exerting a growing influence in many developing ones. Older people are particularly susceptible to a range of conditions, such as cardiovascular disease, blindness and dementia. Nevertheless, this ageing effect is not inevitable and varies across groups and countries. According to the WHO:

> The modifiable risk factors for chronic conditions such as heart disease, cerebrovascular disease, diabetes, HIV/AIDS, and many cancers are well known. Lifestyle and behaviour are *primary* determinants of these conditions with the potential to prevent, initiate, or advance these problems and their associated complications. (WHO, 2004b; emphasis added)

As such, effective health promotion policies have the potential to significantly improve lifelong health and reduce the epidemiological impact of population ageing. Even with such programmes in place, rapid increases in chronic diseases will probably be unavoidable and represent a major challenge for healthcare systems in developing countries. Many of these healthcare systems have patently failed to meet the health needs of younger population structures. The next sections consider different options for responding to this new challenge.

Development and the emergence of modern healthcare systems

During the late 19th century, much of the progress in population health in countries like Britain was due to factors such as improved nutrition, sanitation and education. These developments are not normally considered part of a modern healthcare system. Despite this, the 19th century also saw a rapid extension and professionalisation of modern medicine, promoted by technological progress and the growing status and influence of doctors (Hamlin, 1994). These new health services went on to make increasingly significant contributions to population health through the 20th century. Nevertheless, some authors argue that they have encouraged a 'medicalised' view of health, which is too heavily focused on disease, cure and illness, rather than taking a more holistic approach (Illich, 1976; Bilton et al, 1996).

The emergence of modern, scientific medicine in the West had considerable influence over the early development of colonial healthcare models, which viewed other medical traditions as backwards and potentially harmful (Lyons, 1994). Colonial healthcare systems made important contributions to population health in some developing countries, particularly in infectious disease control. However, provision was mainly geared towards key economic sectors, such as colonial administrators or workers in mines and plantations. Also, many health interventions were repressive in nature, such as imposing 'sanitary segregation' between native and colonial populations. As such, colonial health policies provided a template for future patterns of health provision in many developing countries, including privileged provision for key occupations such as civil servants, a heavy urban bias in service infrastructure and a low official regard for non-western forms of medicine.

The mid-20th century was a period of considerable optimism, reflected in ambitious programmes to control or eradicate various types of infectious disease, such as smallpox, polio and malaria (Dowdle, 1998). At the same time, most developing countries invested heavily in advanced hospital services, closely modelled on those of the West, and in establishing large cadres of western-trained doctors (Blas and Limbambala, 2001). This phase of health policy was in keeping with wider philosophies of modernisation and development of that time, which advocated that developing countries follow the experiences of the West as closely as possible. Predictably, most developing countries quickly faced substantial resource constraints, which limited the extension of these expensive hospital services. Rapid population growth meant that these services only reached a small, privileged minority: typically richer groups in urban areas. As such, the inequalities in health provision established under colonial regimes were further entrenched.

In some developing countries, social insurance programmes also contributed to this pattern of inequality. Chapter Three discussed the emergence of Bismarckian social insurance schemes in Western Europe and their global diffusion, with reference to pension policies. Most of these social insurance schemes had an important health component, offering workers compensation for accidents, sick pay and privileged access to medical care. As with pensions, it is possible to identify distinct models of social health insurance in developing countries. Some countries, such as Indonesia, Thailand or Ghana, limited provision to relatively privileged groups of civil servants. Others sought to extend protection to influential groups of private sector workers with occupation-specific schemes. This approach was particularly influential in Latin America, leading to parallel health systems for insured groups (usually run by social security ministries) and for those lacking protection (run by health ministries) (Abel and Lloyd-Sherlock, 2000). In all developing countries, services for unprotected groups tended to be less well resourced, more limited and of inferior quality to those offered to the rest of society. For example, in 1994, Mexico's health insurance programme for oil workers spent 20 times more per person than the Ministry of Health (Gómez-Dantés, 2000). These divisive social insurance programmes gave rise to fragmented and inegalitarian health services, which have since proved difficult to reform.[5]

By the 1970s, concerns about the high cost and limited value of specialised hospital services led to the emergence of primary healthcare as a major international health doctrine (Phillips, 1990). This emphasised health promotion, prevention, basic services and universal access. It was also linked to a wider WHO-sponsored agenda of universal access to health services, known as 'Health for all by the year 2000'. Despite considerable optimism during the 1980s, the impact of primary healthcare was relatively limited in most developing countries (Rifkin and Walt, 1986; Hall and Taylor, 2003). Its priorities were of limited interest to social insurance schemes and were sometimes resisted by doctors (who felt threatened by a less medicalised health model) and international drug companies (whose profits depended on specialised services).[6]

By the 1990s, primary healthcare had become largely overshadowed by two emerging global health agendas: reproductive healthcare and concerns about the AIDS pandemic. At the same time, the growing influence of neoliberal ideology gave rise to a new set of policies for organising and financing health systems, known as health sector reform. These sought to promote efficiency, following broadly similar principles to the World Bank-inspired pension reforms (World Bank, 1993b). Among other things, health sector reforms recognised that the state played an increasingly limited role in the provision of health services in many developing countries. As with pension funds, health insurance schemes had often proved financially unsustainable, leading to deficits and deteriorating services. Increased economic instability saw reductions in health ministry budgets, reducing already limited provision for uninsured populations. In poorer countries, a growing number of NGOs sought to compensate for declining state capacity. More generally, there has been a dramatic expansion of private healthcare services. A recent World Bank report on chronic disease concluded that the growing prevalence of these conditions can only be addressed by shifting provision away from the public to the private sector (Adeyi et al, 2007).

On the surface, the general models and philosophies that influenced the development of health services in developing countries were broadly similar to those of the West. These included early public health interventions, the expansion of hospital infrastructure followed by attempts to reprioritise basic services, concerns with reproductive health and more recent neoliberal strategies to improve efficiency. However, the nature of health services on the ground varies sharply between countries. Table 4.5 shows the vast differences in per capita health spending between high- and low-income countries, ranging from just US$3 a year in Burundi to US$4,499 in the US. Clearly, the capacity of countries like Burundi to provide health services to any of its population, young or old, is extremely limited. These variations in health spending roughly mirror overall levels of national wealth, rather than population ageing. For example, the population of the US is rather less aged than Russia's and only marginally more than Argentina's. As such, it is essential to understand the expansion of modern healthcare as part of a wider process of economic and social change. The next section examines the consequences of this development for older people.

Table 4.5: Average per capita estimated health expenditure (US$), selected countries, 1997–2000

Country	Spend (US$)	Country	Spend (US$)
Argentina	658	Indonesia	19
Brazil	267	Russian Federation	92
Burundi	3	South Africa	255
China	45	Thailand	71
Ghana	11	UK	1,747
India	23	US	4,499

Source: World Bank (2004: 256–257)

Health services for older people in developing countries

> Older people are a big headache and a waste of resources. The biggest favour you could do as an older people's organization is to get them out of my hospital. (Kenyan hospital manager, cited in HelpAge International, 2001: 10)

For many developing countries, the 20th century gave rise to health systems that failed to reach large sections of their populations, especially the rural poor. At the same time, models of provision were usually highly inequitable, curative and 'medicalised'. Services for older people were particularly limited. Health systems had been established at a time of high fertility and low population growth, and so were rightly focused on the needs of younger age groups such as mothers and children. This focus was reinforced by the later emergence of reproductive healthcare and concerns about AIDS and sexual health. At the same time, considerations of 'human capital' stressed the economic benefits of investing in the health of key groups of workers (Bloom and Canning, 2000). In some countries, this focus on 'worker health' was reinforced by occupation-specific social insurance funds.

By the late 20th century, fertility transition and population ageing meant that older people were starting to account for a significant share of the burden of disease in middle- and some low-income countries. Most developed countries had already seen a major reorientation of their health services towards chronic diseases and the needs of their older populations (NHS, 2001). This has been much less evident in the developing world, however. For example, where primary healthcare programmes have been implemented, their focus has been almost exclusively on mother and child health (Lloyd-Sherlock, 2004). The influential Millennium Development Goals include several health targets, including reducing maternal and child mortality, as well as 'combating' AIDS and other infectious diseases. This has encouraged international development agencies and NGOs to remain heavily focused on the three so-called 'killer diseases': AIDS, tuberculosis and malaria. By contrast, chronic diseases that account for a much higher share of mortality in many developing countries continue to be relatively neglected (Adeyi et al, 2007). As a result, more attention has been paid to the direct and indirect impacts of diseases such as AIDS on older people than on cardiovascular disease or cancers.[7] Influential global health policy documents make very little specific reference to the needs of older people. The World Bank's influential flagship publication *World development report: Investing in health* (World Bank, 1993b) makes virtually no mention of older people; nor does its more recent *World development report 2004* (World Bank, 2004), which includes a chapter on healthcare for the poor. Similarly, the specific attention paid to older people by organisations like the WHO and most NGOs has been minimal. Consequently, geriatric medicine and specialised services for older people remain very limited in most developing countries.

There is more than one reason for the continued neglect of older people's health needs in developing countries and global health forums. To some extent, healthcare organisations are influenced by their own historical priorities and it is not easy to change these quickly. There are, however, signs that negative attitudes towards older people and ageism are pervasive in health policy. While on-record statements as blunt as that made by the Kenyan hospital manager at the start of this section are rare, more subtle and implicit versions of this view are quite widespread. For example, much of the recent literature on chronic disease in developing countries takes pains to stress that these conditions are not restricted to older people. According to one influential study: 'Chronic diseases in developing countries are not just diseases of the elderly.... Chronic diseases affect a much higher proportion of people in their prime working years than in developed countries' (Yach et al, 2004: 2616). The implication is that these diseases are particularly important because of their impact on 'productive younger groups'.

This assumption is clearly reflected in the indicator that is most widely used to compare the values of different health interventions: the Disability-Adjusted Life Year (DALY). This tool claims to neutrally assess the impacts of interventions on individual longevity and quality of life. However, DALYs include an explicit bias away from older people to groups whose 'social value at that time may be greater' (Murray, 1994: 438). As a result, a year of life gained at the age of 70 counts for only

46% of one gained at the age of 25 (McIntryre, 2004). This has had important effects on policy priorities in developing countries where resources are limited. For example, in 2001, the influential WHO Commission on Macro-Economics and Health identified 49 priority interventions for low-income countries, none of which has specific relevance for older people (Hanson et al, 2003). A recent survey in the UK found that more than half of doctors who cared for older people believed that the National Health Service is 'institutionally ageist'. It found that 66% claimed that older people were less likely to have their symptoms investigated and 72% claimed that they were less likely to be referred to surgery or chemotherapy (Help the Aged, 2009). Similar research is not available for developing countries.

Apart from the view that older people are less productive than other age groups and therefore less deserving of healthcare, it is sometimes claimed that interventions for older people tend to be costly and of limited efficacy. For example, it has been argued that population ageing in developing countries will lead to a

> morbidity burden [that] can quickly overwhelm fragile and often underfinanced health infrastructures already unable to meet fully the prevention and treatment needs of a younger population with relatively low-cost, easy to prevent, easy-to-treat illnesses. Inappropriate application of costly technology could easily result: accompanied by the diversion of resources from existing primary care services…. (Bicknell and Parks, 1989: 59)

These concerns reflect debates in developed countries, which, in their more extreme form, make apocalyptic predictions about population ageing and collapsing health and welfare systems (Petersen, 1999). The question is whether the health needs are necessarily expensive to treat, or whether cost-effective interventions are available. To some extent, this depends on whether health systems take a curative and highly medicalised approach, or place greater emphasis on lifelong health promotion and prevention.

The implications of these two different approaches for older people's health are particularly clear in the case of chronic illnesses such as hypertension. This condition significantly increases the risk of stroke, heart disease, kidney damage and blindness, especially for people in later life. There is a range of alternative strategies for dealing with hypertension. Primary prevention involves reducing the prevalence of hypertension throughout life, with policies that discourage smoking, improve diet and promote exercise. However, few developing countries have made significant progress in this area (Feigin, 2007). For example, a recent survey of stroke and heart disease patients in low- and middle-income countries found that over a quarter believed that physical activity was harmful to health (Mendis et al, 2005). Similarly, large industrial interests have undermined efforts to curb smoking and educate people about the risks of tobacco in many countries (Jha and Chaloupka, 2000). Secondary prevention involves controlling hypertension to reduce the risk of stroke and heart attacks. This is usually achieved through various drug therapies, ranging from low dosage aspirin costing a few pennies a month to more specialised hypertension drugs costing around US$10. For all but the poorest developing countries, this represents an affordable and simple policy option, yet a range of studies has found that a high proportion of people diagnosed with hypertension do not even take aspirin (Walker et al, 2000; WHO, 2005a). Together, primary and secondary prevention strategies have led to significant falls in the incidence of stroke in most developed countries. By contrast, the cost of dealing with acute health episodes such as stroke and heart attacks is extremely high. A study of six developing countries found that the cost of the clot-busting drugs most commonly used to treat stroke ranged from US$1,200 to US$2,300 per treatment. This did not include other costs, such as hospitalisation (Pandian et al, 2007b). Consequently, only a very small number of cases from the richest and most privileged groups receive effective treatment.

This example demonstrates the need to substantially reorientate health policies in developing countries away from curative, largely hospital-based care towards policies that promote good health through the lifecourse. Maintaining physical and mental fitness throughout life, including during old age, has been shown to have significant effects on the onset and progression of many forms of chronic disease and mental health conditions (Woodrow, 2002b). These policies would benefit all population groups, young and old. In some ways, then, population ageing simply highlights the unsustainability and ineffectiveness of established healthcare strategies in developing countries.

More generally, there is considerable scope for mainstreaming older people's needs into primary healthcare (PHC) for developing countries. There is evidence that PHC services lend themselves well to building bridges between hospitals services and care provided at home and in the community (Moon, 2002). At the same time, basic, clinic-based services can ease the pressure on hospitals, by providing an element of triage and improving referral procedures. A study in the UK found that 20% of hospital bed days for older people were 'probably inappropriate', and would be unnecessary if more intermediary care services were in place (UK Department of Health, 2001). In developing countries, where hospital infrastructure and specialist health services are very limited, these concerns are especially valid. As well as health promotion and prevention interventions, there is scope for PHC to mitigate the impact of incurable health conditions. Palliative healthcare (reducing suffering from terminal conditions) and concerns about dignified end-of-life care have emerged as key health policy concerns in developed countries. Other than limited initiatives for people with AIDS, they receive virtually no attention in the majority of developing countries, (Seale, 2000; Harding, 2006). At the same time, PHC programmes have the potential to educate older people and their families about widely misunderstood conditions such as depression and Alzheimer's, and this may facilitate their coping.

Older people and access to health services

Even where services of relevance to older people exist, this does not automatically mean that all older people enjoy good access to them. This section considers whether older people enjoy the same levels of access to health services as other age groups. It also examines inequalities of access within older populations. It focuses on two key forms of access barriers: structural mechanisms and sociocultural factors. The first mainly refers to the functioning of healthcare systems, including how they are financed. The second focuses on informal processes of decision making, particularly in households.

Most countries have constitutions that claim to guarantee good health for their entire populations and recognise that all groups are entitled to equal levels of access to these services, regardless of age or other criteria. In reality, all countries, rich and poor, need to prioritise and ration the provision of healthcare. One key mechanism for doing this is through financial arrangements. For example, where older people are required to pay directly for health services, this will often lead to substantial access barriers for all but the richest. In many developing countries, private healthcare provision is much more widespread than government services. As well as high-quality services for the rich, private providers include a large number of mainly unregulated services for the 'lower end' of the market (Zwi et al, 2001). The costs of these private health services are usually substantial, particularly for older individuals who are likely to make frequent use of them (Lima–Costa et al, 2002). As such, high levels of health spending can be a major source of impoverishment and economic vulnerability for households containing older people (Kawabata et al, 2002).

In some cases, older people are also required to pay in full or in part for government health services. These payments are usually referred to as 'user fees' and have been widely promoted as part of health sector reform strategies for sustainable health financing in poor countries (Fiedler, 1993). In theory, user fees may generate additional revenue or 'rationalise' health service usage. In practice, they have often been shown to be inequitable, even where exemptions are supposedly in place for vulnerable groups (Russell and Gilson, 1997). For example, a survey of older people in Ghana found that most were unaware that they were exempt from paying user fees for services from public hospitals, and this had greatly reduced their access (Ahenkora, 1999). Similarly, research from South Africa showed that user fees had a disproportionate impact on utilisation by older people, even though this country boasts a relatively generous pension programme (McIntyre, 2004). A survey of older people in China reported that the introduction of user fees was the main reason why they did not visit doctors or attend hospitals (Jayasinghe, 2006). Recently, organisations such as the World Bank have distanced themselves from user fees, recognising that they are both inequitable and ineffective at generating significant additional revenues, although they are still advocated in a new guise of 'pro-poor copayments' (World Bank, 2004).

Social insurance and private insurance also have particular effects on older people's access to services. In those developing countries that contain substantial social insurance schemes, large inequalities between insured and uninsured older people may arise. In Mexico, for example, insured older people have significantly higher utilisation of formal health services than other older people. For their part, uninsured older Mexicans make greater use of traditional services and self-medication (Borges-Yañez and Gómez-Dantés, 1998; Pagan and Puig, 2005). Private health insurance has been expanding quickly in parts of the developing world, particularly Asia and Latin America (Sekhri and Savedoff, 2005). This is likely to increase general inequalities in population health, and may have particular effects on older people. Ideally, private health insurance funds prefer not to enrol older people, since older people are more likely to make claims and therefore reduce fund profits. Without effective regulation, private funds may exclude older age groups or insist on excessively high premiums (see Chapter Seven for examples of this).

A separate set of access barriers relates to sociocultural factors that may have particular affects on older people. Research from Asia and sub-Saharan Africa found that older people sometimes made little use of services such as cataract treatments, even when they were provided almost free of charge (Donoghue, 1999).The study found that barriers to access included poor knowledge about the service, the low status of many older people in their communities and a widespread belief that poor vision was a natural part of the ageing process. There are indications that these barriers are significant for large numbers of older people in developing countries. For example, there is strong evidence that utilisation of health services is linked to education, and so low levels of literacy among older populations will have a significant effect (Abel-Smith, 1994). Household decision making has a major influence on the use of health services, and so the status of older people within households can be important (Berman et al, 1994).The limited available research suggests that households tend to place more emphasis on the needs of key breadwinners or young children than on older people (Laslett, 1992; Moody, 1993). For example, a study from Uganda (where few services are available free of charge) reported that levels of utilisation for the under fives were roughly double those for people aged 65 and over (Xu et al, 2005). In some cases older people themselves may place a low value on their own health needs, compared with other family members' (Kespichayawattana and VanLandingham, 2003).These attitudes may also be present among health professionals, leading them to informally discriminate against older patients.[8]

The interplay of structural and sociocultural barriers can be seen in a survey of older people's healthcare utilisation in Vietnam (Oahn, 2002). By developing world standards, Vietnam has a good healthcare infrastructure, although older people are now required to pay user fees to access many of the healthcare services (World Bank, 2001; Khe et al, 2002). As in other countries, older people's health needs have received little attention from primary healthcare providers, and there is a shortage of health workers with appropriate geriatric training.The survey found that around 30% of older people who reported acute illnesses over the previous month had not sought care, from either formal providers or other sources outside the household. In 24% of cases, the cost of health services was cited as the main reason for not seeking care. However, 13% respondents claimed they were 'too old to go'. Over half the respondents claimed that their sons were the main decision makers about the use of healthcare services. Only 32% of older men and 23% of older women identified themselves as the main decision makers. The Vietnamese experience suggests that even if healthcare systems are well developed, and even if they provide a wider range of services for older people, these will fail to meet their needs unless appropriate financing strategies are in place.

There are grounds for expecting that in many developing countries older women will be particularly affected by both structural and sociocultural barriers to healthcare. For example, lower rates of lifetime formal sector employment will limit women's health insurance entitlements and will also mean that they have less access to personal pension income to meet healthcare costs. In some countries, older women have lower levels of formal education than men, which will further restrict their access to healthcare. At the same time, specific forms of informal and cultural discrimination against women may continue to operate against them in later life (Sen and Östlin, 2007). The evidence about patterns of illness and healthcare needs among older men and women is quite complex, however. On the one hand, older men usually experience higher rates of mortality than older women, due to a combination of genetic factors and risk behaviours. On the other, many studies report that older women consistently report significantly higher levels of ill-health and lower levels of functioning than older men (WHO, 2000; Zimmer et al, 2003; Palloni and McEniry, 2007).[9] Similarly, patterns of health service utilisation are complex and vary markedly across countries. Older women do not consistently report lower levels of utilisation of health services than older men, and in some cases their rates are higher (Ofstedal and Natavidad, 2003; Yount et al, 2004; Barreto et al, 2006). While gender inequalities in healthcare among older people are sometimes significant, they are variable and complex and so generalisations should be avoided.

Case studies: health in later life[10]

It would be impossible to capture the many issues discussed in this chapter and the varied experiences of older people in a small number of case studies. The two cases outlined here are intended to illustrate some of the complex effects of health and illness on older people's lives. They refer to people from very different socioeconomic backgrounds and locations, highlighting the danger of generalising about older people and health across developing countries. Despite these sharp contrasts, there are still important points of similarity across the two stories. Both reveal complex cycles of illness and vulnerability and each case demonstrates how health problems of other family members can have major effects on older people themselves.

Elizabeth

Elizabeth is 77 years old and lives in a village in Masaka District, southwestern Uganda. This is a relatively impoverished region, dominated by small subsistence farms. By 2000, around 8% of its adult population were estimated to be HIV-positive, a condition that remains highly stigmatised in Uganda.

When asked about her health, Elizabeth did not refer to specific conditions, but described herself as weak "from the head to the knees". Over the past three years, she had been suffering from constant pain in both her legs and now had limited mobility: "Even where there is a burial I sometimes no longer reach [sic]. You imagine not reaching your friends and you feel depressed having lost contact with them." She said that the pain often reduced her to tears, and had made her feel like an old woman for the first time in her life.

Elizabeth claimed she had been in very good health for most of her life, until 2006 when she broke a leg when building her house. She first went to a traditional healer who tried to heal her leg with a mixture of herbs and clay. After a month or so, she lost faith in this treatment and went to a local clinic, which referred her to a district hospital for an X-ray. Sometime after she broke her leg, she began to experience pains in the other one; she puts these down to 'old age', rather than a specific condition such as arthritis. Elizabeth was able to obtain pain relief for her legs from a local clinic that was supported by an international medical agency. However, she claimed that the clinic staff were sometimes hostile to her and threatened to withhold the medication.

Elizabeth's various health treatments were paid for by a nephew, who also provided her with some economic support: "God found a gift for me, a son of my brother." During her life, Elizabeth had given birth to just one child – a daughter who had since died. Elizabeth did not explain the circumstances of this child's death, but was concerned that her nephew did not meet a similar fate: "I pray very hard that I die before him and he attends to my burial; not myself burying him." Elizabeth was worried about her growing dependence on her nephew. Shortly before the interview, she had required hospitalisation because of "dizziness and fever". She had been reluctant to ask her nephew to pay for this, but was eventually forced to do so.

Elizabeth had nursed several people through serious illnesses; "but now I think God realises I do not have the strength to do nursing". Nevertheless, she still provided general care and support for another nephew who was suffering from an unspecified condition. Elizabeth felt that this was her personal responsibility, since the man's biological parents were both dead. She cooked for him and reminded him to take his medication when he had too much to drink.

Bima

Bima was a high-ranking member in the Indonesian civil service, from a middle-class family based in Jakarta. He first became aware he had hypertension when he was 45 years old and suffered a minor stroke. Bima was treated in a government hospital exclusively for civil servants for two weeks and prescribed anti-hypertensives. These were provided free of charge through the civil service health programme. However, they were not effective in lowering his blood pressure and Bima did not trust locally produced drugs. Instead, he purchased imported drugs, but these were expensive, taking up about half of his household's income. To cover these extra costs, the family sold both their cars, sold land and drew on savings. Bima was advised to improve his diet, lose weight, take exercise and develop a less stressful lifestyle, but found it difficult to put this into practice. According to his wife, he had a fatalistic attitude towards his health, despite a family history of hypertension and strokes: "He just wasn't used to doing exercise, and was reluctant to change. He preferred to rely on medication instead".

When he was 52 years old, Bima required surgery for a blocked heart artery and was treated free of charge in the country's leading heart hospital. Ten years later, he suffered his second stroke, which was more serious than the first. Again, he received high-quality emergency treatment in a specialised hospital. Bima was left partially paralysed and mentally impaired. The family paid for frequent physiotherapy and acupuncture sessions, as well as a full-time live-in nurse. Combined with the costs of the drugs, this took up the vast bulk of the household income. By this stage, Bima's children had successful careers and his wife had set up her own business, working out of her house. Nevertheless, they sometimes needed to rely on help from friends and the wider family. Despite the support of the live-in nurse, his wife found his condition very demanding and stressful: "I was lucky if I got four hours' sleep a night.... He would call me every few minutes just to see if I was around.... He felt lonely and scared." This took a serious toll on her own psychological health.

Five months after his second stroke, Bima suffered a third attack and was hospitalised for two weeks. By now, Bima was becoming increasingly depressed, bad-tempered and aggressive, sometimes hitting the nurse or scratching and biting his wife. She found this extremely distressful and was forced to pay the nurse in compensation. Over the following months, Bima lost the ability to speak and started to refuse food and drink. Nevertheless, with intensive nursing and care from his wife, he survived for three years, before dying peacefully at home with his wife and children present. "Despite being ill for such a long time, he had not developed bedsores.... It was as if he had only been ill for a short time, and so I felt that I had done all I could for him."

Bima's wife remains distressed by the loss of her husband and the unpleasant, prolonged nature of his illness. However, she takes some satisfaction from believing that she did everything that was possible to help him. She is also comforted by her devout religious faith. Now aged 63, she is committed to continuing her business, so that she will be financially independent when she is older. After her husband's experience and the loss of many other friends and relatives to stroke, she is determined to maintain a healthy lifestyle of her own. However, she recognises that this is not always easy to do in modern Jakarta: "People spend a lot of time sitting in cars, in traffic jams. You can join the gym, but it's expensive and you have to find the time to do it." Recently, she herself developed high blood pressure and was hospitalised.

Conclusion

This chapter shows that individual ageing is associated with an increased risk of specific health conditions and of reduced functioning, but that these effects are more elastic and less inevitable than is commonly supposed. In most countries, the majority of older people enjoy a better health status than their parents or grandparents did at a similar age. This is due to the growing range of effective therapies for conditions such as cancer, which no longer represents the automatic 'death sentence' it used to. However, these curative interventions are expensive and less readily available in developing countries, where resources are scarcer. Health in later life can also be improved by addressing a wide range of lifecourse effects such as nutrition and exercise. In developed countries, health systems have placed less emphasis on these, despite the evident affordability and benefits of policies that improve diets, reduce smoking and encourage exercise. In developing countries, where large numbers of older people do not have adequate access to curative services, the need for lifelong health promotion is even greater. The continued emphasis on curative health services reduces the scope to promote healthy ageing and increases the costs of treating older people.

There are several reasons for the continued neglect of lifelong health promotion. First, threatening the interests of large tobacco and food industries is a major political challenge, especially for developing country governments. At the same time, there are large political and institutional obstacles to shifting the established emphases of health service providers. Identifying specific policies that succeed in promoting lifelong health is not a simple task, since it requires changes to attitudes, behaviours and lifestyles. These are less tangible than treating illnesses once they have already occurred. Also, it should not be assumed that interventions that prove effective in developed countries can be successfully translated to different socioeconomic and cultural settings. Instead, lessons may be taken from other experiences in developing countries, such as efforts to change attitudes towards risk and sexual behaviour in the face of the AIDS epidemic (Barnett and Whiteside, 2002).

This chapter also shows that health providers often discriminate against older people. In richer countries, this can be seen in the 'institutional ageism' that permeates clinical decision making. In poorer countries, it can be seen in the limited extent of geriatric services and an ageist bias in cost–effectiveness indicators such as DALYs. Older people from poorer groups face particular difficulties in overcoming a range of access barriers, leaving many facing the prospect of untreated conditions and an unnecessarily premature death.

Overall, this chapter shows that changes associated with development have generally benefited the health of older people. However, these benefits fall short of what might have been achieved with more balanced policies, and not all older people have benefited to the same extent. The capacity to sustain these health improvements is questionable, especially in settings of rapid population change and scarce resources. Unless there are radical shifts in global health policy, future increases in chronic disease and reduced functioning associated with later life will be very fast.

Notes

[1] The World Health Organization defines health as 'a state of complete, physical, mental and social well-being and not merely the absence of disease or infirmity' (WHO, 2003).

[2] There is an emerging body of research on disability in developing countries, but few links have been made between disability in general and disability associated with later life (Stone, 1999). The disability literature has much to offer those interested in ageing and development, particularly in areas such as community-based rehabilitation and the social construction of impairment.

[3] For example, the same study found that in Taiwan only 12.4% of women aged 75 and over reported difficulties walking, compared with 33.4% in Thailand (Zimmer et al, 2003).

[4] The reasons for this variation remain unclear, but may relate to the genetic profiles of different populations.

[5] Social health insurance also contributed to the focus on specialist hospital care, instead of basic services and health promotion, which remained mainly the responsibility of under-resourced health ministries.

[6] Chowdhury (1995) provides an interesting account of the role of the international pharmaceutical industry and essential drugs in Bangladesh. Garfield (1989) describes the hostility of many medical doctors to a radical primary healthcare programme implemented in Nicaragua.

[7] Good studies of older people and AIDS include Knodel and Saengtienchai (2004) and Seeley et al (2009). Chapter Six explores the issue with reference to South Africa.

[8] This has been identified as an important issue in developed countries (Singh et al, 2005), but remains unresearched in low- and middle-income countries.

[9] Interestingly, patterns of gender difference vary across countries. For example, in Thailand, reported rates of heart disease among older women was more than three times that for older men, yet in the US, women reported a lower rate (Zimmer et al, 2003). The reasons for these variations are not well understood.

[10] The names of the informants in this section have been changed to preserve their anonymity.

FIVE

Later life and social relations: family, migration and care

Introduction

Informal networks and social relations are central to the wellbeing of all age groups, but are particularly important for older people and young children. As societies undergo modernisation and development, the nature of these social relations will shift, sometimes abruptly. These changes have profound consequences for the lives of individuals and they also feed back into wider development. For example, China's dramatic fertility decline since the 1980s has reshaped families and this will have complex and substantial impacts on that country's future. Chapter Two introduced the idea that modernisation is usually harmful to older people since, among other things, it reduces their social contacts and promotes their isolation. In fact, it is very dangerous to make such generalised claims, since processes of modernisation are very diverse and older people face widely differing circumstances. This chapter explores these issues in more detail. It begins by examining trends in family structures and patterns of living arrangements, and then considers their implications for older people. These developments are located within a wider setting of social change, including an analysis of the effects of migration on older people. The chapter closes with a discussion of the provision of long-term care, including institutional care homes.

Throughout the chapter, particular attention is paid to gender issues. Gender dynamics play a major part in shaping social relations and underpin the functioning of households and other informal institutions. In almost all societies, the majority of caregiving is provided by women, either on an informal basis (looking after relatives) or as salaried workers (in care institutions, hospitals or as hired home carers). Consequently, where development leads to changes in women's social and economic roles, this may have important effects on older people. Personal experiences of later life are highly gendered in a number of other important ways. For example, in some countries, women's limited lifetime access to paid work and restricted pension entitlements mean that they are especially dependent on the support provided by children and other family members when they reach old age. More often than not, older women outlive their spouses, which may leave them vulnerable to social isolation.

Social relations can be understood as a key component of what is sometimes called 'informal social protection'. Social protection refers to any actions that reduce vulnerability, risk and deprivation, and the concept has emerged as a key policy focus in international development (Barrientos and Hulme, 2007). These actions may include 'formal' mechanisms, such as large-scale pension programmes, as well as 'informal' ones, provided by households and communities. In Chapter Three, we saw that older people in developing countries usually obtain most economic support from sources other than pensions. For some older people, paid employment may provide a continued livelihood, but for many (particularly women and the oldest old), families and social relations are often the only means of protection. With reference to social protection, it is helpful to distinguish between three different forms of support. **Material support** refers to transfers of income or other goods (such as food or clothing); **instrumental support** refers to the provision of general assistance with activities of daily living, such as dressing, eating or bathing; and **psychological support** refers to emotional aspects of social relationships. Each of these aspects of support is important for different aspects of wellbeing in later life, although policy makers and social protection research tend to focus on material and economic ones. This chapter seeks to develop a more balanced approach.

Data on social relations in later life are quite limited, especially for developing countries. There are, however, clear indications that experiences are very diverse. For example, older people are often just as likely to provide different forms of support as they are to receive them. In fact, for some older people, social relations and family obligations may be a cause of vulnerability rather than a source of support. To illustrate this diversity, the chapter concludes with a number of detailed case studies, taken from a range of different development settings.

Development and changing social structures

Individual experiences of social relationships should be understood as part of wider trends in social structures affecting all age groups. These result from a complex interplay between population change, development and cultural factors. This section examines these wider social trends and then focuses more directly on older people. Before continuing our analysis, it is important to clarify a number of key terms that are widely used to describe social structures.

Households consist of a single person or group of people living together in the same residential unit. Some definitions require that households participate in shared practices, such as eating together on a daily basis.

Family is a much less precise term than 'household'. Broadly, it refers to small groups of closely related people who have a strong sense of shared identity, which sets them apart from non-family members. Often, families are categorised as:

- 'nuclear': usually two-generation families containing parents and unmarried children;
- 'extended': usually containing several generations and a wider range of relatives and sometimes spanning across numerous households.

In reality, families are much more diverse than these simple categories imply (Fulcher and Scott, 2007). The forms families take and the ways they are understood vary greatly across different cultures. However, most families are characterised by close personal relationships and, theoretically, strong norms of obligation and mutual responsibility.

Kinship usually refers to wider networks of people connected by common descent or marriage. Just as a single family can straddle several households, a kinship network will usually include more than one family. This is particularly important when family members have migrated but remain in contact. Understandings, practices and obligations relating to kinship systems vary widely across different cultures.

Households, families and kinship networks are highly dynamic arrangements and subject to change over time. This has important consequences for all age groups, old and young. There are a number of widely held views about these changes. First, it is claimed that industrialisation and other aspects of development usually lead to a shift away from extended to more nuclear family structures. There is considerable evidence for this transformation in Europe and North America (Ruggles, 1994). However, patterns of change are not always as simple as commonly assumed. In pre-industrial Britain, for example, nuclear families were already the dominant form (Laslett and Wall, 1972). At the same time, there have been historical variations in family and household structures between different socioeconomic groups, and rural or urban settings. While average household sizes have fallen in most developed countries, extended families and kinship networks have been quite resilient in some cases such as Italy (Murphy, 2008).

These important changes in social structures have been influenced by wider population and development experiences. Fertility transition means that women have fewer children and so families and kinship networks are likely to shrink. Where fertility has fallen quickly (which is the case in many developing countries), these changes to social structures may be abrupt. Table 5.1 compares the number of live births reported by different age groups of women in Brazil. It shows that 43% of women aged 70 and over had six or more children, compared with just 11% of women aged between 40 and 44. One consequence of this is that household sizes have fallen sharply: from four in 1981 to three in 2004 (IBGE, 2008).

Table 5.1: Number of reported live births for women by age category, Brazil, 2000

	40–44	50–54	60–64	70+
0 children (%)	10	10	10	12
I child (%)	11	9	8	8
2 (%)	29	19	12	10
3 (%)	22	19	12	10
4 (%)	11	12	11	9
5 (%)	6	8	9	8
6+ (%)	11	23	38	43
	100	100	100	100

Source: IBGE (2008)

Other aspects of development have also contributed to changing social structures. Historical analysis of the US experience shows that urbanisation and shifts in livelihoods from family-centred farms to wage labour based outside the home played an important role in the emergence of nuclear structures (Ruggles, 2001). At the same time, it has been argued that modernisation leads to the replacement or reduction of families' former roles, such as child socialisation and welfare provision, by the state (Giddens, 2005). In many developing countries, urbanisation, migration and economic change have been particularly rapid and so may reinforce the impact of fertility decline on social structures. A comparative survey of 10 East and South East Asian countries found that all had experienced significant declines in average household size during the 1980s and 1990s (Quah, 2003). However, since families, households and kinship networks are also shaped by cultural factors, it should not be assumed that all developing countries will follow the experience of the developed world. For example, despite rapid increases in national wealth and urbanisation in Saudi Arabia, the TFR remained at around four per woman in 2000.

In developed countries, the emergence of nuclear families was associated with industrialisation and urbanisation. In more recent decades, new shifts in social norms and practices have occurred, leading to further changes in social structures. Important post-industrial shifts include rising rates of divorce and remarriage, and increasing numbers of children living with just one parent. These have led to a growing diversity of family forms and a general shift away from nuclear households to solitary living. For example, between 1961 and 2001, the proportion of people in Britain living on their own rose from 11 to 29% (Social Trends, 2006). There are indications that these changes are now occurring in a growing number of developing countries (UN-DESA, 2003a). In Brazil, divorce rates remain much lower than in most developed countries, but increased by 200% between 1984 and 2007 (IBGE, 2008). Similarly, many countries in Africa have seen a sharp rise in the divorce rate (Ohenaba-Sakyi and Tayki, 2006).[1]

Older people's living arrangements

How have these general trends in social structures affected older people? Table 5.2 shows available data on older people's living arrangements for a range of developing countries. It demonstrates considerable diversity, such that an older woman in Malawi was twice as likely to live alone as her counterpart in Colombia. In all countries, there are important differences between older women and older men, with women usually more likely to be living alone and less likely to be living as a couple. This reflects the greater probability that older women will outlive their spouses than the reverse situation. In most cases, a substantial number of older people live with young children or grandchildren, but not with adult children. The number of older people living just with grandchildren in Malawi is strikingly high. This arrangement, sometimes called a 'skip-generation household', is largely caused by the loss of adult children to HIV/AIDS.[2] However, even in countries with a relatively low prevalence of HIV/AIDS such as Indonesia, significant numbers of older people live in skip-generation households. In this case, a key factor is high rates of migration by young adults who leave young children behind with grandparents (Schröder-Butterfill, 2004).

General analyses by the United Nations conclude that the proportion of older people living with one or more children is declining globally, and especially in developing countries (United Nations Population Division, 2005). However, reliable data demonstrating these trends over

Table 5.2: Living arrangements of people aged 60 and over, selected developing countries (%)

Country and year	Sex	Alone	Couple only	With at least one adult child*	With young child** (and no adult child)	With grandchild (and no children)[3]	Other
Turkey 1998	Male	4	35	42	15	1	4
	Female	12	24	54	5	1	4
Indonesia 1997	Male	2	22	42	23	6	5
	Female	12	13	54	6	6	9
Malawi 2000	Male	8	16	17	35	18	6
	Female	14	8	28	13	31	6
Colombia 2000	Male	7	13	50	14	5	11
	Female	7	9	61	4	6	13

Notes: * Aged 25 and over.
** Aged up to 25.

Source: United Nations Population Division (2005)

long periods of time are unavailable for many developing countries. Table 5.3 shows a relatively gradual shift in older people's living arrangements in Indonesia and Turkey over two decades. If these trends are representative of other developing countries, then we may expect steady increases in the proportion of older people living alone and reductions in the proportion living with children. Nevertheless, the proportions of older people living without relatives in most developing countries remain substantially lower than in the developed world. For example, by 2006, a third of people aged 65 and over in the UK lived alone, rising to a half for older women (ONS, 2008). As such, while some developing countries are moving towards more western patterns of living arrangements, most still have a long way to go. The speed and direction of future trends are not entirely predictable. Where rapid fertility transitions occurred over the past 30 or 40 years, the main effects of this shift on older people's household arrangements may yet be felt. Countries such as China and Brazil may therefore see sudden and unprecedented changes in living arrangements in future decades.

Some commentators have suggested that the high proportion of older people living alone in developed countries is mainly due to the wider provision of pensions and other welfare services (Karagiannaki, 2005).

Table 5.3: Living arrangements for people aged 60 and over, Indonesia and Turkey (%)

		Alone	Couple only	With child	With grandchild (and no child)	Other
Indonesia	1974	5.5	12.8	66.1	7.2	8.4
Indonesia	1997	7.3	16.9	62.8	6.1	6.9
Turkey	1978	5.9	16.7	69.5	3.0	4.9
Turkey	1998	7.5	26.4	60.7	2.0	3.4

Source: United Nations Population Division (2005)

This links in with arguments about pensions potentially discouraging family support for older people (see Chapter Three). However, historical evidence from the US shows that the rise in solitary living by older people began well before the development of an embracing welfare system (Ruggles, 2001). Likewise, comparisons across developing countries with different degrees of pension provision do not reveal obvious differences in older people's living arrangements. In South Africa (which has a near-universal pension), around 8% of people 60 and over lived alone in 1998, compared with 22% in Ghana (where only a small minority receive pensions) (United Nations Population Division, 2005). In Brazil, the extension of pension coverage during the 1990s coincided with increases in the average size of households containing older people (Camarano, 2004). One explanation for this may be that younger relatives were attracted by the prospect of sharing this pension income.

Living arrangements and older people's wellbeing

Living alone or without adult children is generally seen as detrimental to older people's wellbeing (Cowgill, 1976). The argument goes that older people are often highly dependent on families for economic and other forms of support and that living apart from relatives is likely to reduce this support. According to the United Nations:

> Co-residence with adult children is an important element of the flow of support between family members. This is particularly so with respect to informal support that depends on physical proximity such as assistance with activities of daily living. (United Nations Population Division, 2005: xvii)

There is considerable evidence that many older people receive substantial amounts of economic assistance from family members, especially in developing countries where pension schemes are limited (Aboderin, 2004; Ofstedal et al, 2004; Scott, 2008). This dependence is likely to grow through later life, as older people's capacity for salaried labour becomes increasingly impaired. Similarly, the care needs of older people with restricted physical and mental functioning are often met by family members, even in developed countries (Brodsky et al, 2003b; OECD, 2005). More broadly, surveys from different cultures show that most older people place a high value on maintaining regular contact with children and other relatives (van der Geest, 2004a; Lloyd-Sherlock, 2007). In keeping with this, most studies show that older people living alone are more likely to suffer from loneliness and depression (United Nations Population Division, 2005). Since data on living arrangements are easier to collect and more generally available than more complex data on economic and social circumstances, they are sometimes used as an indirect 'proxy' indicator of older people's wellbeing.

Although there is some truth in these general observations, they are based on a number of simplified assumptions about older people and household dynamics. First, it should not be assumed that flows of economic, instrumental or psychological support within households and families are always one-way from younger generations to older ones. In many cases, older people provide at least as much material support as they receive, even when they do not have pensions to share (Guo, 2000; Schröder-Butterfill, 2004). Often, women's caring roles continue into later life, as the care needs of children give way to the needs of grandchildren or frail and ailing husbands. As such, it is more helpful to view household relations in terms of interdependency, rather than in terms of who supports whom. Also, the mere presence of an adult child in the same building as an older person is not a guarantee that this child will provide support when required. For example, children who remain living with their elderly parents may be less economically successful than those who succeeded in establishing an independent household. This may include children who are unemployed, disabled or substance abusers (Lloyd-Sherlock and Locke, 2008). In the worst of cases, older people may be exposed to abuse by other household members. Studies from developed countries estimate that between 4 and 6% of older people living at home experience some form of abuse (WHO, 2002b). In most developing countries, elder abuse remains largely ignored, despite growing awareness of violence against women and the vulnerability of young children (WHO, 2005b).[4]

Simple assumptions about living arrangements are also challenged by research findings that wealthy older people are more likely to live alone (Ramos, 1992; Da Vanzo and Chan, 1994). Some older people express a strong preference for solitary living, which they associate with independence, privacy and personal autonomy. This may be particularly the case for older people who still enjoy relatively good health and functioning. Conversely, for the poor, co-residence may result from a lack of affordable housing options and entail overcrowding, especially in urban settings. This in turn may promote household tensions and generational conflict over control and ownership of the home (Sokolovsky, 2001).

There is growing evidence that patterns of support and exchange within families are strongly affected by gender dynamics. One key issue is the rise in female salaried economic activity that has occurred in some, although not all, developing countries (ILO, 2007). The generalised assumption is that this will reduce support for older people, since most care is provided by women (Cowgill, 1976). This need not always be the case, however. If female employment is well remunerated, increased household income will boost their capacity to offer material support for older members. If fertility levels are falling, increased female work time may be offset by the reduced care needs of young children. Also, well-paid women may hire cheaper, lower-skilled carers to meet the instrumental needs of older family members. Even so, paid carers may not be able to compensate for the decline in psychological and emotional support resulting from the absence of close relatives. This scenario may only reflect the experiences of a minority of working women, as for many, employment opportunities are more limited than for men and are less well remunerated (ILO, 2007). For poorer families, increased female salaried work is more likely to result from survival needs than reduced fertility, and it is usually less well paid. Here, any potential benefits for older people are less obvious. Overall, then, it is evident that the implications of changing female employment patterns are complex and context-specific.

Taken together, the various strands of evidence show that it is dangerous to generalise about links between older people's living arrangements and their wellbeing. It may well be the case that older people who live with adult relatives usually experience less vulnerability and enjoy a better quality of life than those who do not. As such, the higher proportion of women who live alone may mean that they are particularly disadvantaged in some ways. However, there are many important exceptions to this general rule. Table 5.4 identifies a number of factors that *may* influence the extent and direction of

Table 5.4: Potential influences on the direction of intergenerational support at the household level

Factors that may promote household support for older people	Factors that may promote older people's support for other family members
Older person's needs for material, instrumental and psychological support	Younger household members with a poor economic situation compared with older members
High status of older person in the household, perhaps due to significant perceived contributions made to other family members in the past	Specific needs of younger household members, due to health problems, addiction or disability
Older person owns assets (such as land or housing) to bequeath to younger household members in exchange for support	Skip-generation households with young grandchildren
State policies that encourage support, such as cash benefits for carers	Capacity of older members to provide different forms of support (health status, access to pension income, etc)
Strong and resilient cultural norms of family support, reinforced by community structures	Cultural norms that encourage continued parental responsibility for children and offspring
Presence of adult household members with financial resources and time to provide needed support	

intergenerational support within households. It should not be assumed that one or a combination of these factors has an automatic effect on support patterns, but they do give an indication of broad tendencies. All things being equal, a frail older person who is perceived to have made major family contributions in the past, who continues to own valuable assets, who has several prosperous children nearby and who lives in a culture that places a high value on old-age support is likely to receive substantial family support. Similarly, an older person who has a significant independent income and lives with needy family members may be required to support them. In many cases, these stylised scenarios may resemble real experiences, and policy decisions often assume that this is the case. Nevertheless, family dynamics are complex and do not always conform to such simple and predictable models of behaviour, as illustrated by the case studies at the end of the chapter.

The effects of living arrangements on older people's wellbeing also depend on older people's wider social relationships outside the household. These are especially important for the 'younger old' who enjoy greater mobility outside the home. Some studies have shown that close relationships outside the household can sometimes compensate for the absence of a spouse or child in the home (Wenger et al, 1996). There is consistent evidence that older people with better social networks report having a better quality of life and health status (Nilsson et al, 2006; Gray, 2009). Research from Thailand shows that the effects of increases in solitary living among older people have been partly compensated for by continued material support from non-resident children (Knodel et al, 2007). Improved transport and communications technologies may promote older people's capacity to maintain meaningful relationships with people outside the home. Despite this, research from Europe suggests that 'intimacy at a distance' does not always make up for increased rates of living alone (United Nations Population Division, 2005).

As well as kinship interaction, wider involvement in the community and outside organisations can be key elements of older people's 'social capital'. In developed countries, older people tend to be more involved in voluntary activities than other age groups are, and this can make an important contribution to psychological wellbeing and active ageing (Greenfield and Marks, 2004). Studies from Korea and the US report that rates of volunteering are particularly high for older people who live alone, suggesting that these activities may be part of a strategy to compensate for reduced psychological support at home (Kim et al, 2007).[5] In poorer countries, there is fragmentary evidence that some older people play important roles in community organisations. For men, this is often based on their seniority status as village heads or local leaders (McIntosh, 2009). For women, this may represent a continuation of community activity into later life. In most cases, however, these opportunities are only available to a small minority of privileged or well-educated older people.

Migration and social relations in later life

Migration can take many different forms, including international and more local flows, as well as temporary, circular or permanent relocations, asylum seekers and refugees. It is estimated that the total number of international migrants increased from 75 million in 1960 to 175 million in 2000 (UN-DESA, 2003b). Reliable data on internal migrations (that is, movements within the same country) are not available at the global level. There are, however, theoretical and empirical grounds for predicting that countries experiencing rapid social and economic development are likely to see equally rapid rates of internal migration. Development usually involves large transfers of population and workers from rural to urban areas or from less to more dynamic regions of a country. This is particularly apparent in China, where rapid economic growth since the 1980s led to a surge increase in internal migration from about 26 to 126 million people between 1988 and 2004 (IOM, 2008).[6] It is estimated that around 70% of China's internal migrants are aged between 16 and 35, which has important effects on the age structure of both their places of origin and their destinations.

Migration has varied implications for older people's social relations and wellbeing. Traditionally, migration has been portrayed as a threat to older people's status, promoting their social isolation from distant younger family members (Cowgill, 1976). In countries such as Indonesia, labour migration is a significant cause of skip-generation households, as seen in Table 5.3. In other countries, such as the Philippines, mass overseas migration has led to the emergence of 'transnational families' as an important social structure (IOM, 2008). The view that these forms of migration are harmful for older people is based on the assumption that it interferes with flows of material, instrumental and psychological support from children to older people, and that it restricts older people's wider social networks. In some cases, older people may be required to care for grandchildren left behind by migrant children (HelpAge International, 2009). Despite this, migration may also be beneficial for older people. As seen above, patterns of intergenerational support are complex and so it should not be assumed that a migrant child represents a net economic loss to an older person. Also, migrants may send money home (remittance income) and this may be much more substantial than income opportunities back in their place of origin (Posel, 2001).

Whether this migration is on balance harmful or beneficial to older people will depend on the situation of these older people and the context in which migration occurs. For example, it is claimed that very high levels of international migration away from parts of Eastern Europe and the former Soviet Union did not generate substantial remittance income. A context of low fertility meant that few younger people remained behind, leaving frail older people in a vulnerable situation (Vullnetari and King, 2008; HelpAge International, 2009). By contrast, in settings of relatively high fertility, having some migrant children may be an important source of economic support that does not interfere with instrumental support provided by remaining children (Knodel et al, 2007). Generally speaking, migrant children from poorer families are more likely to be employed in lower-paid and less secure jobs, reducing the overall amount and reliability of remitted earnings (IOM, 2008).

Two other aspects of migration can have particular implications for older people. Migration at younger ages can have important effects on individuals when they reach later life. It often modifies or disrupts family and wider social relationships, and this can increase vulnerability in old age. For example, migrants who leave young children behind with grandparents or other relatives may find that their relationships with these children are damaged for the remainder of their lives (Lloyd–Sherlock and Locke, 2008). Many migrants express a strong wish to return to their places of origin once they reach old age and are no longer in work (van der Geest, 2004c). However, this may not prove either easy or desirable if children and grandchildren now live in their new location. For people who have migrated from remote rural areas to cities, or from poorer countries to richer ones, limited healthcare and welfare services back home may also dissuade them from returning. As such, migrants may be forced to choose between the pain of missing their place of origin and the disadvantages (and sometimes disappointments) of returning home (van der Geest, 2004c).

Older people themselves may of course migrate. Here, it is possible to identify two broad categories: those for whom migration is a positive decision aimed at enhancing lifestyle; and those for whom it is a necessary strategy and who would otherwise prefer not to move. 'Lifestyle migration' has become increasingly common among older people in richer countries, as individuals who no longer have work or family commitments relocate to more desirable (usually warmer) settings (King et al, 2000). For some developing countries, such as Mexico, Thailand and Turkey, this can create important tourism and business opportunities (Balkir and Kirkulak, 2007; Wong et al, 2007). As they grow older and frailer, these 'lifestyle migrants' may be drawn back to the familiarity, social networks and welfare infrastructure of their origins.

The second broad category refers to older people who move because they are struggling to cope where they are. For these, the main objective of migration is usually to be closer to children. Predictably, people in this category tend to be older and frailer than 'lifestyle migrants'. Many undertake this migration reluctantly and struggle to come to terms with their new setting. As populations become more mobile and families more geographically dispersed, larger numbers of older people in both developed and developing countries may find they need to undertake this form of migration. For example, survey data from the US found that almost a third of people aged 85 and over had migrated between 1995 and 2000 (He and Schachter, 2003). A survey of older people living in shanty towns in São Paulo city in Brazil found that a significant proportion had migrated there from distant rural areas when they were already old (Lloyd-Sherlock, 1998). Most of these had come to live with family members who had previously migrated to the city or to enjoy better access to hospital services. Compared with other older people in the same neighbourhood, this group were less likely to be homeowners and had weaker social networks in the city. Most people in this category struggled to adjust to the urban environment, rarely left the house and were highly dependent on other family members for all forms of support.

Long-term care for older people

So far, this chapter has shown that patterns of family support and social relations for older people are highly variable and subject to rapid change. This has important implications for flows of material, instrumental and psychological support to and from older people. These shifting trends have particular implications for older people with limited functioning and long-term care (LTC) needs.

LTC can be defined as 'material, instrumental and emotional support provided formally or informally over an extended period to people in need, regardless of age' (UN-DESA, 2008: 66). A strict interpretation of this definition would include care for healthy young children. However, LTC usually refers to care for people with disabilities and for older people with limited functioning. Despite important parallels between care for children and care for older people, these issues are usually perceived as very different by policy makers and society in general. For both forms of care, a key issue is the balance between family/state responsibility and informal support/institutionalised care. In terms of childcare, there is a strong international consensus that institutional care should be a last resort (Browne et al, 2006). By contrast, institutional care for older people is often seen as more acceptable (at least by the non-old) and has become increasingly prevalent in developed and developing countries (Brodsky et al, 2003a). Both forms of care require complex interactions between families and external agencies, such as social services, to ensure that appropriate forms of support are provided and that vulnerable individuals are not exposed to abuse. Managing these complex interactions, striking a balance between family and external roles, and respecting different cultural norms is a major challenge for policy makers. In almost all societies, women provide the vast majority of care for children and older people, either as unpaid family carers or as salaried employees. For some women, this may lead to a double care role, with these two forms of care coinciding or following on from each other (Chisholm, 1999; Phillips and Chan, 2002). However, since population ageing is almost always associated with fertility decline, increased LTC needs for older people may be offset by decreased care needs for children.

Clearly, the key difference between care for older people and care for children is that childcare is perceived much more positively in most cultures. This may be because genetic programming and maternal/ paternal drives are stronger than any sense of filial responsibility for parents (Daniels, 1988; Noriuchi et al, 2008). At the same time, in some cultures, greater emphasis is placed on the wellbeing of young children than that of older people, and there are indications that younger family members are becoming less prepared to provide help to older relatives with special care needs (Gray, 2009). For example, surveys of Japanese women of childbearing age conducted in 1963 and 1992 found that the proportion who stated that caring for elderly parents was a 'natural duty' fell from 80 to 49% (Clark and Ogawa, 1996). Ideally, population ageing requires a change in the 'caring mindset', so that care for older people comes to be viewed in a similar way to childcare. This is unlikely in the foreseeable future, which leaves older people with LTC needs particularly vulnerable to domestic neglect and unwanted institutionalisation.

In developed countries, increases in the number of very old people with restricted functioning have led to a rapid expansion in residential LTC institutions, such as nursing homes and care homes.[7] In the US, for example, it was recently estimated that there were 18,000 LTC facilities with a population of 1.2 to 1.6 million people (Spillman and Black, 2005). As populations continue to age, there are growing concerns about the costs and long-run financial sustainability of residential LTC. For example, in developed countries with high levels of state involvement in LTC, the cost is already as high as 3% of GDP (OECD, 2005). There are also concerns that the quality of LTC institutions is uneven and that homes are often poorly regulated. More generally, it has been argued that institutionalisation can promote the social exclusion of older people and infringe on their human rights (Clough, 1996). Numerous studies have found very high levels of abuse of older people in LTC homes by staff members (Goergen, 2001; WHO, 2002b). There is also strong evidence that the great majority of older people prefer to remain in their own homes or live with relatives whenever possible (Wilson, 2000).

A combination of cost concerns and criticisms of care homes have prompted policies that seek to bridge the gap between independent living and permanent institutionalisation. These include state interventions that facilitate continued living at home and support informal carers. Table 5.5 presents the more common LTC approaches in developed countries as a continuum, ranging from intensive residential nursing to more limited interventions such as home help or support groups. There has been a pronounced shift away from more intensive approaches, so that home care accounts for nearly a third of state LTC spending in some countries (OECD, 2005).

Table 5.5: Long-term care options for older people

Intensive institutional care	Long-term hospitalisation
	Nursing homes
Less intensive institutional care	Residential homes
	Short stay or respite care
	Sheltered housing
Community services	Day centres
	Nurse visits
Family support	Home help
	Cash benefits for carers
	Support groups for carers

Models of LTC financing vary widely across developed countries. Some, such as Japan and Germany, have developed specific social insurance programmes, while others continue to fund services through a combination of taxation and private fees (Ogawa, 2004; Howse, 2007). Given the reluctance of most governments to substantially increase spending in this area, it is likely that the majority of care will continue to be provided by family members, especially women, and that the quality of services will remain patchy. A more comprehensive response to LTC needs would require a significant reorientation in societal priorities, and this does not appear likely in the next few decades.

LTC is a labour-intensive process and meeting these labour demands represents a growing challenge for developed countries. It is estimated that around 1.4 million people were employed in LTC in the US in 2005 (Browne and Braun, 2008). Of these, about 90% were middle-aged and female, and 20% were foreign-born (Montgomery et al, 2005). There is evidence that the proportion of foreign-born LTC workers in developed countries has increased sharply in recent years (Redfoot and Houser, 2005). One study reports that Filipinos made up 75% of all people employed in in-home care for older people in California in the late 1990s (Tung, 2000). As such, the growing demand for LTC workers has contributed to wider trends in international labour migration, especially of women. Whether this represents an opportunity or exploitation for women workers is a matter for debate, since employment conditions for LTC workers are usually poor. In the US, average wages in 2005 were only 67% those of the general workforce (Browne and Braun, 2008). Despite this, money sent home by relatives working abroad in the care industry is a substantial source of income for countries such as the Philippines (De Parle, 2007).

To what extent does the experience of developed countries represent the future for other parts of the world? In most developing countries, LTC services for older people receive very little attention, from either policy makers or academics. The assumption is that families continue to meet older people's care needs and so the focus of public policy is clearly on pensions and (to a lesser extent) healthcare (Lloyd-Sherlock, 2002b). As seen in this chapter, such assumptions are often based on flimsy evidence and there are good grounds for questioning their universality.

Existing discussion of LTC in developing countries often falls into the trap of generalising about these countries and making simplistic comparisons with the West. For example, a recent WHO survey commented: 'The conditions in the developing world and their initial experience in developing long-term care are quite different [from industrialised countries]' (Brodsky et al, 2003b: no page number). Implicitly, these generalisations suggest that conditions across developing countries are rather similar, including stronger norms of family support and limited resources for institutional caring. This view glosses over the enormous socioeconomic and cultural diversity within and between developing countries. The limited survey data suggest a more complex pattern, with available estimates for the proportion of people aged 60 or more living in institutions ranging from 0.2% in the Philippines to 3.3% in Uruguay.[8] In the absence of systematic surveys, there is strong indirect evidence that many developing countries are facing a very rapid expansion in demand for LTC. Key drivers of this demand are as follows:

- There has been a rapid growth in the number of oldest old, for whom functioning tends to be more limited. Table 5.6 shows that, although the population aged 80 and over still only represents a small share of the total population of regions such as Africa and Latin America, in absolute terms it almost trebled between 1975 and 2000. Asia now contains more people aged 80 and over than any other world region.

Table 5.6: Population aged 80 and over, by world region, 1950-2020

		1950	1970	2000	2020*
More developed countries	%	1.0	1.6	3.1	5.1
	million	8.5	16.0	36.7	63.6
Africa	%	0.3	0.3	0.4	0.5
	million	0.6	1.2	3.1	6.7
Asia	%	0.3	0.4	0.8	1.6
	million	4.9	9.3	30.0	73.0
Latin America and Caribbean	%	0.4	0.5	1.0	1.9
	million	0.7	1.4	5.4	12.5

Note: * Median variant projection.
Source: United Nations Population Division (2008)

- As discussed above, social and economic trends such as greater female participation in salaried labour and increased levels of migration, may reduce the capacity of informal networks to provide care.
- There is growing evidence that attitudes towards LTC are quickly changing in some developing countries. For example, surveys of attitudes about caring for older people in India found a substantial shift over time. In 1984, 91% of adult children surveyed said it was their duty to care for older parents; by 1994, this had fallen to 77% (Jamuna, 2003). The 1984 survey found no children who supported the idea of sending older people to care homes, but by 1994 23% did.

The demographic shift from caring for young children to LTC for older people is especially apparent in countries with rapid fertility transitions such as China, where there are anecdotal reports of schools being converted into old-age homes (Reynolds, 2007). In China, policy makers are becoming increasingly aware of the effects of the one-child policy on the supply of family care for older people. However, direct government provision of services is limited to the richer cities, such as Shanghai (Zhang and Chen, 2006). In other parts of the developing world, the situation is already comparable to the West. For example, in the city of Buenos Aires, Argentina, 9% of people aged 80 and over were living in residential care homes in 2001. Almost all of these care homes are run by the private sector on a for-profit basis. The few available government-managed homes refuse to admit older people with cognitive disorders such as dementia, on the grounds that they are not equipped to deal with such cases. A recent survey of 100 private care homes in the city found that the quality of care was generally poor, with widespread use of restraints and psychotropic drugs to control residents (Redondo and Lloyd-Sherlock, 2009).There are reports that Buenos Aires also contains at least 400 illegal old-age homes, and it is likely that conditions are considerably worse in this unregulated sector (Cronenbold, 2007).

Similar surveys of private care homes are not available for most other developing countries. In many cases, governments manage a handful of homes, but leave the vast majority of LTC provision to unregulated private providers. For example, in 1999, the government of Malaysia ran just two care homes with a capacity of 150 residents (Fon Sim, 2002).Typically, these are supplemented by a small number of daycare centres and community support initiatives, run by local governments and NGOs (Lloyd-Sherlock, 2002b; Phillips and Chan, 2002). There is an urgent need to assess whether the nature of privately managed care homes in Buenos Aires is typical of other parts of the developing world, as this could represent a massive, overlooked cause of abuse and vulnerability for older people.

For rich and middle-class families in some developing countries, institutionalised LTC may be substituted by paying for a live-in carer. This can be facilitated by the availability of cheap female labour and conforms with wider practices of live-in nannies and domestic helpers (Razavi, 2007). For those older people whose families can afford it, this may represent an attractive LTC option. The consequences for poor families are rather different, however. Supplying the care needs of richer families may generate income, but reduces the availability of informal care in poor households (Sarkar, 2005). If no alternative carers are available, this may expose frail older people in these households to neglect.

Both developed and developing countries are struggling to meet the challenge of LTC for their growing older populations, although attention has been mainly focused on the former. This issue will become more acute in coming decades, as demand escalates. In many ways, establishing an effective system of LTC is a much more complex challenge than paying out pensions or providing health services. LTC policies require careful engagement between vulnerable individuals, their families and outside organisations. Richer countries offer some positive lessons for the developing world, especially the shift away from institutional care to a wider range of interventions.There is little evidence that these more progressive approaches are being adopted on a significant scale in developing countries. In terms of financing, contributory social insurance schemes for LTC are not an attractive option for most developing countries, given the widespread problems of equity and inequality in pension and health insurance programmes.

In fact, the financial burden of long-term care may be considerably smaller in many developing countries, as unskilled labour costs tend to be much lower. Rather than a substantial drain on the public purse, the main risk for developing countries is that large numbers of older people will continue to be denied effective and appropriate LTC. This may well already constitute a major, neglected human rights abuse that will only worsen over time.

Later life and social relations: case studies

In this section, a selection of brief case studies from a range of different settings is provided, revealing the diversity and complexity of older people's social relations.

Childless older people in Indonesia

Even in countries with high rates of fertility, significant numbers of people may have no children. Table 5.1 shows that around 10% of women in Brazil reported no live births during their lifetimes. In poor countries, high rates of infant mortality and illness-related sterility increase the prevalence of childlessness. Detailed research from a village in rural Indonesia found that 21% of older people had never had children and 26% had no surviving children. High levels of out-migration meant that 34% had no children living in their community, which may be considered a form of de facto childlessness. Childless older people experienced significantly higher rates of socioeconomic deprivation, since poverty was both a cause and a consequence of childlessness. For childless older people who could no longer work, alternative sources of support were very limited and few had access to state pensions. A more frequent strategy was to 'acquire' children through informal adoption or step-parenting. Older people with children were generally more secure, although not all could rely on these children for support and some were required to raise young grandchildren. (*Sources:* Schröder-Butterfill and Kreager, 2005, 2007)

Intergenerational relations and social exclusion in Argentina

In-depth interviews with older people in a socially excluded neighbourhood of Buenos Aires found that almost all had large numbers of children, grandchildren and great-grandchildren living with them or in close proximity. Despite this, few reported that they received significant economic support from these relatives. In part, this reflected high local rates of unemployment, which reduced the capacity of younger generations to provide support. However, wider social problems, including alcoholism, drug addiction, violence and crime, were also important in framing intergenerational relations. A high proportion of informants lived with relatives who were facing economic, health and psychological difficulties. In many cases, this had substantial impacts on the informants' lives. For example, one informant lived with a seriously disabled daughter and a violent, mentally unstable grandson; another of her children had died in prison. A second informant had been robbed by her drug-addict daughter two days before the interview and was raising several of this daughter's children herself. A third informant lived with a son with mental health problems and learning difficulties, and had lost a second son as a result of political violence. Concerns about the welfare of children emerged as a major theme in almost all the interviews. Many of these concerns arose from major past or present crises, and they had a strong negative influence on the informants' general sense of wellbeing. More successful children had mainly moved away to better neighbourhoods and did not maintain close contact. Rather than a potential source of support, offspring were therefore more likely to be a source of economic and emotional vulnerability. This aspect of later life vulnerability has not been identified in other studies, which may be because of the difficulties of researching violent, socially excluded neighbourhoods (Schröder-Butterfill and Marianti, 2006). Many developing countries are experiencing urbanisation, unemployment and high rates of crime, and so the experiences of these older people may not be exceptional. (*Source:* Lloyd-Sherlock and Locke, 2008)

Shifting attitudes to social relations in Ghana

A study of older people who were interviewed in Accra, Ghana consistently reported that levels of family support had declined substantially during their lifetimes. In part, this was due to the deteriorating material circumstances of the younger generations, as a result of Ghana's poor economic performance. Where resources were limited, the needs of young children were almost always put before those of older people. At the same time, the younger generation had developed new tastes and needs as a result of their exposure to television and new cultural influences. Expenditure on western consumer goods further reduced their capacity to support older parents. There were also signs that wider norms of filial responsibility grounded in religious beliefs and community values had weakened over time. Overall, the study found that a complex interplay of cultural and socioeconomic change meant that older people could no longer rely on their children for assistance. Separate anthropological research in rural districts revealed a more complex and ambiguous picture. It was widely claimed that respect for older people among younger generations had endured. Relationships with grandchildren were particularly important both for general help with daily chores and companionship. Despite this, many older people complained of loneliness and limited contact with their children. (*Sources:* Aboderin, 2004; van der Geest, 2004a, 2004b)

Enduring family support for older people in Thailand

Like many developing countries, Thailand has seen high levels of out-migration from rural districts, and this has led to a decline in average household sizes as well as an increase in the proportion of older people who do not live with children. A survey of rural districts in 2006 found that over 75% of people aged 60 or more had at least one child who was living in a different province. Despite this, 58% still lived with children and only 7% lived alone. Most respondents also had children living nearby: only 15% had none in the same province. In the absence of a well-developed pension system, children remained an important source of material support for most older people in rural areas. This included substantial and regular flows of remittances from migrant children, as well as daily support from children living more locally. Older people in skip-generation households often received substantial remittances in exchange for their care of young grandchildren. At the same time, 60% claimed to have provided financial support to at least one child. Improved communications and transport technology enabled older people to stay in touch with their migrant children. For example, the percentage of older people's households with telephones grew from 5 to 73% between 1995 and 2006. As such, there was no evidence that migration had increased the social isolation of older people. The main negative effect was that people aged over 70 with migrant children reported that economic assistance from these children did not always compensate for the absence of instrumental and psychological support. Despite this, the study shows that family support for older people in Thailand has been quite resilient in the face of migration and other rapid socioeconomic changes. Fertility transition means that future cohorts of older people will have fewer children, reducing the overall pool of family support, regardless of migration. This may place additional pressures on intergenerational relations in the years to come. (*Source:* Knodel et al, 2007)

Long-term care in Japan

Japan has the highest proportion of people aged 80 and over in the world, accounting for 4.8% of its population in 2005. In recent decades, the capacity of families to meet these growing care needs has been weakened by changing patterns of employment, household structures and cultural attitudes. Historically, the government made little provision for LTC needs, and most LTC was provided informally by female relatives. Also, hospitals met a large proportion of LTC demand, partly due to a strong cultural stigma of placing older relatives in specialised care homes. The limited state provision was means-tested, with non-poor older people required to meet the full costs themselves. From the 1990s, the government recognised that unmet demand for LTC was escalating and implemented a number of initiatives, including a dedicated LTC insurance scheme. This has led to substantial declines in the 'social hospitalisation' of older people and large rises in paid home help (which is included in the insurance scheme). Increases in LTC provided by care homes have been more modest, as the government has control over the supply of places and older people are still required to pay a proportion of these costs themselves. There are concerns that these payments may be a serious access barrier for older people from poor families. Also, the state provides few incentives for informal carers: there is no system of caregiver benefits, and inheritance taxes were substantially increased during the 1990s. Recently, immigration controls have been somewhat eased to permit the entry of much-needed foreign care workers. (*Sources:* Ogawa, 2004; Mitchell et al, 2008)

Conclusions

Chapter One showed that falling fertility rates have been a major factor in accelerated population ageing. This chapter demonstrates that fertility transition has also contributed to significant changes in social structures and social relations. These effects have often been reinforced by migration and changing employment patterns. Changes in social structures affect how later life is experienced. They also influence the wider developmental consequences of population ageing. In China, for example, sudden shifts in family structures will probably lead to an explosive growth in demand for state-supported LTC. In other countries, these trends are less abrupt, but there is clear evidence that growing numbers of older people are living alone and that a largely unregulated LTC industry is emerging.

Nevertheless, many factors can modify the links between social structures and older people's wellbeing. Most obviously, effective pension provision may compensate for reduced material support from family members. Maintaining good health in later life enables older people to participate in social networks inside and outside the home, and reduces their need for instrumental support. In countries such as Thailand, continued cultural norms of respect and support for older people appear to have countered some of the effects of social change. More negatively, in settings of high unemployment, overcrowding and social exclusion, family ties may represent a threat to wellbeing in later life. As such, generalisations about modernisation, social relations and older people's status have limited validity. These generalisations may fall into a trap of idealising pre-modern family dynamics, flying in the face of historical evidence (Johnson, 2004). The same can sometimes be said about current policy frameworks, which are often premised on assumptions about intergenerational solidarity and family altruism. This can be seen with reference to claims about social pension sharing (see previous chapter) or optimistic assumptions that co-residence equates with adequate support and wellbeing in later life. In reality, families and households are becoming increasingly complex forms and knowledge about their internal dynamics is very limited, especially in developing countries. Understanding the inner workings of these social 'black boxes' represents a major challenge for both policy makers and academics.

This chapter shows that the effects of many social changes on older people are double-edged, context-specific and variable. For some older people, increases in female salaried employment may lead to significant improvements in material wellbeing. For many, however, the net effects may be clearly detrimental. Likewise, migration may create both risks and opportunities for entire households. Living alone may represent an affirmation of independence or, for women in particular, liberation from a lifetime of domestic responsibilities (Sagner and Mtati, 1999). Yet frail, chronically ill older people abandoned by their families often experience extreme levels of suffering and deprivation. The case studies at the end of this chapter touched on the diversity of these experiences, and several of these issues are revisited in the remaining parts of book. The chapter on South Africa (Chapter Six) considers the effects of AIDS and social pensions on older people's social relations; the chapter on Argentina (Chapter Seven) includes analysis of old-age LTC costs; and the chapter on India (Chapter Eight) examines social relations in contexts of rural poverty, making particular reference to gender and widowhood.

Notes

[1] In some parts of the developing world, there have also been rapid increases in female-headed households (Chant, 2007).

[2] AIDS mortality also explains the high rates of older women living alone in Malawi.

[3] It should not be assumed that all grandchildren living with older people are minors: early childbearing may mean that a significant proportion is already well into adulthood.

[4] Chapter Six returns to this issue with reference to South Africa.

[5] By contrast, studies of more general participation outside the home, in religious organisations and social clubs, found that rates were lower for older people without children (Gray, 2009). In this case, limited access to wider social networks appeared to reinforce the isolation of older people who did not have children.

[6] Data are more reliable for China than many other countries as migrants are required to register their location as part of an 'internal passport' system.

[7] Nursing homes usually provide some medical services on site, with trained staff. Care homes usually do not.

[8] These data are taken from a recent United Nations survey of older people's living arrangements (United Nations Population Division, 2005). The limited number of countries for which data were reported and the datedness of the information (the Uruguay figure is for 1985) indicate the lack of attention given to this issue. Also, the quality of these data is very questionable. Weak regulation and data reporting for care homes in some countries mean that the actual figures for institutional living are significantly higher.

SIX

Ageing and development in South Africa

Terminology relating to race and ethnicity are highly politicised, and the precise definitions applied in this chapter are set out in endnote 1.

Introduction

This chapter provides the first of three country case studies, which complement the thematic chapters in the first part of the book. It begins with a general review of South Africa's long-run social and economic development, making particular reference to aspects that shape the lives of older people living there today. Then, the country's main demographic trends are examined. Population ageing is set in a wider context of fertility transition, as well as shifts in life expectancy, living arrangements and the impact of the AIDS epidemic. Predictably, this reveals large disparities between different racial groups. The chapter then turns to two issues that have received particular attention in recent years: the impact of South Africa's much-vaunted social pension programme and the effects of AIDS on older people. After exploring these issues at a general level, three case study life histories of different older individuals are presented. These cannot be taken as representative of national trends, but provide some sense of the diversity of later life experiences and help to illustrate how wider trends can shape individual lives. The chapter concludes with an overview of the key factors that influence the situation of older South Africans, and highlights the importance of mounting social violence, along with the heavy legacy of apartheid.

Social and economic development in South Africa

The emergence of a modern economy and the evolution of apartheid

The history of South Africa has been framed by issues of race and colonisation, and they continue to shape the country's experiences of population ageing and the lives of older people today. Colonisation began in the 17th and 18th centuries when parts of the territory were incorporated into Holland's growing maritime empire. In the 19th century, British imperialism began to encroach, with the establishment of the Cape Colony in 1806. Many settlers of Dutch origin (known as Boers) moved into the interior of the country to set up independent territories such as the Orange Free State. Despite the spread of white control, large parts of the country remained under African rule, most notably the Zulu Kingdom on the east coast.[1] During the 19th century, significant numbers of migrants from India and South East Asia were brought by the British to work on sugar plantations.

To a large extent, the emergence of South Africa's modern economy dates back to the 1870s and 1880s, when substantial deposits of gold and diamonds were discovered near what later became the cities of Johannesburg and Kimberley (Bienart, 1994). The riches offered by these discoveries were partly responsible for mounting conflict between Europeans and Africans as well as the Boer War, eventually resulting in a unified South African state in 1910. The new mines also created a massive demand for migrant labour (Feinstein, 2005). At that time, mining was highly labour intensive and the areas around the mines were sparsely populated. A variety of factors, including restricted economic opportunities in rural areas and government policies (such as increasing levels of taxation, which led to a need for cash income), stimulated large flows of young male migrants. Fears of theft and a desire to maintain 'worker discipline' encouraged the housing of migrants in basic, single-sex compounds. African mine labour was exclusively male, leading to highly gendered patterns of migration, as well as the development of a substantial commercial sex industry around the mines. To a large extent, women, children and older people were left behind in the villages. This led to a geographical pattern of economic and social relations that has persisted ever since – large-scale temporary labour migration from relatively poor rural areas to the industrial centres such as Johannesburg; a significant proportion of female-headed households in rural areas, as well as 'skip-generation households' where older women are responsible for raising grandchildren left behind by migrants; and gender relations frequently characterised by conflict and violence (Preston-Whyte, 1988; Mazur, 1998; Jewkes and Abrahams, 2002).

Theoretically, the creation of the new unified South African state as part of the British Empire might have offered opportunities to improve economic and political opportunities for Africans. Previously, Africans and Asians had enjoyed a limited range of political rights in the British-run Cape Colony. However, a British imperial commission in 1905 reported that: 'Conferring on blacks political power ... or weakening in any way the unchallenged supremacy of the ruling race was out of the question' (South African Native Affairs Commission, 1905, cited in

Bienart, 1994: 69). As a result, non-white people were almost entirely excluded from political participation.

In 1913, the Native Lands Act prohibited African ownership of land outside demarcated reserves. Although Africans accounted for two thirds of the population, these reserves occupied only 7% of land, much of it of inferior quality. Over the following decades, the farming economy became increasingly polarised between a highly subsidised, white-owned commercial sector reliant on cheap African labour, and a backwards, largely subsistence sector. At the same time, mining companies were obliged by the state to maintain a 'colour bar', which restricted Africans to unskilled work, and which meant that they were paid a fraction of that received by their white counterparts (Feinstein, 2005). This system of discrimination was subsequently extended to all areas of the formal labour market, ensuring that even unskilled white people had access to privileged employment opportunities.

Economic discrimination against Africans was paralleled by increasingly draconian social sanctions. In 1948, South Africa achieved political independence from the British and its new government openly embraced the policies of apartheid with a wave of legislation. Notable examples included the 1950 Population Registration Act, which mandated the classification of people into racial groups on the basis of their skin colour, and the 1950 Immorality Act, which banned inter-racial marriages. Of particular significance for the country's long-run social development was a series of measures seeking to enforce racial segregation and limit the permanent presence of Africans in urban areas. One direct consequence was that most older Africans were effectively banned from living in urban areas.[2] Many Africans were forcibly resettled to the already overcrowded reserve areas (later known as homelands or Bantustans). According to Feinstein (2005: 194): 'The majority of households in the reserves were only part-time farmers, predominantly women or elderly persons ... poverty-stricken rural communities were increasingly dependent on remittances from migrant workers, pensions and other income transfers' (Feinstein, 2005: 194). Those Africans permitted to remain in cities were obliged to live in 'township' neighbourhoods, which contained few amenities, and African business activities in the townships were very restricted (Meredith, 2005).

In the mid-20th century, only a minority of Africans received any formal education, and this was largely provided through church and mission schools. With the 1953 Bantu Education Act, the government took over the education system and established a system of separate schools for different racial groups. Among Africans there was further subdivision along broadly tribal lines. The government discouraged the use of English or Afrikaans (the language of the Boers) in African schools, arguing that teaching children in their mother tongues would promote literacy (Feinstein, 2005). At the same time, funding for African schools was restricted to taxes levied on Africans themselves; inevitably a minimal level. This led to huge funding inequalities between schools for white people and ones for other races. A lack of language-specific books and teaching materials and the language needs of the modern economy added to the exclusion of Africans from many forms of employment. While the new education system saw substantial increases in the number of Africans attending schools (whatever their quality), a survey in 1970 found that the majority of Africans had only attended school for three years or less (Feinstein, 2005).

Health policy was equally framed by the inequalities of apartheid, as reflected in both the scarcity and poor quality of health services in the Bantustans (Seedat, 1984). In 1982, the entire budget of KwaZulu Bantustan (with a population of over three million) was equivalent to that of a single hospital in Johannesburg (De Beer, 1984). This obliged many rural Africans to seek care from traditional providers. In the cities, separate hospitals were established for different racial groups, with wide variations in service quality (Baldwin-Ragaven et al, 1999). The cost of services was a particular problem for Africans, due both to their poverty and to their limited inclusion in health insurance schemes.[3]

From the 1920s, the government pursued a policy of promoting manufacturing by increasing taxes on foreign imports as well as large direct subsidies. Industry responded impressively, so that by the late 1940s it accounted for more than double the share of GDP derived from mining. It had also overtaken mining in terms of employment. Unlike the gold and diamonds produced by the mines, most manufactures were for domestic consumption. As such, the continued poverty of most Africans represented a severe market limitation. At the same time, manufacturers' growing needs for skilled workers led them to question aspects of the colour bar and call for the extension of education to Africans (Feinstein, 2005). However, this was seen as a challenge to the core principles of apartheid and was strongly resisted by the government.

South Africa's mining economy and the subsequent extension of manufacturing brought the country relative prosperity, especially in comparison with the rest of Africa. To a large extent, this was driven by abundant supplies of cheap African labour as a result of apartheid policies. However, the country's post-war economic growth (an estimated annual GDP increase of 2.2% between 1950 and 1973) did not match the performance of many countries in Asia and Latin America (Feinstein, 2005). From the 1970s, the country's performance continued to decline, with an average annual GDP contraction of 0.6%, between 1973 and 1994. It was becoming increasingly apparent that the apartheid system could not provide a platform for sustained economic growth. At the heart of apartheid was a key contradiction: a desire to enforce racial separation versus a need for cheap African labour in white farms, factories, mines and homes. Increased international disapproval led to trade sanctions and a decline in foreign investment, which was essential for the continued extension of manufacturing (Jones and Inggs, 1999). The colour bar and education system led to a shortage of skilled labour, so that companies were obliged to employ white people for most skilled work, paying relatively high salaries. The white farming economy remained heavily subsidised and uncompetitive.

The white-dominated government's inability to halt this economic decline was a major, if indirect, factor behind its eventual demise. It is estimated that the number of unemployed people rose from under half a million in 1960 to nearly six and a half million in 1996 (Feinstein, 2005). This both fuelled political unrest and called into question the social sustainability of the growth model. Following the 1976 Soweto Revolt, African resistance to the regime became increasingly organised, led by a new generation of well-educated, radical activists (Simkins, 1999). During the 1980s, overt colour bars were largely abandoned and most of the legislation promoting segregation was rescinded. Some efforts were made to move towards a more egalitarian education system, although the average amount spent on a white pupil was still seven times that spent on an African. By 1986, many of the economic institutions and key policies of apartheid had been dismantled. However, there were few signs of a political accommodation between the white-dominated government and political demands of other racial groups. It was not until 1994 that the African National Congress (ANC) came to power with a landslide election victory and white rule effectively came to an end.

South African development since 1994

When Nelson Mandela, at the age of 75, took office as President, the country was one of the most inegalitarian in the world, and this inequity was largely constituted on racial grounds. In 1994, average personal incomes for Whites were more than 8.5 times higher than those of Africans (Feinstein, 2005). The United Nations Development Programme observed that the white population enjoyed a standard of living comparable to that of Spain, yet for Africans, standards were below those of several African countries (UNDP, 1994). Only about half the economically active population had formal sector jobs and it was estimated that the formal sector could only absorb around 6% of new entrants to the labour market (Meredith, 2005).

Among non-Whites, there were understandable expectations of radical government intervention that would dramatically turn around the deep inequities left behind by apartheid. However, the administration that Mandela and the ANC inherited was heavily in debt, and there were fears that dramatic shifts in economic policy would discourage overseas investment and prompt mass out-migration of skilled white workers and white-owned capital. While the new government strove to create new opportunities for Africans, the main beneficiaries were a small minority of well-educated Africans (Iheduru, 2004). Decades of neglect in education and training meant that most Africans lacked the skills and qualifications needed to gain from the end of overt discrimination. Progress in improving basic services in rural areas, where most older Africans lived, was relatively slow. As a result, income inequality actually increased during the years of ANC rule (Herbst, 2005).

Similarly, the ANC government has struggled to radically improve healthcare for poor Africans, especially in the face of HIV/AIDS. The first significant discovery of HIV/AIDS cases occurred in 1986. By 1990, surveys of pregnant women were reporting HIV rates of around 0.7%, climbing to 2.2% in 1992. It is thought that South Africa's legacy of apartheid in terms of migrant labour, divided families and prevalent violence provided the ideal 'risk environment' for the rapid extension of HIV/AIDS (Barnett and Whiteside, 2002). Despite this alarmingly fast rate of spread, the government was slow to respond. To some extent, this could be explained by the disruption caused by political transition and the many challenges facing the new, inexperienced ANC government. Yet even by the late 1990s, as the epidemic intensified, AIDS policy became increasingly incoherent and obstructive, culminating with President Mbeki's notorious claim that HIV and AIDS were entirely unrelated (Schneider, 2002). Public outcry, both from within South Africa and internationally, persuaded the government to belatedly extend anti-retroviral drugs from 2003. By this time, rates of HIV prevalence were estimated to have reached around 10%, and AIDS was accounting for over half a million deaths each year. While it is unlikely that a more effective government response would have averted the epidemic, the overall toll of death and illness could have been significantly less. As seen below, this failure has had major consequences for many older Africans.

Following the regime change, fees for basic government health services were abolished and efforts were made to reduce the massive geographical imbalances in health infrastructure inherited from apartheid. While some progress has been made, the shift towards a more orthodox neoliberal economic model led to cuts in funding for public healthcare. This has hamstrung efforts to upgrade the quality of services in the former Bantustans (Protasia and Torkington, 2000). At the same time, the declining quality of public health services in urban areas has led to a rapid growth in private health insurance and provision (Gilson and McIntyre, 2007). These private health plans are unaffordable for most South Africans, particularly older people, against whom private health insurance has a particular bias. Continued problems of leadership in the Ministry of Health have thwarted any reforms towards a unified and more equitable healthcare system.

Since the ANC took office, South Africa's economy has performed relatively well, particularly given the less than promising scenario it faced in 1994. This has enabled substantial rises in spending on education and social benefits, including pensions (see below). Gradually, significant progress is being made in improving the basic infrastructure of the townships and rural areas. However, progress in improving access to decent, reliable employment has been negligible. Average unemployment rates are officially over 40%. In some rural areas, rates of close to 70% have been reported (Hosegood and Timaeus, 2006). This means that many older people in South Africa have one or more unemployed children, which has important effects on families and intergenerational relationships.

In part due to high levels of unemployment, South Africa suffers from particularly high rates of crime and violence. Other contributory factors include the brutalising effects of the labour migrant system and state repression, as well as the turmoil surrounding political transition (Shaw, 1995). Violence has also been associated with a history of high rates of alcoholism among Africans, white people and coloured people and, more recently, dramatic rises in drug abuse (Seedat, 1984; Parry, 1998). As will be seen, violence and insecurity are key concerns for most older people in South Africa, shaping social relations, especially with younger generations.

Demographic trends and population ageing

Rather than a single, national trend of demographic transition, it is more useful to look at the experiences of racial categories separately. Even before the formalisation of apartheid, the demographic profiles of these racial groups were very different. For example, between 1940 and 1950, the TFR for white women was 3.5, compared with 6.5 for all other racial groups (Chimere-Dan, 1993). Under apartheid, population policy was predictably preoccupied with boosting the relative size of the white population (Baldwin-Ragaven et al, 1999). As well as encouraging European immigration, this involved pro-natalist policies exclusively for white mothers, including welfare payments and tax benefits. By contrast, policies towards Africans were framed by a desire to reduce fertility levels as quickly as possible, with well-funded family planning programmes providing free contraceptives (Swartz, 2002).[4] This led to a rapid convergence in fertility rates between the different racial groups (Table 6.1). By the 1990s, fertility among black South Africans was substantially lower than rates recorded for most other sub-Saharan African countries.[5] Since the political transition in 1994, population policies have shifted towards reproductive healthcare agendas, emphasising the importance of issues such as female empowerment and sexual health, rather than birth control per se. This agenda has struggled to deal with the growing AIDS epidemic and widespread sexual violence against women.

Table 6.1: Total fertility rates by official race categories, 1960–98

	1960	1970	1980	1990	1998
African	6.6	5.4	4.6	3.7	3.1
Coloured	6.5	5.1	3.2	2.9	2.5
Asian	3.8	4.1	3.1	2.7	No data
White	3.5	3.1	2.4	1.9	1.9

Source: Swartz (2002: 549)

Africans have historically experienced much lower levels of life expectancy than other racial groups. Official data on racial variations in life expectancy were not published during the apartheid period, but differences between Africans and Whites during the 1940s were around 20 years (Seedat, 1984). Little was done to reduce this gap: by 1997, life expectancy at birth was 77 years for white women, compared with only 55 years for black women (Kinsella and Ferreira, 1997). Most of this variation in life expectancy was due to differences in infant mortality.[6]

Despite these high rates of infant deaths, as well as the best efforts of population policies, the relative share of the white population fell from 21 to 9% between 1936 and 2001 (Table 6.2).

Table 6.2: Racial composition of population (millions)

	1936	2001
African	6.6	35.4
White	2.0	4.3
Coloured	0.8	4.0
Asian	0.2	1.1

Source: Statistics South Africa (2001); Kokayi Khalfani and Zuberi (2003)

As discussed in Chapter One, fertility rates exert a much greater effect on population ageing than mortality trends do. Table 6.3 compares levels of population ageing for the different racial groups. Higher rates for Whites and Asians are due to their longer histories of low fertility. Predictably, population ageing has been less pronounced for Africans and coloured people. Even so, the speed of African fertility transition since the 1970s means that population ageing for this group is more advanced than for most other African countries. As ageing among Africans accelerates, the future racial composition of older age groups may increasingly resemble that for the population as a whole (although this effect will be complicated by the impact of HIV/AIDS). Table 6.4 shows that, despite the lower rates of demographic ageing among Africans, they still account for the lion's share of the population for all older age groups.

Table 6.3: Age distribution by racial grouping, 2001 (% of total racial group population)

	50–59	60–69	70–79	80+
African	5	4	2	1
White	12	8	5	2
Coloured	7	5	2	1
Asian	10	5	2	0.4

Source: Statistics South Africa (2001)

Table 6.4 also reveals a substantial gender disparity, with women over-represented among the oldest age groups. Although similar disparities are found in most countries, in the case of South Africa there are some specific causes for greater risk of male mid-life mortality. These include

Table 6.4: Racial composition for different age groups, 2001

	50–59	60–69	70–79	80+
Total	2,843,300	1,853,200	999,000	428,300
% Male	46	40	37	32
% Female	54	60	63	68
% African	68	69	68	71
% White	18	19	22	23
% Coloured	10	9	7	5
% Asian	4	3	2	1

Source: Statistics South Africa (2001)

especially high rates of accidents and homicide; in part, another legacy of apartheid (Hosegood and Timaeus, 2006). Another factor has been high rates of mortality from silicosis and other respiratory illnesses among miners (McCulloch, 2002). All things being equal, these gender disparities could be expected to result in higher levels of widowhood and solitary living among older women. Data from the 1996 Census show that 39% of women aged 60 and over were widowed (Mba, 2005). In the South African context, however, where many women with migrant spouses are already de facto widows, the consequences of actual widowhood may be less obvious (Rosenblatt and Nkosi, 2007). It was recently estimated that nearly half of all African households were female-headed (May, 2003).

The prevalence of migrant households also complicates analysis of household form and living arrangements, since to some extent the same household may be 'stretched' over a rural and an urban location. Table 6.5 reveals significant differences in living arrangements for older people by racial category. First, predictably, older white people are much more likely to live alone than are other races. Over time, the proportion of older people living alone has been gradually rising, and it has been suggested that this may be as much due to their own preferences than to 'abandonment' by younger family members (Merli

Table 6.5: Living arrangements of people aged 60 and over by racial grouping, 1996 (%)

	Nuclear	Single	Extended or augmented
African	20.6	6.0	73.4
White	54.8	19.2	26.0
Coloured	25.4	5.3	69.3
Asian	30.9	4.0	65.1

Source: Adapted from Mba (2005)

and Palloni, 2006). The small numbers of African older people living alone is, in part, due to low marriage rates, with mothers tending to remain with their own parents rather than set up a separate home with a partner (Hosegood and Timaeus, 2006). This both reflects and reinforces the role of older women as carers of grandchildren. Second, there is evidence that South Africa's extensive social pension scheme, discussed in more detail below, has encouraged younger relatives to co-reside with older pensioners (Sagner and Mtati, 1999). Also, the cost of establishing an independent household, especially for unemployed children in urban areas, should not be overlooked.

The category 'extended or augmented households' refers to a variety of forms, including skip-generation households. It has been estimated that at least 15% of Africans aged 60 and over were living in skip-generation households (living with a grandchild aged under 15, but no adult children) (Noumbissi and Zuberi, 2001). As with widowhood, the prevalence of de facto skip-generation households may be much higher if some migrant household members are absent for long periods of time. For Asians and coloured people, lower rates of labour migration and AIDS mean that skip-generation households are very uncommon, with nuclear or three-generation households the norm. While it is dangerous to make simple assumptions about the relationship between living arrangements and many aspects of older people's lives, these patterns are likely to have important implications for intergenerational relationships.

In 1982, the percentage of white South Africans living in state-subsidised or private old-age homes was the highest in the world, at 11% of the population aged 65+ (Seedat, 1984). By contrast, state and private provision for other racial groups was minimal. Since the political transition, the number of homes for older Africans has increased, but they receive little state support and are mainly run by voluntary organisations (Protasia and Torkington, 2000). According to one voluntary worker, interviewed by Protasia and Torkington:

> The government does not want this type of home for elderly people. It says that in our culture elderly people are the responsibility of the community. They must be left in their houses and relatives and friends must look after them.... But when we leave them at night criminals come in and not only rob them but also beat them up, rape them and in some instances, kill them. (Protasia and Torkington, 2000: 143)

Despite the strictures of the apartheid regime, around half of African older people were living in cities by the mid-1990s (Mba, 2005). Predictably, there were large racial discrepancies in urbanisation: for older Whites and Asians, the figure was over 90%. The fact that so many older Africans were able to live in urban areas points to the difficulty of enforcing this aspect of the apartheid system as much as to its eventual relaxation. However, for many older Africans the dismantling of apartheid meant that they at last had a legal entitlement to urban residence and were no longer vulnerable to expulsion.

AIDS, health and older people

South Africa's long-run experience of economic and political development had complex consequences for social relations. In particular, it made the country highly vulnerable to diseases such as HIV/AIDS. The speed with which the epidemic has spread across South Africa has been exceptional. Surveys of pregnant women in 1990 reported a HIV rate of 1%, rising to 8% in 1994 and 28% in 2003 (Merli and Palloni, 2006).

Although HIV/AIDS infection is especially common among people aged 15 to 40, the number of older people who are HIV positive is far from negligible (Table 6.6).[7] Given the poor health infrastructure in rural parts of South Africa and a tendency to misdiagnose the cause of death among older people, it is possible that these figures understate the real prevalence rate. The data suggest that older men are especially vulnerable to infection, perhaps reflecting gender differences in sexual networking in later life. The rapidly growing availability of anti-retroviral drugs is now increasing the likelihood that some people with HIV will survive for longer periods and into old age. Despite the availability of age-specific prevalence data, HIV/AIDS health education programmes and health services largely ignore the risks of infection and illness for older people (Hosegood and Timaeus, 2006).

As well as being at risk of infection or illness, older people can be significantly affected by HIV/AIDS less directly. Particular attention

Table 6.6: Estimated HIV prevalence by age group, 2005

	Men	Women
15–49	8.2	13.3
50–54	14.2	7.5
55–59	6.4	3.0
60+	4.0	3.7

Source: Shisana et al (2005)

has been given to the role played by older people as carers of children dying of AIDS and surviving orphans (HelpAge International, 2005). It has been estimated that South Africa contained as many as 1.2 million AIDS orphans in 2005, and that up to 40% of these children lived with their grandparents (HelpAge International, 2003; UNAIDS, 2006). This suggests that a very high proportion of older people, especially Africans who have been worst hit by the epidemic, have been left with the sole responsibility for raising young children.

While this picture is broadly accurate, it needs qualifying in a number of ways. First, caution should be exercised with regard to terminology: many poorer grandparents may be aged in their forties and so their status as 'older people' is debateable. Likewise, the UNAIDS definition of 'AIDS orphans' refers to anyone aged under 15 who has lost either parent to the disease. This will include a number of orphans with a surviving mother or father, who may be in a position to provide care. Second, as a result of labour migration, older people were already playing a major role in childcare before the AIDS epidemic struck, and skip-generation households were already prevalent in rural areas (Merli and Palloni, 2006). As such, care of AIDS orphans should not be presented as a complete break with the past, but should be located in a wider context of grandparenting. Third, evidence about the impact that caring for AIDS orphans has on older people is not entirely clear. To some extent, it can be taken as read that the financial responsibilities of feeding, clothing, nurturing and educating young children will be substantial. On top of these economic effects, older people face major physical and emotional demands. As such, most policy documents describe these 'AIDS grandparents' in heroic terms:

> Our grandmother is so wonderful. She helps us in so many ways. She feeds us, dresses us and brings us up properly. When we see her, we see our mother. If she were not here, we would have been scattered around other families and would not be treated in the same way. We are so grateful that she is still with us. (Catherine, aged 15, the eldest of eight grandchildren being cared for by Irene, 80 years old, in Malawi; cited in HelpAge International, 2003: 2)

Hopefully these stories may be the norm, rather than the exception. However, there is little in-depth research to test their universal applicability, to assess whether older men and older women play similar roles, or to explore how older people may interact with other surviving kin in assigning responsibilities.

As well as caring for AIDS orphans, older people may also be tasked with caring for children who are in the terminal stages of the disease. There is evidence that older people play a major role in providing this support. A high proportion of people who become ill with AIDS are temporary labour migrants, and lack family support systems near their places of work. When the illness becomes severe, these people typically return to their rural places of origin to receive care and support from older relatives (Hosegood and Timaeus, 2006). A study of 3,000 older people in KwaZulu-Natal over a two-year period found that 20% had lost at least one younger adult household member, and at least 12% had lost one through AIDS (Hosegood and Timaeus, 2006). All the same, HIV/AIDS is not the only major cause of young adult mortality: around 30% of deaths among 15- to 29-year-olds are attributed to violence and accidents (Statistics South Africa, 2007).

The potential impacts of losing an adult child to AIDS or other causes are complex (Knodel et al, 2003). As well as the burden of caring for this child and any surviving orphans, there can be a wide range of effects. Among most Africans, a combination of religious beliefs and tribal custom mean that large and expensive funerals are considered essential, even among poor households. Avoiding a 'proper' funeral would be considered a sign of disrespect for the deceased and lead to a loss of face in the local community. A survey of 771 households affected by HIV/AIDS found that the average cost of a single funeral was around four times the household's monthly income (Steinberg et al, 2002).[8] A number of formal and informal savings organisations have evolved to help meet these costs: it is estimated that between 20 and 30% of households belong to an informal burial society (Scheepers, 2006). Even so, funeral costs add significantly to the economic vulnerability caused by HIV/AIDS.

At the same time, losing a child to AIDS may signify the loss of a breadwinner or household carer. This issue has been highlighted in countries such as Thailand, although the consequences may be rather different in South Africa (Knodel and Saengtienchai, 2004). For example, it was estimated that over 40% of people of 'working age' were unemployed in 2004 (Statistics South Africa, 2004). As a result of falling wages, many children in work may be unable to make significant contributions to other household members. Rather than receive financial assistance from children, most older people receive pensions and, in many cases, share this income with younger family members (see below). Consequently, the death of a child to AIDS or another cause may not represent a net economic loss. There is no evidence that AIDS mortality reduces the supply of care for older people. While there has been a growing tendency for older people to live alone, research suggests that this may reflect a desire for independent living rather than a loss of family support due to AIDS mortality (Sagner and Mtati, 1999; Merli and Palloni, 2006).

It is likely that the wider health and psychological impacts of losing one or more child to AIDS will be at least as significant as the financial implications, although this is an area that has been scarcely researched. As well as the physical demands and emotional trauma of caring for a terminally ill child, the potential exposure of older people to secondary infections, such as tuberculosis, from the sick child may be significant. Also, general stigma and negative community reaction to HIV/AIDS may increase older people's social isolation at a time when they most need support.

AIDS policies have focused on two areas of relevance to older people. First, a range of schemes have sought to reduce economic vulnerabilities through a range of cash transfer programmes (see below). Second, efforts have been made to support older people in their caring roles, particularly by NGOs (HelpAge International, 2007). In recent years, a particular focus has been on educating older people about anti-retroviral drugs, so that they can encourage their children to stick to the drug regime. Generally, AIDS policies have focused on older people as carers, rather than on addressing their own welfare needs. There is little sign of this focus shifting.

Another concern about policy is the extent to which the understandable emphasis on AIDS has deflected policy attention away from other issues of greater direct relevance to older people. While AIDS prevalence among older people is far from negligible, the leading causes of death, illness and disability among this group are heart disease, stroke and cancer (Statistics South Africa, 2007). A study in rural KwaZulu-Natal province in 2000 found that 95% of deaths for people aged 60 and over were unrelated to HIV/AIDS (Hosegood et al, 2004). A major health survey conducted in a rural district of a former homeland found that stroke was the leading cause of mortality for older people (Kahn et al, 2006). The survey criticised the quality of healthcare provision for people at risk of stroke, noting that only a quarter of those with hypertension were receiving any treatment whatsoever. Even among those receiving treatment, around half still had elevated blood pressure. By contrast, research with poor older people in urban districts found much higher levels of awareness of blood pressure and better access to free medication (Lloyd-Sherlock, 2009). These geographical discrepancies reflect the failure of the ANC government to overcome the legacy of apartheid in terms of health services for older people.

Pensions and social protection[9]

As in most other countries, it is helpful to distinguish between non-contributory 'social' pensions, and separate contributory schemes providing for specific sets of workers. South Africa has an extensive and long-established state social pension system. Limited means-tested benefits were first made available to older white people and coloured people in 1928 (van der Berg, 1997). In 1944, this non-contributory scheme was extended to Africans, albeit with substantially lower benefit values. At first sight, the extension of pensions to Africans in 1944 appears to be out of keeping with the wider ethos of apartheid and minimal state provision for non-white people. As in other countries, the emergence of a modern system of social security reflected an interplay between specific political concerns and structural economic interests (see Chapter Three). On the one hand, the state was looking to appease nascent African union movements at a time of generalised labour shortage, due to the participation of many white people in the Second World War. On the other, the proposal was enthusiastically received by the mining industry, which recognised that the payment of pensions to miners' households would enable them to pay lower wages, and would eliminate any responsibility for workers once they had retired (Sagner, 2000). The scheme also strengthened controls over population movement, since retired African miners were required to return to the homelands to receive the benefit. In 1993, on the eve of transition from white rule, social pension values were finally equalised for all racial categories.

South Africa's current system of social pension provision has been a focus of international interest for both researchers and policy makers working in ageing and development. To a large extent, the scheme has been put forwards as an example of 'best practice' for other developing countries to emulate (HelpAge International, 2004). The social pension is funded through general taxation and costs around 1.5% of GDP. Benefits of around US$3 a day are paid to all men aged 63 and over and women aged 60 and over. To qualify, older people must pass a means-test, based on their own income and their spouses' (but not other relatives'). Currently, the scheme pays out around two million benefits. It has been independently evaluated as efficiently administered and effective at reaching the country's most economically vulnerable older people (Committee for the Enquiry into a Comprehensive System of Social Security for South Africa, 2002). Research has shown that the pension has a significant impact on income poverty rates, as well as other aspects of economic vulnerability (Barrientos et al, 2003b). Around three quarters of eligible older people are thought to receive the social pension, although there are large access disparities across different districts (Noble et al, 2006).

It has been claimed that the social pension does not just benefit older people, but is pooled across entire households (Ardington and Lund, 1995; Barrientos et al, 2003b). Indeed, in settings of high unemployment, older people may represent the only reliable source of household income A study of a rural district of KwaZulu-Natal Province found that 29% of households contained at least one person of pensionable age (Hosegood and Timaeus, 2006). Consequently, household pension pooling may potentially benefit a significant proportion of South Africa's poor. Since many older women perform a major grandparenting role, the social pension may be particularly beneficial for young children (Mohatle and de Graft Agyarko, 1999; Duflo, 2000; Case, 2001). As such, the pension has been identified as an important tool in addressing the economic vulnerability of AIDS orphans (HelpAge International, 2008).

While the evidence for pension pooling is fairly robust, there are indications that this process is not entirely straightforward. For example, comparisons between Africans and coloured people show that pension sharing is much less widespread among the latter group (Moller and Ferreira, 2003). Also, high levels of alcohol consumption among men and gendered attitudes towards family responsibilities may mean that older males are less likely to share their pensions. A separate issue is whether older people share their pension income willingly or are coerced or bullied into doing so. Research has found that many older people feel 'severe normative pressure' to pool their benefits (Sagner and Mtati, 1999: 393). Several studies refer to widespread violence and physical abuse of older people, which is partly linked to obtaining the benefit by force (Burman, 1996; Protasia and Torkington, 2000). A more general concern is whether the social pension is mainly applied as a policy to improve older people's wellbeing or whether it is seen as a tool for investing in the welfare of other family members. Pooling pensions does not preclude older people from benefiting personally: for example, by increasing their status within a household and increasing access to general care from family members. Nevertheless, there is a degree of conflict between these two policy objectives.

Further debate relates to how social pensions are spent. Some studies claim that by receiving a reliable income, pensioners are able to access cheap loans and other forms of credit, rather than relying on loan sharks. It is claimed that the combination of the pension income and access to credit has enabled older people to invest in productive micro-enterprises (Ardington and Lund, 1995). As such, social pensions might be a 'springboard' for economic development. In the same vein, injecting cash income into poor rural areas may be a major stimulus for community development: lively monthly markets occur in villages on the day the pension is paid out. However, these effects can be double-edged. There are reports that many pensioners have borrowed to such a degree that they have become trapped in cycles of debt and are compelled to hand over their entire benefits to their creditors (Kirk, 2001). From my own observations in Northern Province, pension markets may be an opportunity for local enterprise, but a sizeable part of this activity involves alcohol consumption and debt collection.

Overall, the social pension programme has had a substantial impact on the wellbeing of older people in South Africa, particularly poor Africans. Consequently, it represents something of an exception to the negative effects of pension provision in other countries, as discussed in Chapter Three. The social pension has come to be seen as an important plank in South Africa's anti-poverty and social protection programmes, and has strong political support. The country has a growing range of other cash benefit schemes for the poor, including benefits for disability, child allowances, foster care grants to financially compensate carers of orphans and special grants for people with AIDS. Together with the social pension, these schemes pay out around 10 million benefits – representing almost a quarter of the entire population (Nattrass, 2006). There is some evidence that large numbers of people aged in their fifties receive disability grants for chronic diseases such as hypertension, heart conditions and diabetes. These are then converted into old-age social pensions, when the person reaches the appropriate age (Lloyd-Sherlock, 2009). Older carers may directly receive foster grants and child allowances, and they may also benefit indirectly if this money is shared across households. A survey of poor households comprising African and coloured older people found that social pensions accounted for around 40% of income, but other transfers accounted for a further 24% (Moller and Ferreira, 2003). There is little available information about the extent to which these other benefits are pooled across households and support all members, including older people.

A separate system of contributory retirement schemes exists alongside the social pensions and anti-poverty programmes. South Africa saw a rapid proliferation of contributory occupation pension plans during the 1920s. The expansion of the manufacturing industry from the middle decades of the 20th century caused affiliation to these company schemes to rise to over nine million workers (van der Berg, 1997). Initially, membership of these funds was exclusively white, but the need for cheap, skilled industrial labour led to the incorporation of substantial numbers of Africans by the 1980s. Nevertheless, as the majority of black people lacked secure formal sector employment, most relied on social pensions, rather than company schemes. By 2000, over 60% of white men and 40% of white women aged over 60 received an employer-provided private pension; for Africans, coverage was rather less than 10% (Lam et al, 2006).

By 2004, contributory pension funds were paying out around 1.1 million benefits – roughly half the number of social pensions (van den Heever, 2007). Unlike many other developing countries, most schemes are still organised into occupational funds for specific firms and industries, each with different terms of financing and entitlement, and membership is voluntary (van den Heever, 2007). Pension values are extremely variable, with average replacement rates of only 24% of final salaries. As a result, many formal sector workers face a significant reduction of income upon retirement, although benefits are still worth considerably more than the social pensions. Many of these programmes pay out a single lump-sum, rather than a monthly benefit, leaving retirees to spend or reinvest the money as they wish.

The contributory pension system suffers from many of the problems identified in Chapter Three. In particular, concerns have been raised about the regulation of the many funds. There are currently around 13,500 separate funds, of which most have fewer than 100 members, which is likely to inflate administration costs and pose a major challenge for regulation (Hendricks, 2009). One study calculated that administration charges varied from 27% to as high as 43% of total fund income (Rusconi, 2004). Pension fund regulation is in the hands of the Public Investment Committee, which has been criticised for being secretive and largely unaccountable (Hendricks, 2009). At the same time, the pension system has become increasingly inequitable, due to the introduction of progressively more generous tax subsidies, now equivalent to around 1.2% of GDP (van den Heever, 2007).

Finally, South Africa has a separate set of pension provisions for civil servants, dating back to the colonial period. During apartheid these schemes were reorganised so that each homeland ran its own separate civil service fund. These programmes have been heavily criticised for substantial political interference and unsustainable terms of benefit (van der Berg, 1997). Despite being notionally contributory, civil service pensions were substantially funded out of general tax revenues. Following the political transition, the various funds were amalgamated into a single fully capitalised scheme, which now provides around 230,000 retirement benefits a year (Hendricks, 2009). The management of civil service pension assets has been privatised, and concerns about the effectiveness of the private fund administrator have prompted some government departments to withdraw from the system. There are also claims that generous pension entitlements for current civil servants were part of an early retirement package offered to white workers by the ANC government in order to free up senior government posts for Africans (Hendricks, 2009).

Given the problems facing contributory pension programmes for civil servants and private sector workers, there are growing calls for a large-scale pension reform. Taken together, tax subsidies for contributory schemes and direct tax support for civil service pensions are greater than government funding for the social pension programme. As such, there is much scope to make the pension system as a whole more equitable. The government recently set out plans to replace these fragmented schemes with a three-pillar pension model, similar to that proposed by the World Bank (Fisher-French, 2007). There is, however, little indication that any such reforms will be implemented in the near future.

Three lives[10]

Nokuthula

Nokuthula is 58 years old and lives in a shack in the established African township of Langa in Cape Town. She was born in the Eastern Cape, in a district that used to be part of Transkei homeland. Her parents were poor smallholders who grew maize. Nokuthula was unable to complete primary school because her father died and her family could no longer afford the fees. There were no jobs in Transkei, so she went to live with a sister in Cape Town. "It was so difficult at that time because I didn't have a pass. The police would start chasing you if you didn't have a pass. If they caught you, they would beat you, put you in the van and just take you to jail....They threatened you all the way."

Nokuthula found occasional work as a domestic cleaner for wealthy white families. "They treated you like an animal, I can say … I did try to stay because I was so desperate, but I couldn't get used to it." She also worked as an office clerk, but then:"they employed a coloured lady, instead of me. But at that time you can't argue, you can't say anything." Nokuthula married when she was 30 and had two daughters. Her husband had a stable job in a hotel, and they were able to buy a small house back in Transkei (they were not allowed to own property in Cape

Town). For the past 20 years, Nokuthula has been working in the same petrol station. Her husband stopped working 14 years ago because of heart problems and was provided with a disability grant. He is now aged 66 and the grant was converted to an old-age pension a year ago. Both daughters still live with Nokuthula and neither is in work. She describes one daughter as "a bit slow". The other one likes going out at night, and was recently stabbed at a party. Nokuthula is extremely worried about what will become of her children. She would like to go back to live in Transkei, but is waiting for her daughters to settle down and find steady jobs. Nokuthula knows she will be entitled to a pension when she is 60 but plans to wait until she is 65, since she earns twice that amount at work. She was diagnosed as a diabetic seven years ago. She could get free medicine at the local government health clinic, but her long working hours prevent this: "You have to take the whole day in the clinic every time. You can just go there from seven o'clock in the morning up to four o'clock." Instead, she pays around £10 a month for her medicine, although she still goes to the clinic for occasional check-ups.

Nokuthula feels that life in South Africa has become much better since the political transition: "I feel like you can say whatever you want to say now, you're free for anything." Her salary (£150 a month) is considerably higher than it used to be. Eight years ago her firm tried to sack her and replace her with someone younger and cheaper, but the union interceded on her behalf: "and that was that". Nevertheless, Nokuthula's main concern is that the neighbourhood and the city as a whole have become much less secure in recent years: "You can't be sure if you're safe at home or on the way anywhere. There are robberies and just horrible things going on around.... Everything's unhappy." Nokuthula was recently assaulted when she was travelling to work on a train. She dreams that when she goes back to Transkei she will at last be able to return to school to finish her education.

Daisy

Daisy is 68 and lives in a pleasant suburb of Cape Town. She was born in Scotland and migrated to South Africa with her husband and two young children in 1968. Her husband "got a job just like that, with a good company. In those days, they were encouraging people to come over." Daisy had one further child in South Africa, and worked as a part-time sports teacher. She and her husband divorced in 1979 and she then took on a secretarial job. Under South African law she was only entitled to limited financial support from her former husband.

"It was a struggle, but then I worked at it." Daisy went on to work as an office administrator, but was forced to stop work when she was 60, the standard retirement age. She was later allowed to return to her post to fill in for a colleague who had died of a 'virus'. Daisy eventually retired when she was 65. She started to receive part of a British pension when she was 60, but felt she needed to continue working in order to cope financially. She also received a retirement lump sum from her occupational pension plan and invested it with a local broker. However, the manager of the investment company disappeared with all the funds. She continues to receive a monthly payment of 1,300 Rand from this fund, but is unable to access the principle to reinvest elsewhere. Daisy feels very bitter about this and is sceptical that the manager will be brought to justice: "He's out on bail, living it up."

Since 'retiring', Daisy trained as a masseuse, as well as in business management, and took a university degree: "I got honours at my grand old age ... I never knew what I was capable of doing." Initially, she worked as a masseuse, but as the economic situation deteriorated in 2008, her clients 'dried up'. Daisy then 'took herself off' for a few months to the UK, where she worked as a private carer for wealthy older people. She plans to do the same again in a few months, as she was able to earn a substantial amount. She uses part of this money to pay for her granddaughter's university fees (£3,000 a year). The job also gives her an opportunity to visit relatives, and she enjoys the challenge and contact with other people.

Daisy remains in excellent health, has an active social life and tries to go to her gym twice a day. She has a private health plan from her former employer, and continues to pay 500 Rand a month into it. Daisy didn't think that she would still be on her own 30 years after her divorce, but is comfortable in her own space. Two children live in Cape Town and a son is in Johannesburg. She is particularly close to her son and would like to be able to see more of him. Daisy is not confident that her children will meet all her care needs as she gets older: "They're not the same as they are in the UK.... They're not used to seeing that close family ... I don't want to be a responsibility to them." Her son had a successful career, but could not progress because of "different things happening in the country, because he's white – you know what I'm saying". He is now training as a plumber.

Daisy herself feels she could no longer get work in South Africa due to both her age and her colour, although she is very positive about the end of white rule. She feels that the country is less well run and more dangerous now: "I've seen things have deteriorated." Over the years, she has upgraded the security for her house, including burglar bars, spikes on the walls, an alarm and a camera system.

Thomas

Thomas is 66 years old and lives in a coloured township of Cape Town. He was born in a neighbouring district and his father was a railway worker. Thomas attended school from the age of six through to 15, when he took up an apprenticeship in a local furniture factory: "The principal of the school got me the job. He got two jobs for me: one as a messenger boy and the one in the factory." Thomas remained with the same firm for 40 years when he retired. When he was 21 he married a local woman and set up his own home. They went on to have two daughters and a son. When he was 26, Thomas moved to the house where he still lives now. Although they did not consider themselves wealthy, he feels they had enough income to cover their general needs: "It was alright then. Of course you wanted to have more and the money was little, but you could get more." Thomas's wife died when he was 36 and he went on to marry again a few years later.

Thomas retired when he was 55, because his firm relocated to a distant part of the city. He initially received unemployment insurance, but this stopped when he started to receive a social pension, aged 65. His second wife, who worked in a clothing factory, was able to retire and obtain a social pension when she was in her early sixties. Despite receiving these two pensions, Thomas feels that they are much less well-off than they used to be and that life is a struggle: "You get your [pension] money and you go to a shop and you come back with nothing, all your money is gone. Just the basics."

Thomas has a range of health problems, including diabetes: "My health? [laughs] They just don't know what is going on behind this body." He receives diabetes medication free of charge from a nearby government clinic. Despite this, Thomas has little faith in government doctors, so prefers to pay for private consultations, which he struggles to afford. He finds he is becoming increasingly forgetful and confused, and blames this on his diabetes: "If I get up and go to the room to fetch something, when I get there I don't know what I'm looking for."

Thomas's three children all live locally and he now has nine grandchildren and four great-grandchildren. They come to visit him and his wife once or twice a month, but he is reluctant to ask his children for financial help: "We try and sort our problems out ourselves." His eldest daughter separated from her husband a few years ago and spent about two years living with them: "She lived here like a queen.... We treated her very nicely, but she left here because of another man and she was unappreciative."

Thomas observes that his neighbourhood has changed considerably over the 40 years he has been living there. On the one hand, the basic infrastructure has improved: "There were no tar roads, all the others were sand." On the other, there has been an increase in crime and insecurity: "One evening there were these drug dealers hanging around, and I was worried because I can't run now. And I just walked past them, and as I passed they greeted me, 'Good evening Mr Smit.'"

Conclusions

As discussed in Chapter One, patterns of economic, social and political development vary widely between countries and should not be viewed as a single pathway of modernisation. South Africa's complex history demonstrates this powerfully. This chapter shows that it would be impossible to understand the current experiences of older people in South Africa without reference to the country's unique development trajectory. This includes the emergence of a large and relatively well-resourced state welfare apparatus that has been able to establish an embracing set of pension and other cash benefit programmes. These programmes have had a significant impact on older people's economic wellbeing. They may also have affected other aspects of older people's lives, potentially raising their social status in households and communities. It has been argued that the social pension has had a major impact on how old age is perceived and understood in South Africa, with later life increasingly associated with pensioner status (Sagner, 2000). The social pension has also reinforced cultural norms of older people as carers of vulnerable family members and grandchildren.

However, experiences of old age in South Africa are not just framed by pension provision, and must be located in a wider context of social division, inequality, violence and the AIDS epidemic. The personal testimonies of Daisy and Thomas, both of whom receive pensions, reveal that social pensions do not eliminate deprivation in old age or override longstanding racial economic differences generated by apartheid and colonial rule. One study found that over 30% of older Africans had incomes below half the poverty line in 1999, compared with only 7% of Whites (May, 2003). Contributory pensions receive large direct and indirect state subsidies and disproportionately benefit white South Africans. Likewise, the legacy of apartheid education policies continues to affect the lives of older Africans, most of whom were denied a proper education during their early lives. According to the 2001 Census, less than 30% of older Africans had completed primary school and less than 5% had a complete secondary education (Lam et al, 2006). In 2002, a survey of older Africans and coloured people asked 'what was the one factor that would have made your life better': over 47% referred to a better education (Moller and Ferreira, 2003).

Violence and the explosive AIDS epidemic are more indirect legacies of apartheid, but are equally important for older people of all races. Information about violence and abuse of older people is very limited, but there are indications that it is prevalent. Research on women of all ages found that around half reported some experience of gender violence (Jewkes et al, 1999). One survey of women in 1998 found that 7% admitted to having been raped at some point in their lives (Jewkes and Abrahams, 2002). Protasia and Torkington (2000) provide substantial anecdotal evidence of violence against older people and suggest that the police services do little to prevent such behaviour. Another recent survey found that most older people perceived problems of crime and violence as worsening in the early 2000s (Moller and Ferreira, 2003). Linked to this, there is much scope for improving the lives of older people through policies that more robustly address problems of alcoholism among older males.

It would therefore seem that experiences of old age in South Africa are complex and double-edged. To a large extent, they are framed by race: most older Whites have more in common with counterparts in developed countries than with their African neighbours. Even among Africans (who make up the bulk of the older population), there are large socioeconomic differences between those in rural areas and those in urban areas (Moller and Ferreira, 2003). Although the vast majority of older people receive pensions and many are exposed to violence, this chapter shows that it would be misleading to portray them as passive dependants or as burdens on development. Most older people continue to make important contributions to their own welfare, as well as that of others. As well as through caring and pension sharing, a significant proportion of older people remain economically active (Lam et al, 2006).

Older people's adult lives have straddled the apogee of apartheid, its demise and political revolution. For many, this has been a challenging and disorientating experience. Drawing on life histories with Africans in an old-age home, van Dongen (2005: 538-539) observes that: 'Older people in South Africa are the flesh and blood of what younger generations want to forget: oppression, lack of freedom, submissiveness, servility and compromise'. She claims that older people's apparent association with a 'shameful past' has reduced their status among younger age groups.Yet many older Africans (not least, Nelson Mandela) have lifetime experiences of struggle against violence and injustice. If South Africa is to throw off the negative legacies of apartheid, younger people must draw on the lessons of the past and have much to learn from those who lived through it.

Notes

[1] This chapter uses the artificial racial categories that have been officially applied in South Africa. These (as all racial categories) are essentially a social construction, but their importance in the country's development has been such that they are essential tools for analysis. The term 'white' refers to people with European settler origins; 'African' refers to indigenous, dark-skinned groups; 'coloured' refers to people of mixed race; 'Asian' mainly refers to the descendants of indentured labourers brought from South and South East Asia. The term 'black' has traditionally referred to non-white people in general, although the political interpretation altered somewhat with the inception of Black Economic Empowerment in the 1990s.

[2] To be entitled to live in urban areas, Africans had to demonstrate that they had been born there (this was very unusual) or were in full employment. Those who lost work were quickly 'relocated' to rural areas (Feinstein, 2005).

[3] In 1977, 76% of white people were covered by health insurance schemes, compared with only 3% of Africans (Seedat, 1984).

[4] There is evidence that African women were sometimes coerced or misinformed about contraception (Baldwin-Ragaven et al, 1999).

[5] For example, the TFRs for Zambia and Tanzania in the 1990s were both over six (United Nations Population Division, 2008).

[6] In the poorest parts of the country, reported levels of infant mortality were as high as any found in sub-Saharan Africa. One study of a poor rural reserve in 1964 estimated that up to half of all children failed to survive until their fifth birthday (Leary and Lewis, 1965).

[7] A separate survey conducted specially with older 55-year-olds found rates of around 7% for both men and women (Human Sciences Research Council, 2002).

[8] Other studies have found costs to be even higher (Roth, 2001).

[9] This section links in closely with the wider discussions of pension programmes found in Chapter Three. Readers who are not familiar with general pension policy and terminology may find it helpful to refer back to that chapter.

[10] The names of the informants in this section have been changed to preserve their anonymity.

SEVEN

Ageing and development in Argentina

Introduction

Argentina is a relatively wealthy country, with an embracing welfare system and an aged population structure. As such, it may offer insights relevant to the future for other developing countries. Despite this, it is widely accepted that Argentina's economic performance over the past 70 years has been poor and erratic. The causes of this decline are complex, but this chapter will seek to assess whether population ageing has played any role in hindering growth. The chapter will also consider how this gradual decline has affected experiences of ageing and the lives of older people. It follows broadly the same structure as the other country case studies in this book. First, it provides a brief overview of Argentina's economic and social development. This is followed by an analysis of demographic trends, including fertility transition and population ageing. The chapter then focuses on a number of key themes. In this case, they cover potential economic impacts of population ageing, as well as the provision of social security and health services, and the care economy. These more general analyses are complemented by three life histories of older Argentines, which reveal the diversity of old-age experiences and the different ways in which national factors intersect with personal biographies.

Social and economic development in Argentina

In the first half of the 20th century, Argentina was one of the richest countries in the world. In terms of development and social welfare, it was seen as much closer to Australia, Canada and New Zealand than to its Latin American neighbours (Platt and Di Tella, 1985). By the end of the 20th century, decades of extreme economic instability and growing social inequality had relegated Argentina to 'developing country' status. The scale of Argentina's relative decline was dramatic: in 1950, average per capita incomes were still 84% of the Organisation for Economic Co-operation and Development's, by 1987 they had fallen to only 43% (Della Paolera and Taylor, 2003). The Argentine experience demonstrates that development should not be understood as an inevitably linear and irreversible process. Current cohorts of older people were born into a prosperous country and lived through its decline, which will have shaped the courses of their lives and their situation in old age. As such, Argentina provides an unusual, but enlightening case study of ageing and development issues.

The first colonial Spanish settlements were established in Argentina in the mid-16th century. From that time until the country achieved independence from Spain in 1810, it was a sparsely populated, impoverished colonial backwater (Lewis, 2002). The most developed region was the north of the country, which provided food and supplies for colonial mines in Peru and Bolivia. For most of the colonial period, European ships were not permitted into Buenos Aires, stifling its development. Following independence, the fortunes of Buenos Aires and northern Argentina reversed, reflecting a profound reorientation of the country's economy. Argentina might have lacked the precious stones and minerals that had originally drawn the Spanish to Latin America, but it possessed one resource in abundance: the vast, fertile plains of the Pampas. This large area, centred around Buenos Aires, has a temperate climate and is ideally suited for livestock ranching, as well as the production of wheat, corn and other western staples.

From the mid-19th century, several factors combined to initiate what would become one of the most sustained periods of rapid economic growth the world has ever seen. These included domestic political stability and massive increases in demand for meat and cereals in the fast-industrialising economies of Europe, particularly Britain. Between 1876 and 1900, exports of wheat grew from 21 to over two million tons, and there was a similar increase in the volume of fresh beef exports (Lewis, 2002). The Argentine boom was supported by huge inflows of foreign investment, funding the development of infrastructure such as railways linking the Pampas to Buenos Aires. While cattle-ranching and wheat farming were not as labour intensive as South African mining, Argentine development still required large inputs of population (Castro, 1991). As with South Africa, the economic epicentre was sparsely populated, mainly by nomadic indigenous groups. Unlike South Africa, most of these were killed in a genocidal military campaign between 1879 and 1880, leaving the Pampas region a white, settler economy. From the 1870s, huge numbers of European migrants came to Argentina, drawn by the attractions of easy money and free ocean passages paid by the government. Between 1880 and 1930, net immigration was over three million, accounting for around half the country's total population growth (Sánchez-Albornoz, 1974). The largest concentrations of immigrants were from Italy (55%) and Spain (26%). This wave of immigration had a profound impact on the demography of Argentina: for example, in 1914, 63% of the urban population were foreign born.

Between 1880 and 1930, the Argentine GDP grew at an average annual rate of 5% a year (Diaz-Alejandro, 1970). This transformed the economy and society of the Pampas region and, in particular, Buenos Aires, which emerged as a prosperous cosmopolitan metropolis, more comparable to New York and Chicago than Mexico City or Lima. The protracted export boom enabled the development of an incipient social welfare system, with investments in sanitation, public health and education. Between 1869 and 1947, the total rate of illiteracy fell from 73% to just 12%.[1] In the larger cities, there was a growing network of state and charitable hospitals, offering a relatively comprehensive range of services (Recalde, 1991). The export boom also spurred political change. European migrant workers brought with them new political ideologies, including revolutionary bolshevism. An increasingly prosperous and educated population started to pressure landowning elites to establish a more democratic system of rule. In 1916, Argentina held its first recognisably democratic presidential elections, based on universal male suffrage (voting for women was not introduced until 1947). Beyond Buenos Aires and the Pampas, the pace of economic, social and political change was much slower, leading to marked regional disparities, which have endured ever since.

Between the First World War and the 1929 Great Depression, the Argentine export boom began to lose momentum. The precise reasons for this are complex and the subject of sometimes heated debate, but contributing factors included the loss of key European markets and the exhaustion of fertile virgin Pampas farmland. Further export growth required raising output per unit of land in an increasingly competitive international marketplace. The main policy response was to shift the focus of development towards manufacturing, as part of what became known as 'import substituting industrialisation' (ISI). According to this strategy, local industries were offered large amounts of state support in the form of subsidies and protected local markets (by taxing manufactured imports). It was hoped that these protected industries would eventually be able to compete internationally without state support. By 1947, one and a half million Argentines were employed in industry, almost as many as in agriculture (CEPAL, 1959). At the same time, there was a rapid growth in public sector employment, which trebled between 1930 and 1955. As with the export boom, the new industrial model was mainly focused on and around Buenos Aires, leaving other regions to languish (Sawers, 1996).

The new industrial development model considerably strengthened the political influence of the urban working class, and this contributed to the political emergence of Peronism in the 1940s. Juan Perón's first period of rule, from 1944 to 1955, is still seen as a political, social and even cultural turning point in Argentina's development. Before his rule, notionally democratic politics had been dominated by elite and urban middle-class interests. Perón drew his support from mass, populist appeals to the urban working classes and rural poor, forming a tight political alliance with labour unions. Although social welfare programmes were already quite well developed in Argentina, Perón came to be associated with the establishment of a generous and embracing welfare state. This included significant extensions in health insurance and pension provision. The industrial development of Buenos Aires and other large cities such as Rosario and Córdoba attracted large flows of rural migrants, especially from poorer provinces to the north. These were joined by migration from neighbouring countries such as Bolivia and Paraguay. By contrast, overseas immigration from Europe became much less significant from the 1930s (Torrado, 1994).

Argentina's new industrial development strategies never yielded the sustained high levels of growth generated by the previous export boom. Local industries remained heavily dependent on state support and struggled to become internationally competitive. Their expansion was hindered by a lack of conveniently located raw materials and the small size of Argentina's market. Powerful unions meant that labour costs were substantially higher than in other industrialising economies. Also, the political continuity of the export boom had given way to an increasingly unstable situation. In 1955, Perón was ousted by a military coup. The following decades saw a succession of short-lived regimes, some democratic, some military, including a disastrous second period of Peronist rule in the early 1970s. This political instability was underpinned by profound differences of opinion about the best path for Argentine development: whether the country should return to its liberal heyday of rural exporting, or whether it should continue to pursue state-led industrialisation. By the 1970s, inconsistent economic policies and inefficient industries meant that the ISI model of development had effectively run out of steam. Both the country's politics and economic performance became increasingly unstable, leading to the notorious 'Dirty War' of 1976 to 1983, when a repressive military government murdered up to 30,000 of its own citizens.

By the late 1980s, the social consequences of Argentina's poor economic performance were becoming more obvious. In 1970 (the first year for which data are available), only 5% of households in Greater Buenos Aires had incomes below the official poverty line; by 1985 this had reached 22% (Table 7.1).[2] Falling industrial employment contributed to a growing informal economy, paralleled by a rapid expansion in shanty towns on the peripheries of the larger cities (Yujnovsky, 1984). At the same time, increasing pressures were put on funding for social welfare programmes and some were cut back (Minujin, 1992). In 1989, Argentina experienced the first of several hyperinflationary episodes, which dwarfed its previous economic crises. In the same year, Carlos Menem, a Peronist, was elected president, marking a significant new phase in Argentine development.

Table 7.1: Estimates of household poverty for Greater Buenos Aires, 1970–2005

Year	% of households below poverty line	Year	% of households below poverty line
1970	5	1990	25
1975	9	1995	18
1980	11	2000	21
1985	22	2005	23

Source: Lloyd-Sherlock (1997a); INDEC (2008)

Menem remained in office until 1999 and oversaw a radical shift in policy towards right-wing neoliberalism. Subsidies for inefficient industries were cut, trade barriers were removed, state-owned enterprises were privatised and efforts were made to reduce labour costs. Most significantly, strict measures were introduced to control inflation, by linking the local currency to the US dollar. Initially, the new policies worked: inflation was virtually eliminated, exports increased and privatisations generated substantial revenue for the government. By the mid-1990s, Argentina's international reputation had been transformed from an economic disaster to a 'poster-boy' for the benefits of World Bank neoliberal policies (Blustein, 2005). Yet in spite of rapid economic recovery, unemployment remained high and it was evident that the benefits of the new model were not trickling down to the poor (Table 7.1). As part of the new policy model, several aspects of the welfare system, including pension programmes, were either downgraded or privatised.

The neoliberal boom lasted until the late 1990s when a combination of factors began to undermine the new development strategy. Eliminating inflation led to an overvalued *peso*, reducing the competitiveness of exports. The privatisation programme lost momentum, as the government ran out of assets to sell. Menem's political position weakened and the unions became increasingly adept at defending wages and labour conditions. In 2001, the neoliberal revolution ended just as abruptly as it had begun. The government was finally forced into devaluing the *peso*, unleashing a massive economic crisis. In a single year, GDP fell by 28%, while unemployment and the poverty rate both doubled (Fiszbein et al, 2002). Since then, the economy has recovered from most of these losses and exports have benefited from rises in global food prices. There is, however, little evidence that the Argentine economy has broken free of its long-term cycle of decline and instability. Since 2002, the country has elected Peronist presidents, who promise to return to the core Peronist welfare traditions of the 1940s.

Argentina's unusual economic trajectory raises a number of important issues relating to population ageing and development. Early 20th-century prosperity enabled the creation of a fairly embracing welfare state, including contributory social insurance pension funds and a range of healthcare programmes. In more recent decades, this welfare infrastructure has been increasingly under pressure, which will have had particular effects on groups such as older people. At the same time, some have argued that the costs of maintaining these social policies have contributed to Argentina's lack of international competitiveness (World Bank, 1997; IMF, 2004). This links into wider debates about the potential economic burden of population ageing (see Chapter One).

The country's changing fortunes will have done much to shape the lives and experiences of its older population. Current cohorts of older people reached adulthood in the 1950s and 1960s, when industrial and public sector employment were readily available and wages were still high (Roxborough, 1993). In the main, they were well educated and politically active, either as Peronists or in opposing factions. As they progressed through adulthood, many will have experienced increasing economic insecurity and a gradual decline in living conditions. This cohort will have reached old age at a time of welfare privatisation and retrenchment. High levels of unemployment and a growing informal economy mean that, as in South Africa, many of this cohort's children and grandchildren will be facing economic distress, with implications for patterns of family support and intergenerational relationships. More broadly, older people in Argentina today reached adulthood at a time of relative optimism – few foresaw the extent of national decline that occurred in the latter decades of the 20th century. For most of this cohort, these expectations of a more prosperous future were never realised, and this was paralleled by a shift from idealism to disillusion and political disengagement.

Population dynamics and development in Argentina

Argentina experienced demographic transition considerably earlier than most other developing countries. Sustained falls in fertility began around the end of the 19th century, closely following mortality declines (Table 7.2). By 1947, fertility had fallen to levels not seen in Latin America as a whole until the 1990s. The shortness of the lag between mortality and fertility decline limited the growth of the local population, increasing the importance of immigration for the country's development (Table 7.3).

Table 7.2: Indicators of demographic transition in Argentina and Latin America

	Total fertility rate, Argentina	Total fertility rate, Latin America	Crude death rate, Argentina	Crude death rate, Latin America
1895	7.0	NA	29.8*	NA
1914	5.3	NA	19.7**	NA
1950–55	3.2	5.9	9.2	15.5
1960–65	3.1	6.0	8.8	12.3
1970–75	3.2	5.0	9.0	9.8
1980–85	3.1	3.9	8.5	7.8
1990–95	2.9	3.0	8.2	6.6
2000–05	2.4	2.5	7.7	6.0

Notes: * Average for 1890–95.
** Average for 1910–15.
Sources: Lattes (1974); United Nations Population Division (2008)

Table 7.3: Total population and per cent foreign born, Argentina

	Population	% foreign-born
1897	4,124,000	25
1914	8,162,000	30
1947	15,894,000	15
1960	20,611,000	NA
1970	23,748,000	NA
1980	28,094,000	7
1990	32,581,000	5
2000	36,896,000	4

Sources: Lattes (1974); UN Population Division (2008)

The early onset of demographic transition was essentially a consequence of Argentina's export boom of 1870 to 1930. Rapidly increasing prosperity, along with improvements to sanitation and extensions to public health infrastructure, underpinned improvements in life expectancy, especially for young children. For example, the proportion of children born in Buenos Aires who died in their first year of life fell from 33% to 7% between 1870 and 1930 (Nari, 1996). The export boom also promoted urbanisation and access to education, which are commonly associated with reduced fertility. By 1914, two thirds of the population were literate and over half lived in cities. These effects overrode population policies, which sought to slow the fertility decline in response to fears of depopulation and that the local population might be 'swamped' by the waves of immigrants (Rock, 1991). Despite these sentiments, modern contraceptives, including condoms, were readily available and being widely used in Buenos Aires and other cities from the 1920s (Nari, 1996).

The effects of demographic transition on Argentina's population growth and age structure were heavily modified by mass immigration. The great majority of immigrants were working-age adults and few arrived with families. Since fertility rates in Italy and the other host countries were significantly lower than in Argentina before the 1920s, it is likely that immigrants had fewer children than the native population. This would have accelerated the overall pace of fertility decline (Pantelides, 2006). The impacts of the export boom and large-scale migration were much less evident outside Buenos Aires and the Pampas. This led to large regional disparities in demographic trends. For example, total fertility did not start to fall in the northeast until the 1950s and several Argentine provinces still had TFRs of over four in 1980. Life expectancy at birth in Buenos Aires was 68 years in 1960, 11 years greater than for north-western Argentina.

Rapid and early fertility transition led to rapid and early population ageing. Table 7.4 shows that the total number of people aged 60 or more roughly trebled between 1950 and 1980. More recently, Argentina has seen accelerating growth of its oldest old, so that in 2008 the total population aged 80 or more reached one million. Regional variations in fertility, life expectancy and migration produced sharp internal differences in population ageing. For example, by 1960, 9.5% of the population of Buenos Aires city was already aged 65 and above, compared with only 2.5% of the northern province of Jujuy. Given that political and economic power was heavily concentrated in Buenos Aires, this may have increased the potential impact of ageing on development priorities. Table 7.5 shows the large variations in population ageing

Table 7.4: Population ageing in Argentina, 1950–2000

	60+ (%)	80+ (%)	60+ (000)	80+ (000)
1950	7.0	0.5	1,208	82
1960	8.8	0.6	1,818	119
1970	10.7	0.8	2,571	191
1980	11.9	1.1	3,345	298
1990	12.9	1.4	4,208	459
2000	13.3	1.7	4,988	712

Source: United Nations Population Division (2008)

Table 7.5: Regional comparisons of population ageing and education, 2001 (%)

	Population aged 65+	Illiteracy rate for men aged 65+	Illiteracy rate for women aged 65+
Total	10	6	6
Buenos Aires city	17	1	1
Jujuy	6	14	32
Santiago del Estero	6	13	18

Source: INDEC (2008)

across Argentina in 2001. It also gives some indication that experiences of old age varied sharply between regions: older people living in Buenos Aires were almost all literate, while in poorer provinces a significant proportion, especially of women, were not.

Unlike most other developing countries, Argentina has been experiencing population ageing for a long period. It is therefore instructive to assess how this trend may have affected the country's general development experience. Put crudely: has the growing population of older people been a significant factor contributing to Argentina's poor economic performance?

Assessing the economic impacts of population ageing

Chapter One argued that identifying obvious links between demographic change and economic growth is extremely difficult, even in developed countries where population ageing is relatively advanced. First, population ageing needs to be located in a wider context of demographic change, including reductions in mortality and fertility. Most studies of international development stress the economic advantages of rapid fertility transition, since this slows overall population growth and reduces pressure on available resources. High levels of fertility are associated with large numbers of young children, who are usually economically unproductive and absorb significant amounts of resources. It follows that, all things being equal, Argentina's rapid progression towards low fertility rates would have boosted the country's economic performance. In fact, it has been argued that Argentina's fertility transition did not happen quickly enough. Taylor (1992) claims that the main reason Argentina fell behind economies such as Australia and Canada was because its birth rates were significantly higher. He argues that large numbers of children boosted per capita consumption, hence reducing domestic savings rates, which, in a context of scarce international capital, restricted economic growth.

It is also possible to develop equally plausible arguments that Argentina might have benefited from higher fertility rates. This was clearly the view of policy makers during the export boom, giving rise to pro-immigration and pro-natalist policies (Castro, 1991). Slow population growth limited the supply of workers, increasing labour costs compared with competing economies and boosting the bargaining power of labour unions. It also reduced the size of the domestic market, which became increasingly important during the years of ISI. As a result, Argentina fell behind countries like Mexico and Brazil, both of which experienced rapid population growth and economic booms between the 1950s and the 1970s.

Given these different effects, it is difficult to weigh up the overall impact of rapid fertility decline on Argentina's economic performance. The same can be said for the impact of population ageing. Table 7.6 summarises widely held views about the most likely effects of population on economic performance. Put simply, all of these effects suggest that population ageing is bad for the economy. Chapter One provided a detailed assessment of these potential effects and concluded that they are usually more complex and less predictable than is commonly assumed.

Table 7.6: Standard views about the economic impacts of population ageing

Effect	Standard view
Dependency rates	Population ageing increases the share of population that does not work, reducing its overall productivity
An ageing workforce	Older workers are inherently less productive than younger ones
Resource allocation	Older people consume disproportionate amounts of public and private resources (pensions, health services and care). This reduces resource availability for more productive investments
Savings	People divest savings in later life, which depresses the overall savings rate

In the case of dependency ratios, rising numbers of older people must be offset against changes in numbers of children (and Argentina still contains around twice as many people aged under 18 than over 60). Also, assumptions about the rate of economic activity of different age groups must be put to the test, particularly in settings where productive employment opportunities are limited. Table 7.7 shows that Argentina's old-age dependency rate increased substantially between 1950 and 2000. It also shows that in 1950 a substantial proportion of older Argentines were in work or seeking employment, but by 2000 this had fallen sharply. This decline in old-age economic participation was mainly due to the extension of pension schemes. Since relatively few older people were working, the productivity effects of an ageing workforce (which are themselves highly contentious) are unlikely to be significant. A combination of demographic ageing and declining later life activity rates will have significantly increased the share of the population who are 'economically inactive'. Nevertheless, comparing the old-age dependency ratio to the total dependency ratio shows that falling proportions of children have partly compensated for this effect.

Table 7.7: Dependency rates and labour force participation, 1950–2000

	1950	1975	2000
Old-age dependency rate*	6.4	12.0	15.5
Labour force participation for population aged 65+ (%)**	30.9	16.1	11.5
Total dependency rate***	53.2	58.2	59.8

Notes: * Number of persons aged 65 and over per 100 persons aged 15 to 64.
** % of age group either in employment or actively seeking employment.
*** Number of persons aged 65 and over plus number aged 0 to 14 per 100 persons aged 15 to 64.
Source: United Nations Population Division (2002)

The links between a growing inactive population and economic performance are neither automatic nor simple. First, it is necessary to consider whether jobs would have been available for a larger working population. In the case of Argentina, unemployment and underemployment increased significantly from the 1970s and have remained stubbornly high, suggesting that the country would have struggled to accommodate more workers.[3] Second, levels of consumption among the inactive population need to be assessed. Hypothetically, if Argentina devoted no resources to its inactive population, this group could be considered as neither productive nor a burden. By contrast, if older people are unproductive *and* absorb large amounts of resources (through public policies such as pensions as well as private transfers at the household level), population ageing is likely to have a large economic effect. The following sections attempt to gauge this effect, examining resource consumption by older people in three areas: pensions, health policy and LTC.

Social security and pension provision for older people

By the 1950s, Argentina had established an extensive set of pension programmes. Over time, these became increasingly expensive to run, and by the late 1980s they absorbed funding equivalent to 8% of the country's GDP. In 1990, as Argentina experienced an acute hyperinflationary crisis, government support for the social insurance system accounted for a quarter of all public spending (Bucerius, 2003).[4] Undeniably, the high cost of supporting the pension system made a significant contribution to a mounting fiscal deficit, which was itself a major cause of the wider economic crisis. This would appear to be powerful evidence that the resource requirements of ageing populations can have significant economic effects. The rest of this section considers how Argentina reached this critical juncture and the extent to which population ageing was to blame.

In 1904, Argentina became the first Latin American country to adopt a Bismarckian social insurance programme, when a compulsory retirement fund was established for government workers (Lewis and Lloyd-Sherlock, 2008). Over the following decades, separate schemes were set up for other influential occupations, including railwaymen (1919) and bank workers (1923). The early years of Perón's first government, in the mid-1940s, saw a substantial extension of state pension schemes, with the creation of contributory funds for industrial workers and the commercial sector. In 1954, schemes were established for the self-employed and rural workers, although only a small minority of these groups ever became affiliated. As a result, the proportion of the economically active population included in the national pension system rose from 4% in 1944 to around 65% in 1954 (Ross, 1989).

The expansion of pension provision broadly coincided with the onset of population ageing: by 1950, the country contained over a million people aged 60 or more. By this time, several influential academic and political figures were warning of the need to respond to a growing older population, with measures including pension provision (Bunge, 1940; Germani, 1955). Rather than as a direct response to population change, however, the rapid expansion of the pension system is usually explained in terms of political machinations between the government and trades unions. During the 1940s, Perón established a close alliance with the labour movement, whereby the government offered trades unions a range of welfare benefits in return for their political loyalty (James, 1988). As part of this, some labour leaders were offered key roles in state agencies responsible for supervising the pension funds.

There is no evidence that the labour unions were motivated by general concerns about providing for future cohorts of older people. Instead, their main goal was to obtain generous retirement packages for their own memberships. In this, they were very successful: the new pension schemes included an 82% final salary replacement rate and attractive early retirement packages (Feldman et al, 1988). At the same time, worker contributions were relatively low, ensuring the schemes' popularity. Over the long run, this would lead to a large imbalance between resources being paid into these pension funds and their financial liabilities. Initially, however, the pension funds seemed to be awash with money. The main reason for this was that very few people inscribed in the newly established funds had yet reached retirement, and so the ratio of contributors to pensioners was still very high.

Extending the pension system was just as attractive to the Argentine government as it was to the unions. First, it ensured the political support of the labour movement, which was essential to its ISI strategy. Second, extending the pension system had brought in large numbers of new contributors who bailed out the deficits of the older funds. Many of these old funds were organised on even more generous principles than those set up under Perón, and this had quickly undermined their financial positions. For example, by 1939, the railway scheme had less than half of the funds needed to cover its long-term pension obligations (Lewis, 1993). Broadening the net of participation initially boosted the overall ratio of contributors to pensioners and kept the pension system afloat. The resulting temporary surpluses represented a large pool of funds that the government could draw on to finance its increasingly ambitious ISI projects.

The 1950s and 1960s saw no significant changes to the pension system, other than the centralisation of separate pension funds into unitary state agencies. This stability reflected the enduring power of the labour unions and the importance of a cooperative, efficient workforce for the pursuit of ISI development. Despite this continuity, the financial position of the pension system was transformed, as growing numbers of workers started to reach retirement age. Between 1950 and 1965, the number of benefits being paid out rose from 188,000 to 1,086,000. Many workers took advantage of early retirement, so that by 1966 over a quarter of pensioners had retired aged under 50 years old (Feldman et al, 1988). Past surpluses had been poorly invested, generating low and even negative rates of return, and levels of contributor evasion were very high. Inexorably, the pension system as a whole began to suffer from large and growing financial deficits.[5] During the 1970s and 1980s, the number of pensioners continued to rise and the financial crisis deepened. The average value of pensions fell increasingly short of the official 82% replacement rate, reaching only 43% in 1986. Efforts were made to increase contributions and the age of retirement, but these were resisted by both employers and unions. A growing informal sector and falling wages made further inroads into the shrinking pool of contributions.

By the 1990s, it was clear that the pension system required a radical overhaul. The collapse of the ISI growth model and an associated reduction in the power of the labour unions ended the political alliances that had underpinned existing arrangements. In 1994, as part of Menem's neoliberal revolution, a sweeping set of reforms was introduced. These included increases in contribution rates, raising the age of retirement (to 65 for men and 60 for women), reducing the official replacement rate to around 60% and gradually increasing the minimum number of contributions from just 15 years to 30 (Rofman, 2004). At the same time, the system was restructured along the lines of the Three Pillar Model discussed in Chapter Three. Workers were required to choose between a government-funded scheme or to join privately managed individual savings plans. By 2006, around 80% of formal sector workers had been enrolled into the new private plans.[6]

Following the economic crisis of 2001, there was a re-evaluation of the 1994 pension reform. Increases to the retirement age and, in particular, the minimum years of contributions were leading to sharp falls in coverage. Between 1993 and 2003, the proportion of people aged 65 or more lacking a pension rose from 23 to 37% (Rofman, 2004). Coverage rates for poorer income groups, those most in need of state support, were particularly low.[7] As the labour market had become more informalised, it was estimated that more than half of older people would lack a pension by 2025. Benefits had not kept pace with inflation, leading to effective replacement rates of around 40%. Although the private funds had generated good returns on their investments (averaging 11% a year between 1994 and 2003), there were mounting concerns about their exposure to sudden economic shocks. The loss of contributors to the government system meant that there were fewer funds for the state to cover its ongoing pension liabilities. The shortfall was met by substantial tax transfers, which accounted for 66% of pension fund income by 2003 (Roca and Bourquin, 2007). In other words, contributory pension funds were increasingly subsidised by the taxpaying society as a whole. As the new government sought to demonstrate its traditional Peronist credentials, there was increasing pressure to develop a more effective welfare system for older people.

One option would have been to develop an extensive programme of social pensions, as has been done in several other developing countries. Argentina already had a limited programme of non-contributory pensions, paying out 115,000 benefits in 2003, covering around 4% of the population aged 60 and over (Bertranou and Bonari, 2005).[8] Instead, the government decided to radically reform the contributory pension system. Previously, people who had not made the required 30 years of contributions needed to pay off all the outstanding contributions before they would be eligible for a benefit. This represented an insurmountable barrier for most older Argentines. From 2005, people with insufficient contributions were allowed a pension, with the value of their benefits reduced to cover the cost of the missing payments. In effect, these pensioners continue to contribute to their pension after retirement, although the rate of these contributions is unlikely to cover the funding shortfall.[9] The 2005 reform had an immediate impact on the pension system, as many people with few or even no lifetime contributions were now entitled to a discounted pension. Between 2004 and 2007, the number of contributory pensions paid out rose from 3.3 to 4.3 million (Roca and Bourquin, 2007). It is now claimed that over 90% of older people in Argentina have access to either a contributory or a social pension, possibly the highest coverage in Latin America.[10] The 2005 reform was accompanied by a series of other measures seeking to undo the policies of the 1990s. As the Argentina economy started to recover from the 2001 crisis, average benefit values were allowed to rise substantially. In 2007, the government enabled people affiliated to private funds to return to the government system. This led to a substantial fall in private fund membership, from around 12 to 10 million in a single year.

The impacts of population ageing on the financial status of Argentina's pension system have been complex and indirect, and have changed over time. For most of the 20th century, the effects were minimal. Early retirement, contributor evasion, the misuse of early surpluses and unfeasibly high pensions (especially for more influential occupations) had a much larger and more direct impact on pension finance. Rather than a consequence of demographic change, the growing pension crisis was driven by a combination of political short-termism and institutional failure. In more recent years, it is arguable that population ageing has become a more significant factor. The main driver of extended pension coverage and rising benefit values was no longer political management of the labour unions, but recognition that the 1994 reforms had failed to guarantee income security for a high proportion of older people. The economic welfare of older people had become a serious political issue in its own right: people aged 60 or more account for over a fifth of Argentina's voting-age population. As population ageing continues, it is likely that the maintenance of an acceptable old-age safety net will remain a high political priority.

Health policy for older people

Since the 1990s, total health spending in Argentina has accounted for around 7% of GDP. In absolute terms, this represented US$524 per person each year in 2008, considerably higher than other countries in the region.[11] In Chapter One we saw that population ageing does not *inevitably* lead to sharp rises in health spending, and that its impact is sometimes exaggerated and oversimplified. Nevertheless, since Argentina has high health spending and an aged population structure, it is valid to assess the extent to which they are linked.

Ideally, the impact of population ageing on health spending would be assessed by identifying the share of total health spending devoted to older people and how this has changed over time. In practice, this is impossible for several reasons. As in most countries, health budget data are broken down into services and types of provider, but are rarely disaggregated into specific age groups of patients. Second, the health sector is highly fragmented and decentralised, with a wide diversity of providers and financing mechanisms. This impedes data capture and comparison. Third, the quality of budget data is very uneven, especially for the growing private health sector.

A second approach would be to compare the health needs of older people to the rest of the population and assess how they have changed over time. If these needs are substantially greater, then it might be concluded that older people account for a higher share of the health budget. Again, there are a number of problems with this method. First, it should not be assumed that there is a simple relationship between the health needs of different population groups and the amount of healthcare resources devoted to them. In most countries, richer groups usually receive a larger share of health spending, despite enjoying better health than the poor. Older people may face particular discrimination compared with younger age groups. Second, good comparative data on the health status of Argentina's older population and other age groups are not available. General epidemiological data show that older people have a similar health profile to that of developed countries, with relatively high prevalence of hypertension, heart disease, diabetes and osteoarthritis (Vassallo and Sellanes, 2000). Given the size of the older population and these high rates of chronic disease, it can be assumed that they account for a large share of demand for health services. Whether these demands are adequately met, is quite another matter. The rest of this section focuses on different parts of the health sector, analysing factors that have affected their expenditure and the extent to which they provide effective services.

All health systems are complex, but Argentina's is particularly so. The health sector can be broken down into three broad areas: decentralised publicly funded services managed by the Ministry of Health, a separate set of union-run social insurance funds (numbering over 200) and privately financed healthcare. Argentina also has a health insurance fund that is exclusively dedicated to pensioners: PAMI.[12] Table 7.8 shows the relative importance of these sectors, in terms of budget.

Table 7.8: Distribution of health spending by sector (%)

	1997	2008
Ministry of Health	23	23
Union funds	30	31
PAMI	11	7
Private insurance and other private payments	41	40

Sources: Vassallo and Sellanes (2000); *Tiempo Pyme* (2008)

At first sight, PAMI would appear to offer good value for money. Pensioners made up around 10% of the population in 1997, and PAMI represented 11% of health spending. By 2008, its share of the health budget had fallen sharply to 7%. In fact, PAMI has been widely criticised over the years and has come to be seen as one of Argentina's most notoriously corrupt and inefficient state agencies (Bonvecchi et al, 1998; Redondo, 2004). By the mid-1990s, it emerged that PAMI had massive debts, which reached somewhere between US$2 billion and US$4 billion by 2000.[13] As with the contributory pension system, PAMI's financial crisis made a significant contribution to public sector debt and the country's economic instability. It would therefore seem to provide further evidence of a link between population ageing and reduced economic performance. Yet, just as with pensions, the huge level resources devoured by PAMI were much more the result of failures of governance and institutional mismanagement.

PAMI was first set up in 1971, possibly inspired by the creation of MEDICARE, the world's first social health insurance scheme for older people, in the US six years earlier (Redondo, 2004). Creating PAMI made good political sense to a military government, which was seeking to placate labour unions. The scheme relieved the union-run health funds from the responsibility of providing care to members after they had retired. Although these union funds continued to receive the same levels of resourcing through compulsory worker contributions, levels of demand for their services fell sharply. Labour unions were able to divert the large funding surpluses to a range of other activities, ensuring their continued political influence.

PAMI is funded separately from the union funds, with compulsory contributions levied on wages and pension benefits. Since it is exclusively for pensioners, older people without a benefit are excluded. PAMI does not provide services directly; instead, it contracts them out to a wide range of private organisations. Despite being part of the national social security system, PAMI itself is not a state agency and theoretically has the same independent status as the union funds. During the 1970s and 1980s, the scheme grew rapidly in terms of both membership and financing. By 1994, it provided services for over three and a half million people (over 10% of the total population) and managed an annual budget of over US$2 billion (Lloyd-Sherlock, 2003). But PAMI was also massively in debt, with a US$400 million shortfall between income and expenditure by 1994. To cover this deficit, members' contributions were topped up with substantial government funding. Despite these additional resources and several expensive (World Bank-funded) reform initiatives, PAMI's debts continued to grow.

It is widely recognised that the major factor driving PAMI's indebtedness was extreme administrative inefficiency. By 1983, it was employing 12,000 staff, a high proportion of whom were political appointments filling largely fictitious posts (Redondo, 2004). Despite several attempts to reduce staffing levels, these remained largely unchanged by 2001. More generally, PAMI has suffered from high levels of corruption. A labyrinthine system of contracts with service providers created opportunities for malpractice. One study identified 26 different categories of corruption in PAMI (Bonvecchi et al, 1998). As a non-state entity, it is shielded from public scrutiny, but it was heavily exposed to political influence. PAMI directors were usually political appointments, and they often mobilised PAMI's resources to further their own political careers, offering a wide range of welfare services that were outside PAMI's own remit.

A substantial proportion of PAMI members were not older people, with around a quarter aged under 60 by 1998. In large part, this was because of early retirement. It also resulted from politically motivated decisions to extend PAMI entitlements to new groups, including military veterans and women with seven or more children. All children aged under 21 of PAMI members were entitled to use its services, accounting for around half a million people. By contrast, until 2005 a significant share of the older population was denied access to PAMI services, since they were not pensioners. As such, it would be misleading to view PAMI as essentially a health fund for older people.

The limited available research shows large gaps between the services PAMI purported to offer and actual delivery, in terms of both quality and quantity. The range of statutory services listed in PAMI's own 'Digest' went well beyond those offered in most developed countries, yet spending per person was less than a 10th of MEDICARE's (Lloyd-Sherlock, 2003). Third-party providers were mainly paid a fixed amount per member, which encouraged widespread under-servicing. A virtual absence of regulation and information management permitted very uneven levels of quality. For several months during 1998 and 2002, PAMI suspended all payments to service providers and for essential drugs. As a result, a significant proportion of PAMI members made no use of the system, preferring to pay privately (Redondo and Salzman, 2000). In other words, despite the huge resources it absorbed, PAMI did not provide effective health services for its membership.

Since 2002, PAMI has seen a new set of reforms and these appear to have been more successful. Contracting has been simplified, to avoid some of the more obvious forms of corruption and inefficiency, and the total workforce has been scaled down somewhat. While PAMI still has substantial accumulated debts to services providers, it has been able to generate a large financial surplus in its current account. The relative ease with which PAMI was able to slip back into surplus indicates the degree of inefficiency and corruption it had previously suffered. Whether this has been done at the expense of further downgrading health services for older people is less clear: there are few signs that PAMI has been able to develop a more systematic and transparent model of service delivery.

For those older people who can afford it, private health insurance has become increasingly popular over the past decade. Data on the private insurance sector are extremely limited and incomplete: by 2008, an official register of firms and insurance plans had yet to be established. Older Argentines face particular barriers accessing private health insurance. First, they are required to pay much higher premiums than other age groups. A recent study of 40 plans found that people aged 72 paid more than double those aged 42 (Economy Ministry, Republic of Argentina, 2003). A separate survey reported that many private insurers refused cover for people aged over 60, and those that did would only accept new members with a clean bill of health. Premium levels varied from US$60 to US$419 a month, and the quality of care was highly variable (Lloyd–Sherlock, 2001b). In 2008 new legislation required that being aged 65 or more should not be sufficient grounds for denying membership of a plan, and that payments should not rise excessively with age (Cufré, 2008). Given the almost complete absence of regulation of the privately financed sector, little can be said about the range or quality of services on offer. There are media reports that some of the cheaper plans provide a very limited package. Even after the 2008 law, private insurance remains unaffordable for the great majority of older people.

The union funds and the Ministry of Health account for around half of Argentina's total health spending (Table 7.8). In the case of the union funds, the creation of PAMI has meant that almost none of this funding is dedicated to older people. The union sector is extremely fragmented, notoriously inefficient and had also been subjected to a series of largely failed reforms. These health funds represent a major source of financial and political power to the labour unions and they have been able to resist structural changes (Lloyd–Sherlock, 2005).[14] Reducing these inefficiencies could significantly reduce overall health spending in Argentina, regardless of population ageing.

Theoretically, the Ministry of Health is a provider of last resort for people who do not have cover for PAMI, private plans or the union funds. Provision is highly decentralised and it is not possible to collate systematic data on financing or the level of service offered to older people. It is generally assumed that the overall level of quality is below the other sectors', and the few available studies suggest that the public healthcare infrastructure is poorly maintained and outdated, particularly beyond Buenos Aires (World Bank, 1997). The Ministry's core budget has varied sharply over recent years, but this appears to be more a reflection of political priorities than underlying demographic trends.

To summarise, establishing any link between population ageing and expenditure is impossible even for individual health sectors, let alone for the healthcare system as a whole. Instead, it is clear that the main causes of high costs have been institutional rather than demographic. Argentina's healthcare system is in very poor shape to meet the increased demand associated with population ageing, and this has meant that many older people continue to receive a poor service. More generally, the healthcare system is widely criticised as suffering from a heavy bias towards expensive, specialist, curative services (Escudero, 2003). Much less attention has been paid to measures that can promote good health throughout life, including in old age. For example, Argentina continues to have a much higher smoking prevalence than in most developed countries, and government anti-smoking legislation has been half-hearted (Sebrie et al, 2005). It has been estimated that tobacco-related disease accounts for over 15% of Argentina's total health budget. By developing a more efficient and better-prioritised healthcare system, Argentina could greatly improve the health of all age groups, young and old.

Long-term care needs

As well as pensions and healthcare provision, a third area where older people may consume significant amounts of resources is the provision of LTC. As discussed in Chapter Five, these care needs have tended to receive less attention than pensions and health, but they can be just as significant, in terms of both resourcing and their impact on older people's quality of life. It is also important to bear in mind that many older people actively contribute to the care economy, by looking after young grandchildren, sick or disabled relatives and ageing spouses. Nevertheless, age-related illness, frailty and disability mean that increases in the proportion of older people, particularly the oldest old, are likely to increase demand for LTC. Drawing on survey data from Buenos Aires about older people's health status and functioning, a recent study (Monteverde et al, 2008) assessed their overall degree of dependency in later life. It found that 22% of people aged 60 or more in 2001 experienced some form of dependency. Of these, the great majority experienced either 'high' or 'severe' levels of dependency. There was a clear gender gap, with older men experiencing less dependency (14%) than older women (25%). The study estimated the average number of years that people aged 60 could expect to experience dependency for during their remaining lifetimes: 5.5 years for women and 2.5 years for men.

Despite the high demand for services, it might be concluded that the direct costs of LTC in Argentina are relatively small, simply because the state provides very few services. The first charitable old-age home was established in Buenos Aires in 1857 and several mutual aid societies followed suit over the subsequent decades (Freysselinard et al, 2000). These continued to be the main source of institutional care until the 1970s, since only a handful of state-funded homes were established.

The creation of PAMI in 1971 was an important milestone in LTC provision. As well as managing health services, PAMI was charged with meeting the care needs of its members. It did this by contracting out to private care homes and through the establishment of a range of other services, most notably clubs and daycare centres for pensioners. During the 1990s, as PAMI's deficits mounted, payments to care homes were mainly discontinued, forcing many out of business and leaving their residents in a highly vulnerable condition. In recent years, PAMI has sought to re-establish networks of care homes and to promote training programmes for paid carers. This has been supported by a government agency – the Dirección Nacional de la Tercera Edad – albeit it with a minimal budget. Given the lack of publicly available financial information for PAMI, it is not possible to accurately assess the extent of public expenditure on care services, but it is a very small fraction of the pension and healthcare budgets.

Due to the lack of government involvement, only a very small proportion of people aged 60 or more (2% in 2001) were reported as residents in old-age homes, almost all of which operate on a private for-profit basis (Redondo and Lloyd-Sherlock, 2009). The great majority of older people are left to rely on their families for support: it has been estimated that over 80% of dependent older people receive care on an unpaid basis from a relative (Freysselinard et al, 2000). This informalisation of the care economy has important implications for the quality of care received, for the person providing the care and for the costs of caring.

Leaving care to family members is not costless, since these relatives lose potential earnings from other, salaried forms of employment. Monteverde et al (2008) estimated that the real average cost of providing family care for an older woman would be over US$65,000 during the course of her lifetime.[15] Increasing the proportion of care provided by residential homes substantially reduced the overall care costs, due to economies of scale and other effects. From this it might be concluded that the real cost of informal caring is very high indeed. However, this is based on the assumption that the salaried labour market has the capacity to productively absorb these additional workers, which may well not be the case. As in other countries, it is female relatives (including older ones) who provide the bulk of unpaid care (Esquivel, 2008). Caring for an older relative restricts the potential amount of time women are able to make pension contributions, reducing their own welfare entitlements in old age.

The effects of the care economy on older people are less easy to assess, as little reliable information exists. Most older people express a strong preference to remain in their own homes, and to be cared for by their own relatives. However, low levels of fertility and changing social trends mean that a growing share of older people live alone. According to the 2001 Census, 19% of people aged 65 and over lived alone, and a further 27% lived in nuclear households without children. For people aged 80 or more, the proportion living alone is even higher. Although some of these people may choose to live alone, the data suggest that many struggle to access informal care when they need it. Nor should it be assumed that living with a younger relative is a guarantee of informal support. Several studies reveal much more complex patterns of family dynamics, and in some settings living with children may be as much a source of vulnerability as of potential support (Lloyd-Sherlock and Locke, 2008). There are growing anecdotal reports of family abuse and abandonment of older people. A recent survey of older people in residential care homes found that a significant proportion had been admitted by relatives against their will (Redondo and Lloyd-Sherlock, 2009). Regulation of care homes is lax and there are indications that the quality of services they offer is highly variable (Redondo and Lloyd-Sherlock, 2009). On a more positive note, the extensive network of day centres established by PAMI remains largely intact. These centres provide an important source of support and social activities for older people with high levels of functioning, and could form the basis for a more concerted programme of supporting domiciliary care.

Overview of the economic impact of population ageing

Argentina has seen decades of poor economic performance, it has a large population of older people (most of whom are no longer in paid work) and spends heavily on pension provision and healthcare. At first sight, the links between population ageing and reduced economic dynamism would appear quite evident. The previous discussion suggests otherwise. Argentina's relative decline began in the 1930s, well before it contained large numbers of older people. High levels of spending on pensions and healthcare may have contributed to this decline, especially from the 1960s when large deficits emerged. However, the main causes of high spending were institutional and political in nature, rather than demographic. The impact of ageing on economic dependency must be offset against falling numbers of children and the economic benefits of reduced fertility. Any effects of ageing on savings rates were swamped by decades of high inflation, which acted as a major disincentive to hold onto money. Moreover, the real opportunity costs of reduced economic activity in later life and of the diversion of informal carers from paid work depend on the capacity of the labour market to absorb these extra workers productively. High rates of unemployment and underemployment suggest that this capacity should not be taken for granted. Arguably, slower fertility transition and more gradual population ageing could have increased the labour supply to the extent that worker costs were pushed down, thus boosting growth and the supply of jobs. This, however, is a highly speculative argument, and it ignores the costs of larger cohorts of young children.

Population ageing may have had little to do with Argentina's long-run decline, but its economic significance has increased in recent decades. Had Argentina developed more effective pension and health policies in the past, it would have been in a strong position to face the challenges of ageing today. Instead, problems of poor governance and inefficiency continue to bedevil many areas of social policy, especially in healthcare. The substantial amounts of public resources devoted to these programmes crowd out the possibility of developing a more systematic set of policies supporting the care economy. Increasingly, older people are seeking their health and care needs from a poorly regulated private sector. The recent upgrading of pension policy has boosted the income security of the older population, but questions remain about its long-term sustainability.

As Argentina's older population has grown, it might be expected that it would become more politically influential, especially since the return of democratic rule in the 1980s. Many of today's cohort of older people have past experiences of political activism and most are literate. During the military governments of the late 1970s and early 1980s, a group of older women ran a high-profile human rights campaign, with daily demonstrations outside government buildings. In the 1990s, a small but vocal pensioner lobby organised marches and protests against Menem's pension reforms. Despite these precedents, a substantial political movement representing older people's (or even pensioners') interests has not emerged in Argentina. Pension policy is a very prominent public issue, but the lines of the debate are mainly drawn between traditional Peronists and opposing ideologies, rather than between young and old. Political parties are acutely aware of the weight of older voters and this will have important effects on future policy directions, especially for pensions.

Current cohorts of older people have lived through decades of political turbulence and growing economic uncertainty. Many suffered from the contraction of the pension system during the 1990s, in terms of both coverage and benefit values. The recent pension upgrading will have brought relief and a secure income to many, but this alone does not guarantee a good quality of life in old age. The following three life histories give a flavour of what it has been like to grow older in Argentina. As in the other country chapters in this book, they do not intend to provide a representative view of ageing experiences – these are too complex and too diverse to be captured in a small number of interviews. What they do offer is three very different sets of experiences, taken from three different socioeconomic strata. They provide striking contrasts in terms of access to pensions and other public resources, as well as patterns of family relationships and care. Each informant's life was profoundly shaped by wider national events (such as the rise and fall of the industrial sector and political transitions), but these effects were very different. A common theme that emerges is a growing fear of violence and a difficulty in making sense of the bewildering pace of national change.

Three lives[16]

Anastacio

Anastacio is 83 years old. He was born in the province of Santiago del Estero, about 600 miles to the northwest of Buenos Aires, one of 14 brothers and sisters. He worked on the land from the age of 14 and came to Buenos Aires in search of work when he was 18 (1943). He had no difficulty finding a factory job, and continued to work there until he was 59 (1978): "There was so much work around in the old days. I left my job in one factory, and two blocks away I found another place that was taking people on." Anastacio married a woman from Santiago when he was 28, but they separated shortly after the death of their young child. He later remarried and had a daughter

Anastacio was allowed to retire one year before the usual age, as he had developed bronchial problems at work. Initially, he was not given a full pension, and he had to hire a lawyer to help resolve his claim. Shortly after Anastacio retired, his factory and most of the other ones in his neighbourhood were shut down. At first, he continued work in a small repair workshop but he found this was too much for him. His income consists of a basic pension and the pension of his recently deceased wife (who worked as a cook). Although he does not live in a shanty town or slum, he feels that his neighbourhood has become much less secure in recent years and does not go out at all after dark: "There were 2,000 people working in my factory. Now, there are so many poor people living round here and lots of stealing. It wasn't like that before. Now there just aren't any jobs to be had."

He lives with a daughter, her husband and two young grandchildren, and says that they look after him well: "I don't have any complaints about my life these days." Anastacio's health has deteriorated in recent years. Among other problems, he is deaf and has developed Parkinson's disease. He has been trying to obtain a hearing aid through PAMI for the past three years, without success. Rather than rely on PAMI, he mainly sees private doctors and finds these difficult to afford.

Anastacio feels that Perón did much to improve the lives of people like him, but that his legacy was later undermined, especially during the 1980s and 1990s: "As far as I'm concerned, Peronism was the best thing that ever happened in Argentina. They respected us workers.... Those guys who say they are Peronists nowadays are just nothing".

Susanna

Susanna is 79 years old and was born in a Pampas village about 60 miles from Buenos Aires. Her father was an Italian migrant, who set up a successful family business in the village. After finishing school, aged 17, she trained as a school teacher, qualifying a year later (1947). Initially, she was not able to get a teaching position, as it was necessary to affiliate to the Peronist Party and she was not prepared to do this. Instead, she worked in her father's office, making contributions to the commercial pension fund.

Following a military coup (1955), Susanna was able to start work as a teacher: "The officers were almost all married to schoolteachers who were out of work. So they started to give posts to the older women first. That's how I got my chance." She continued working until she was 47 (1976), when she was allowed to retire on a full pension, worth 82% of her previous wage: "When the military came back into power, many of their wives were still teachers. So they allowed people to retire young, so their own wives would benefit. That worked out well for me, too." Despite this, she feels she was cheated out of her commercial pension entitlement: "The pension fund had told me not to worry, that when I retired they would take into account the seven years I had contributed. But when I stopped working, they just refused to."

Susanna then moved to Buenos Aires, to accompany her four children who were studying at university there. She was able to buy a house in one of the city's most prestigious neighbourhoods, mainly due to money she inherited from her father. All of her children have done very well in life and one now lives in the US. Susanna's husband died of lung cancer when she was 56 and she now lives alone. She says that this is her preference and that she sees her family on a daily basis.

Susanna's children had advance warning of economic crises, which enabled her to withdraw her money from banks and protect her savings: "We were saved twice. Once in the 1970s, because my children worked for IBM and they know about the shock policy in advance....Then [in 2001] I had a daughter who worked in the Banco Francés. She started to see how people were panicking, and told me to get my money out while I still could." Susanna has a number of health problems, including back pain and heart disease. She prefers to pay for an expensive private health plan rather than rely on PAMI or her old union fund: "PAMI is just a joke. They do all those adverts and have numbers you can ring, but I've never been able to get through." Susanna remains very active and is on the committee of her local pensioners' association. She says she is content with her life, but is saddened by the state of the country: "We've lost so many of our traditions; our respect and our courtesy.... I always thought that this was going to become an organised country, but now there's so much instability."

Ana

Ana is 80 years old and was born in Goya, about 500 miles north of Buenos Aires, one of 15 brothers and sisters. She now lives in one of Buenos Aires' most notorious and dangerous slum districts. She attended school until she was eight years old, when her mother took her to work as a nanny for a family in Paraguay. She was not allowed to continue in school and was badly treated by the family. Aged 13 (1939), Ana escaped and came to work as a domestic servant in Buenos Aires: "I didn't know anything. I didn't even speak Spanish, only Guaraní. These days nobody speaks Guaraní anymore – I've completely forgotten it." She stayed with the same family until she was 19, when she married and had her first child. Her husband, "an excellent man", had a good job, working for the Eva Perón Foundation and then for the post office. Ana had five children, and when she was 30 (1956) she started to work in a factory: "It's gone now. Those days there were strikes all the time. It was really frightening. Sometimes people fought each other with knives. I just wanted to get on with the job, but sometimes there were people at the gate who wouldn't let you past. My husband didn't like me being there."

Ana went back to work as a hospital cleaner, but they found it hard to make ends meet, so were forced to live in the slum. In 1976, they were forced to move again after the slum was bulldozed by the new military government, but returned to build a new home there a few years later. Ana's husband died of a heart attack in 1984. She now lives with a daughter who is divorced and suffers from epilepsy, two grandchildren and a son with serious mental health problems: "He doesn't work. He just sleeps and says crazy things. When he has a fit and doesn't take his pills, he has to spend weeks in bed. I have to look after him like a baby." The son is sometimes violent and Ana is afraid to leave him alone in the house.

The family lives off Ana's widow's pension and her daughter's disability benefit, and by selling crafts in a local market. She has substantial debts on money that she borrowed using her pension as a guarantee. Ana says she is in good health, but does not make regular health visits to health clinics. She has been assaulted several times and would like to move somewhere else: "They've attacked me twice recently. Once when I was collecting my pension they threatened me with a gun and took my purse and everything. I know who they are, their names even. Then they broke down our front door and took everything we had in the house. One of them is a neighbour's son, but I was too frightened to go to the police." Ana is very concerned about how her family will cope after her death: "It's a struggle. Life is very hard for women who are trying to support their families on their own. Even though I'm 80, if they offered me a job I'd take it straight away. I won't let things beat me".

Notes

[1] Unlike other developing countries, differences in access to education and literacy between men and women were relatively small (Pantelides, 2006).

[2] Poverty levels for the rest of the country were considerably higher, but reliable data do not exist.

[3] By 2008, the official unemployment rate was 9%.

[4] Pension funds accounted for the bulk of this social insurance budget, although social health insurance schemes were also an important component.

[5] For more details, see the discussion around Table 3.3 in Chapter Three.

[6] The rapid growth of private funds was driven by very heavy investment in marketing. Also, workers who did not take action to remain in the government scheme were automatically transferred to the private one and were not allowed to return.

[7] In 2001, 88% of older people in the richest income quintile had pensions, compared with only 32% in the poorest one (Bertranou and Bonari, 2005).

[8] Argentina also has a system of honorary pensions, which members of the National Congress and Senate award on a purely discretionary and unaccountable basis, with no specific age criteria. In 2003, 140,000 such awards were being paid out.

[9] Beneficiaries 'pay back' on average 40% of their pensions (that is, they get a pension worth 60% of the minimum rate). After five years, the repayments stop and they get a full pension.

[10] This figure may be somewhat exaggerated. Since the political takeover of the national statistics agency in 2006, official figures have become very unreliable.

[11] For example, per capita spending in Brazil and Mexico was US$260 and US$310, respectively.

[12] This scheme is popularly referred to as 'PAMI' (Programa de Atención Médica Integral). In fact, PAMI is just one programme run by a larger pensioner health insurance agency, known as the Instituto Nacional de Obras Sociales para Jubilados y Pensionados.

[13] The precise amount depended on specific interpretations of existing contractual obligations and the degree to which creditors had written off outstanding debts.

[14] Interestingly, government threats to reform these health funds played a large part in persuading the unions to go along with the 1994 pension reform.

[15] This estimate is based on paying family carers below market rates. If they were paid at market rates, the cost would rise to US$75,746.

[16] The names of the informants in this section have been changed to preserve their anonymity.

EIGHT

Ageing and development in India

Introduction

The selection of India for a case study can be justified purely in terms of its large population, which reached one billion in 2000. Although population ageing in India is less advanced than in countries such as Argentina (7% of Indians were aged 60 or more in 2005), the country's sheer size means that nearly an eighth of the world's population aged 60 and over live there. As well as scale, India presents deep-seated and complex patterns of diversity. These can be seen in terms of large development disparities between rural and urban districts and between the different states. They are also evident in strong traditional divisions based on religion, gender and caste, as well as increasing socioeconomic differentiation.

In addition, India offers a valuable case study of both continuity and change. India was granted independence from British rule in 1947, which means that current cohorts of older people have spent most or all of their lives in an independent country. Between the 1950s and the 1980s, economic performance was relatively sluggish, and many early aspirations failed to materialise. By contrast, in recent years India has experienced a dramatic surge in economic growth, based on manufacturing, as well as a dynamic new information technology and services sector. Yet the extent to which this boom is transforming the lives of its population, particularly older people, is questionable. The great majority of older people in India continue to live in rural areas, often in impoverished villages that have seen little economic or social progress during their lifetimes. These experiences contrast abruptly with the dramatic growth in prosperity of a small, new class of young, urban employees. As such, a key issue is why the socioeconomic status of so many Indians changed so little through the 20th century. This is highly relevant for the situation of current and future cohorts of older people. For example, it is estimated that less than 10% of the labour force are presently employed in formal sector activities, greatly reducing the scope for pension coverage (Harriss-White, 2003).

This chapter follows the same broad structure as the other country chapters. It begins with an overview of India's development since independence, before moving on to examine demographic trends and patterns of population ageing. Given India's geographical diversity, particular attention is given to two particular states (Uttar Pradesh and Kerala), which demonstrate substantially different patterns of development and population change. The chapter goes on to explore a number of key themes, with sections on gender and poverty, old age and illness, and pension policies. It concludes with three testimonies from older people, which illustrate the complexity of lived experiences of old age in India today.

Development in India

Unlike Argentina and South Africa, there is no obvious historical point of departure for India's modern development. The arrival of the British East India Company in 1617 and its subsequent annexation of large territories was a key period of change. Nevertheless, many important Indian traditions and institutions predate the country's piecemeal incorporation into the British Empire (Stein, 1998). In 1857, following a large-scale uprising, the British government took over direct rule of the entire territory.[1] This period of direct British rule led to important economic developments, such as the construction of an extensive railway network and the expansion of trade. However, colonial rule was associated with a significant rise in rural poverty, so that by the mid-20th century, India was one of the poorest countries in the developing world (Roy, 2000). Over 90% of the population still lived in rural areas, often engaged in low-productivity subsistence agriculture. Efforts to extend basic health and education services were very limited and only around a fifth of the population were literate at the time of independence (Kingdon et al, 2005). Colonial rule coincided with several major famines and epidemics of infectious disease, resulting in millions of deaths (Dyson, 2005). This period also saw the introduction of important changes to the Indian state, many of which still remain in place. These included a generous civil service pension scheme, which continued largely unchanged until 2004.

Indian independence is strongly associated with the figure of Mahatma Gandhi. Despite this, Gandhi never occupied a formal political post, and he was assassinated by a radical Hindu protestor in 1948. Instead, it was Jawaharlal Nehru who dominated Indian politics following independence. Nehru served as Prime Minister between 1947 and 1964, a post his daughter and grandson would also occupy in later years. His achievement in establishing a unified, secular and democratic state was impressive given the political and social upheaval of independence and partition. In contrast to many post-colonial leaders, Nehru sought to promote the continuity of state institutions, ensuring that the majority of imperial civil servants kept their posts in the new regime (Luce, 2006). Given the overwhelmingly rural nature of India's population and economy, there was an urgent need for major interventions to promote rural development, including large-scale land reform and irrigation. Instead, following the dominant international development philosophies of that period, Nehru focused on state-led industrialisation and massive government projects such as dams and steel plants. As in Argentina and South Africa, this model of industrialisation relied on heavy state subsidies, which came to be associated with corruption and inefficiency. Moreover, Nehru's focus on industry yielded disappointing economic returns. Between 1950 and 1980, the economy grew by an average of 3.2% per year, only slightly faster than the population growth rate. Not surprisingly, then, little progress was made in reducing the burden of widespread poverty, especially in the countryside. Similarly, progress in extending basic services across the population did not match the expectations of the early post-independence years. For example, by 1980, less than half of the population were literate and the infant mortality rate was nearly double South Africa's. In part, these failures were due to rapid population growth, which significantly increased the overall level of need. The blame also lay with low levels of resourcing and the poor delivery of basic services in most Indian states (Dreze and Gazdar, 1997).

In 1967, the relative neglect of the rural sector led to a serious economic shock. India had become increasingly reliant on food imports, so that when international food prices rose, the country faced a major balance of payments crisis. Subsequently, rural development received rather more attention, with widespread modernisation and innovation, as part of a wider international movement known as the 'Green Revolution'. This led to rapid improvements in rural productivity, so that India became self-reliant in food. In the absence of significant land reforms, however, the benefits of this Revolution were mainly limited to richer farmers and more fertile states. As such, its overall impact on rural poverty was small (Lipton and Longhurst, 1989).

By the 1980s, Nehru's industrialisation model had started to lose momentum, leading to a mounting trade deficit and renewed balance of payments problems (Acharya et al, 2005). A lack of investment in basic services and infrastructure such as roads was a major barrier to the country's modernisation. In 1991, a new fiscal crisis sparked by oil price rises led to an unprecedented economic collapse. It also ushered in a radical set of economic reforms, which were to have a dramatic impact on India's economic performance.

Since 1993, the Indian economy has grown at an annual rate of over 6%: far exceeding its performance over the previous decades (Acharya et al, 2005). At the same time, population growth has slowed significantly, enabling substantial rises in per capita wealth. Unlike China, India's economic boom has not been based on rapid industrialisation, or on significant changes in the rural sector. Although there are important pockets of progress in the countryside, most of the rural economy continues to face the problems that have beset it since before independence (Luce, 2006). Instead, the boom has been led by a massive expansion in the services sector, most notably in information technology. This has been made possible by a well-educated and cheap English-speaking workforce, as well as new policies that have opened the Indian economy to the outside world. These policies bear some similarities to the neoliberal reforms that were rolled out in Argentina and other developing countries during the 1990s, and are strongly supported by the World Bank and IMF. They include sharp cuts in industrial subsidies, export promotion and the gradual deregulation of financial markets, as well as recent moves to develop a privately managed pension system. As in other countries, efforts to promote efficiency and reduce corruption in the public sector have met with strong political resistance and progress has been limited (Caiden and Sundaram, 2004).

Economic expansion and a deceleration in population growth have enabled significant reductions in the overall prevalence of poverty in India, although these were slower during the 1990s than during the 1980s. World Bank estimates for 2005 show that 42% of the population were still living below the international poverty line of US$1.25 a day. Despite its rapid rate of economic growth, a higher proportion of its population lived on less than US$2 a day than was the case in sub-Saharan Africa (*The Times of India*, 2008). In absolute terms, India now contains more poor people than at any point in its history, and malnutrition is still widespread in rural districts of the poorer states (Cassen and McNay, 2005).

There are several reasons why the benefits of the economic boom have not been spread more widely. Most importantly, the service sector has not generated sufficient levels of employment, especially for poorly paid semi-skilled workers. For example, it is estimated that information technology only employs around a million people, out of a total labour force of over 350 million (Luce, 2006). With a further seven million employed in manufacturing and 21 million civil servants, the great majority of Indians continue to work in agriculture or in informal activities (Harriss-White, 2003). Beyond the dynamic service industries, major structural barriers and infrastructural bottlenecks remain. For example, rigid labour policies established during Nehru's rule led to higher labour costs than in countries like China, discouraging the recruitment of workers. They also promoted 'informalisation', with large formal sector firms subcontracting work to unregulated enterprises. The boom has led to a widening gap in productivity and earnings between the minority formal sector and the rest of the workforce. It has also contributed to rising income inequalities both between and within states, with poorer regions falling further behind the new centres of economic progress (Cassen and McNay, 2005). At the same time, continued state corruption has undermined efforts to support development through road building and other infrastructure projects (Luce, 2006).

Since the 1980s, there have been a growing number of high-profile government initiatives aimed at reducing poverty and promoting human development in rural areas (Kochar, 2008). Particular focus has been placed on employment generation and nutritional support through subsidised food. Most evaluations of these programmes conclude that they have been poorly targeted and plagued by corruption, so that their general impact on poverty and deprivation has been marginal at best (Cassen and McNay, 2005). In 2005, the latest of a series of employment-based initiatives – the National Rural Employment Guarantee Act – was passed by Parliament. Theoretically, this guarantees poor rural households a minimum of 100 days' paid employment a year. While the fund is well resourced (costing around 1.5% of GDP), continued targeting problems mean that the scheme may be no more successful than previous efforts (Sjoblom and Farrington, 2008).

As well as persistent rural poverty, India continues to face particular barriers in human development for women and other disadvantaged groups. While some progress has been made in reducing gender gaps in literacy, they remain substantial. In 2001, around a quarter of India's male population was illiterate, compared with half of its women. Similarly, gender gaps in infant mortality remain significant (Khanna et al, 2003). These specific forms of deprivation are part of wider structures of exclusion and inequality, which continue to restrict the lives of many women and other disadvantaged groups, particularly in rural areas. These include India's caste system, a form of social hierarchy rooted in Hinduism, whereby individuals are allotted hereditary roles, occupations and statuses. Traditionally, *dalits* (or 'untouchables') have made up the lowest tier in this system, and have been restricted to jobs deemed as unacceptable to their 'superiors', such as street sweeping or collecting human waste. In theory, other castes remain forbidden to have contact with *dalits*, let alone inter-marry with them (Luce, 2006). *Dalits* comprise around 16% of India's population, with a further 8% categorised as belonging to marginalised 'scheduled tribes' (or *adivasis*).[2] Since independence, the government has pursued a policy of positive discrimination for *dalits*, *adivasis* and similar groups, providing fixed quotas of public sector employment and access to university places. Where implemented, these measures have led to some improvement in the status of *dalits* (less so for *adivasis*), but substantial inequalities remain (Borooah, 2005). Traditional forms of inequality based around gender and caste remain particularly entrenched in rural areas, ensuring that women and other low-status groups bear the brunt of rural poverty.

While in many ways India's development since independence has been disappointing, in one key area it has exceeded all expectations. Despite widespread poverty, powerful internal divisions, a poorly educated population and a corrupt state apparatus, India has somehow succeeded in maintaining a pluralist, democratic system of governance (Guha, 2007). The model is broadly based on the British parliamentary system, although important powers have been devolved to states and local governments. For the first four decades after independence, politics were dominated by Nehru's Indian National Congress Party, with a strong agenda of unity and secularism (Luce, 2006). Since then, political structures have become more fragmented, with religious parties such as the Hindu BJP (Bharatiya Janata Party) gaining ground. Although local politics often suffer from corruption and clientelism, national elections are widely considered to be free and fair (Singh, 2003). Democracy has provided spaces for less powerful groups to improve their position: for example, *dalits* have become especially well organised and effective at pressuring state agencies in recent years (Luce, 2006). In some states, such as Kerala, democracy has permitted radical left-wing movements a major role in policy making, with important consequences for rural poverty and human development.

Overall, India's experiences of development since 1947 have only had limited effects on the majority of its population. During the 1950s and 1960s, industrial promotion led to the continued neglect of agriculture. The Green Revolution created opportunities for richer farmers, but did little for the large numbers of rural poor. The recent boom may be transforming India into a global economic superpower, but its benefits have only reached a small minority of its population. Over two thirds of Indians continue to live in rural areas. The extent of change has been particularly limited for older age cohorts, few of whom would have been able to benefit from gradual extensions to basic education or the opportunities offered by the information technology sector. As younger groups migrate to urban areas, India's older population remains disproportionately rural: in 2001, over 71% of people aged 60 and over lived in rural areas (Alam, 2008). Yet, not all of India's regions conform to this disappointing national picture. Given the country's sheer size, varied traditions, increasingly divergent economic patterns and decentralised politics, experiences of all age groups vary profoundly across the different groups and regions. It is not possible to do justice to this complexity within a single book chapter, so specific reference will be made to two particular states. These are Uttar Pradesh, which in many ways represents the wider national experience of rural underdevelopment, and Kerala, which stands out as an exceptional case and may offer key lessons.

Uttar Pradesh is located in the north of India. With a population of over 190 million people in 2008, it is India's most populous state, and is often characterised as broadly typical of the country's less economically and socially developed regions (Dreze and Gazdar, 1997). The economy of Uttar Pradesh remains dominated by agriculture and the bulk of the population continue to live in impoverished villages (Ajwad, 2007). The state has seen some economic progress since independence, notably the introduction of modern agricultural practices during the Green Revolution. However, these have failed to benefit the majority of the rural population, as landholdings were highly unequal. Social and political changes have been even more limited, as traditional attitudes towards caste and gender remain entrenched in village life. Local politics continue to be dominated by large landholding elites, with particularly high levels of corruption and patronage. This is reflected in poorly developed social policies. For example, by 1981, only 10% of villages contained medical facilities, compared with 96% in the state of Kerala (Dreze and Gazdar, 1997). As a result, infant mortality is significantly higher than the national average and the state has the highest rates of maternal mortality in India (Ajwad, 2007). Poverty and social inequalities have given Uttar Pradesh one of the highest rates of fertility and population growth in India. It also contains a particularly high concentration of disadvantaged groups, such as scheduled castes and scheduled tribes.

Kerala is located in the south west of India. Like Uttar Pradesh, it is largely a rural state, with an economy dominated by agriculture. However, Kerala has come to be recognised internationally as a 'success story' for human development (Ramachandran, 1997; Parayil, 2000).

Key indicators of wellbeing, such as literacy and life expectancy, are considerably better than national averages. For example, in 1996, infant mortality was 13 per 1,000 live births compared with 72 in India as a whole (Anand et al, 2000). It would therefore appear that Kerala has overcome many of the social problems affecting other parts of the country. Yet historically, Kerala's economic performance has been sluggish since independence. Per capita incomes are around the national average and unemployment levels are the highest in India. As a result, large numbers of younger adults have migrated to other states or abroad in search of work, usually leaving older family members behind.

The roots of Kerala's social progress are complex. They include an unusual political history, with local rule dominated by the Communist Party and allied organisations. Among other things, this permitted radical land reforms from the late 1950s and increased government efforts to develop basic services. Also, Kerala has fewer traditions of gender and caste inequalities than other parts of India, permitting wider access to education, employment and the benefits of social progress. As a result of its relatively low fertility and high life expectancy, as well as age-selective out-migration, Kerala is now India's most aged state.

Fertility transition and population ageing

India's population was already very large during British rule, reaching around 250 million in 1870 and growing to 350 million by the time of independence (Dyson, 2005). Despite the limited progress in extending health services, there were significant and sustained reductions in mortality from the 1950s. Key factors included government campaigns targeting infectious diseases such as smallpox and cholera, as well as improved food security. Following independence, this decline in mortality led to a surge in population growth rates (Table 8.1).

Table 8.1: India: selected demographic indicators, 1950–2005

	Crude death rate (deaths per 1,000 population)	Population growth rate (%)	Total fertility rate (children per woman)
1950–55	26.0	1.73	5.91
1960–65	20.2	2.04	5.82
1970–75	15.1	2.22	5.26
1980–85	11.6	2.26	4.50
1990–95	9.8	2.08	3.86
2000–05	8.7	1.62	3.11

Source: United Nations Population Division (2008)

As seen in Chapter One, the standard demographic transition model predicts that sustained falls in mortality will eventually be followed by a reduction in fertility rates. In the Indian case, significant fertility decline did not begin until the 1970s, and overall levels continued to be high through to the 1990s. Some studies suggest that fertility may have increased rather than fallen during the 1950s and 1960s (Dyson, 2005).[3] This delayed transition was a key factor in India's rapid population growth, and high fertility remains a major area of concern for policy makers. By the 1960s, population control was viewed as central to the country's development strategy and occupied a prominent place in its five-year plans (Visaria, 2005b). Particular efforts were made to promote female sterilisation and male vasectomy, culminating in the 1976 National Population Policy. Controversially, this policy used various forms of incentive and coercion to promote female sterilisation. Widespread political opposition to these methods led to Indira Gandhi's resignation as Prime Minister the following year (Gwatkin, 1979). Since then, population control policies have been more careful to recognise individual rights and incentive payments have largely been eliminated (Visaria, 2005b). Nevertheless, female sterilisation remains the main method of birth control.

Despite sometimes authoritarian policies, the take-up of effective contraception has been quite slow and limited. In the 1970s, only around 10% of couples were using effective methods, rising to 45% in 2000 (Visaria, 2005b). In rural areas, the prevalence of contraception remains very low, and fertility rates are consequently much higher than in the cities. In these areas, high fertility both contributes to and is fed by poverty and gender inequalities. The persistence of high fertility in rural areas has been explained by a number of factors, such as low levels of female literacy and female employment, as well as limited access to basic health services (Murthi et al, 1997). The impact of female literacy on fertility is evident in comparisons between states such as Kerala and Uttar Pradesh (Table 8.2). A recent survey found that fertility rates among illiterate women in Kerala were identical to those

Table 8.2: Kerala and Uttar Pradesh: selected demographic indicators, circa 2000

	Total fertility rate, 1996–2001 (births per woman)	Female literacy, 2000 (%)	Population aged 60+, 2001 (%)
India	3.64	54	7.0
Kerala	1.62	88	10.9
Uttar Pradesh	4.75	42	4.4

Source: Census of India (2001); Dyson (2002)

of their illiterate counterparts in Uttar Pradesh (National Population Stabilisation Fund, 2007).

The massive variations in fertility between the two states shown in Table 8.2 have wide-ranging implications for other aspects of development and population change. Among these, they lead to different patterns of population ageing. Kerala's success in reducing fertility means that it now has the highest concentration of older people in India. Continued high fertility in Uttar Pradesh has led to continued rapid population growth. While demographic ageing is not as advanced here, the sheer size of its total population means that it contains a larger number of older people (over 10 million in 2001) than any other Indian state. For India as a whole, fertility remains well above the replacement rate of 2.1, so that its population continues to grow by around 17 million a year. As a result, it is estimated that the country's total population will grow by a further 500 million by the middle of the 21st century (Dyson, 2005). By contrast, Kerala has faced below replacement rate fertility since the 1980s. Low birth rates, combined with high levels of out-migration may mean that Kerala's population will fall in the foreseeable future.

Table 8.3 shows population ageing trends for India as a whole. During the 1950s, high fertility and reductions in infant mortality led to a sharp rise in the number of children and hence a fall in the proportion of older people. From the 1960s until the 1980s, there was a steady, unspectacular rise in the proportion of older Indians. Since this occurred in a context of very fast population growth, the numbers aged 60 and over doubled between 1950 and 1980. From the 1980s, there was a marked acceleration in population ageing, which was largely a response to falling fertility rates. This acceleration is projected to increase over the next 20 years, leading to massive projected increases in the total number of older people.

Table 8.3: Population ageing in India

	Population aged 60+ (%)	Population aged 60+ (000)
1950	5.4	20,052
1960	5.2	23,286
1970	5.5	30,081
1980	5.8	40,051
1990	6.3	54,209
2000	7.1	74,083
2025*	11.5	166,348

Note: * Median variant projection.
Source: United Nations Population Division (2008)

Data from the 2001 Census show that the total number of women aged 60 and over was only slightly greater than the number of men. This is at odds with the experiences of most other countries, where later life is clearly feminised. Taking India's population as a whole, there were 108 men for every 100 women in 2001, which represents a substantial sex imbalance (Guilmoto, 2007). The causes of this imbalance are complex and associated with practices of gender discrimination, which lead to higher rates of female mortality in early life. The restoration of parity at older ages is in keeping with the international experience of greater female longevity in later life, which offsets higher female mortality at earlier ages. In Kerala, where gender discrimination is less pronounced, the population aged 60 and over is highly feminised, with 123 women for every 100 men (Moli, 2004).

Table 8.4 shows that, even with population ageing, the demographic 'burden' of large cohorts of children is much greater than the 'burden' of India's older population.[4] Due to falling fertility, the proportion of Indians in dependent groups has fallen since 1961, with a particularly sharp drop in Kerala. By contrast, high proportions of young children in Uttar Pradesh have caused the overall dependency rate to increase. India's national experience represents a potential 'demographic dividend' of low dependency, but its failure to generate rapid employment growth is diluting these potential benefits. In rural areas of states such as Uttar Pradesh, older people have large numbers of children and grandchildren. Whether these represent a source of support or a burden in old age is discussed in the next section.

Table 8.4: Demographic dependency ratios, 1961 and 1991

		Uttar Pradesh	Kerala	India
Youth*	1961	75.6	83.5	76.6
	1991	76.8	49.9	67.0
Old**	1961	11.7	11.3	10.5
	1991	12.6	14.4	11.8
Total***	1961	87.2	94.7	87.1
	1991	89.4	64.3	78.7

Notes: * Population aged under 15 as % of population aged 15–59.
** Population aged over 59 as % of population aged 15–59.
*** Population aged under 15 and over 59 as % of population aged 15–59.
Source: Rajan et al (1999)

Experiences of old age: gender and poverty

The majority of India's population continues to endure poverty and material deprivation, and older people are no exception to this general situation. Nevertheless, some studies claim that older people are less likely to experience poverty than other age groups and are therefore less in need of social assistance (Pal and Palacios, 2006). Table 8.5 summarises results from an influential World Bank poverty survey. It shows that in Uttar Pradesh older people are less likely to live in poor households. This may be because poorer people are less likely to survive into old age than people who have relatively wealthy lives. By contrast, older people in Kerala appear more likely to experience poverty. In this case, higher government investment in basic health and education may mean that people from poorer social groups are more likely to survive into old age.[5] In fact, the main conclusion that can be taken from Table 8.5 is that variations in poverty between states are much greater than variations by age group. Indeed, there are several reasons why this form of simple poverty comparison is more misleading than helpful. First, it is based on a very basic '60 plus' notion of old age, which has little meaning in the lives of many Indians. Second, it assumes that monetary income is an effective indicator of wellbeing in later life. This section challenges both these views.

Table 8.5: Household-level rural poverty (%) for households, 1995–96

	All households	Households containing at least one person aged 60+	Households not containing a person aged 60+
Kerala	15	18	14
Uttar Pradesh	44	42	45

Source: Pal and Palacios (2006)

To some extent, 'old age' is not a particularly helpful category for policy making and academic analysis in India. Many of the material deprivations experienced by older people are shared by their wider households and communities. Some studies observe that traditional ideas about ageing and later life in India are far removed from those found in developed countries (Cohen, 1998; Vera–Sanso, 2006). In part, this may be because only a small minority of the population can expect to retire and receive a pension. Among the rural poor, later life may be defined with reference to declining physical labour capacity, and may therefore set in well before 60 years of age. For women, old age can be associated with having successfully reared and married off their children, rather than a specific age (Vera-Sanso, 2006). Cohen (1998) provides a particularly sophisticated analysis of how notions of old age are culturally embedded and often at odds with the simple categories applied in western gerontology. Also, later life needs to be understood as part of a wider pattern of diversity, interacting with other social identities such as gender and caste. There are many important axes of difference among India's older population, including religion, caste, socioeconomic status and location. The best documented and, arguably, most significant of these divides is between older men and older women.

As seen in Chapter Two most lifecourse experiences are profoundly gendered and this carries through into important gender differences in later life. In the case of India, differences in life opportunities are clearly apparent from early childhood, leading to (among other things) significant gaps in educational attainment and infant mortality rates. Table 8.6 shows substantial differences in literacy rates between men and women, which are especially high for older cohorts. Gender discrimination continues during adulthood via a wide range of complex, culturally embedded processes, including discrimination against women in the allocation of household resources and in access to paid employment. There is some evidence that these discriminatory practices are slowly easing in parts of India, particularly among middle-class urban families. One key factor behind this has been girls' increased access to basic education. Also, in some regions, most notably Kerala, traditions of gender discrimination were always less evident. Nevertheless, for the great bulk of women, life opportunities remain far more limited than for their male counterparts, particularly in states like Uttar Pradesh (Dreze and Gazdar, 1997; Singh, 2007). These experiences of disadvantage then carry through to later life. For example, older women are less likely to have access to paid employment than older men, even in Kerala (Table 8.7).

A key aspect of older women's disadvantage is related to their experiences of widowhood, and these have received considerable

Table 8.6: Literacy rates by age and place of residence, 1995–96 (%)

	Total population		Population aged 60+	
	Male	Female	Male	Female
Total	53	32	41	13
Rural	47	25	34	8
Urban	69	54	66	31

Source: Rajan et al (1999: 34)

Table 8.7: Estimated work participation rates for older men and women, 1991

	India	Kerala	Uttar Pradesh
All aged 60 and above	43	26	34
Men aged 60 and above	65	46	59
Women aged 60 and above	20	10	4

Source: Rajan et al (1999)

academic attention (Chen, 1998, 2000; Adinarayana Reddy, 2004). Widowhood affects a high proportion of older women in India: in 1991, over half of women aged 60 or more were widowed, rising to two thirds for women aged 70 or more (Dandekar, 1996). For men, the figures were only 16% and 21%, respectively. These differences occur mainly because widowed women are usually prohibited from remarrying, while men are free to do so. In all countries and cultures, widows tend to face a number of disadvantages, including a reduced economic status and a higher likelihood of solitude and loneliness. As discussed in Chapter Two, the extent of these disadvantages varies between countries. A number of other consequences of widowhood are less 'inevitable' and result from particular institutional arrangements and cultural practices.

There is general consensus that in India the consequences of widowhood for women are particularly harsh. Several traditional practices contribute to this. First, women are usually expected to live with their husband's family after marriage and remain with this family after widowhood. In most of India, patrilineal inheritance practices predominate, whereby land and other property are usually passed directly from deceased males to their sons, rather than to their surviving wives (Agnes, 1999).[6] At the same time, widows face particular barriers to employment opportunities. As such, many remain entirely dependent on their dead husband's families for support. Widowhood is also highly stigmatised in India, and in some cases women may be accused of contributing to their husband's deaths or of witchcraft (Chen, 1998; Lamb, 2000). This may then make them vulnerable to abuse and abandonment from their deceased husband's relatives.

The abject condition of many Indian widows is indisputable and well documented. There are, however, grounds for arguing that the relationship between widowhood and wellbeing in later life is quite complex. First, not all widows are old. This is partly due to a tendency for women to marry older men: in 1981, the average age gap was seven years (Mari Bhat, 1998). Second, the treatment of widows can be quite variable. For example, in urban areas traditional restrictions are less easily enforced. Lamb (1999) observes that age of widowhood has an important effect on the wellbeing of older women. Younger widows, particularly childless ones, have a particularly low status in their husband's families, leading to a lifetime of extreme deprivation that carries through into their old age. By contrast, becoming a widow in later life is 'not nearly as traumatic, difficult and radical a transition', particularly if they have surviving sons (Lamb, 1999: 552). This group are able to call on their offspring for support and face less stigma. Comparing women who have been widowed at different points in their lives shows the value of locating experiences of gender and widowhood within a wider lifecourse framework.

The focus on widows may have led to the neglect of other groups of vulnerable older people, including women. It should not be assumed that unwidowed older women do not also face particular forms of hardship and vulnerability. Generalised discrimination against women may mean that married wives are just as likely to be denied access to public resources and household goods (Agarwal, 1998). The growing prevalence of chronic diseases may impose a heavy burden of care on married older women with sick husbands. For these women, widowhood may lead to an improvement in circumstances. Similarly, it should not be assumed that older men do not face generalised, as well as age- and gender-specific, forms of deprivation. In some other developing countries, older men often enjoy greater access to pension income and this is a major reason for their relative economic wellbeing. In India, only a small minority of older people, men or women, have access to a pension, and so this gender effect is less significant. To date, there has been almost no research focusing on the situation of older men in India.

In much of rural India, all age groups, young and old, face the daily challenges and hardships caused by poverty and economic insecurity (Ajwad, 2007). In the absence of effective social security provision or adequate formal sector employment, the two key economic and social resources are land and social networks. As such, the leading causes of vulnerability in later life are landlessness and childlessness. Ideally, older men continue to cultivate land as long as they are physically able and then divide it between their sons, who are then obliged to provide them and their wives with regular money and food in return (Dharmalingam, 1994; Dandekar, 1996). In many parts of India, older people would expect to remain with their youngest son, who would traditionally be the last to marry and inherit the house in return for the support he provides (Dharmalingam, 1994). This traditional system of intergenerational support breaks down where older people lack land or sons to inherit it. The centrality of sons (and daughters-in-law) explains the high value placed on male offspring. This both contributes to high fertility rates (as married couples seek to have one or ideally several sons to guarantee their security in old age) and perpetuates discrimination against girls (who do not usually make a direct contribution to their parents' welfare and whose marriage incurs dowry costs). As part of this, the status of women in rural areas is closely tied to their reproductive 'success' in producing male heirs. Women who fail to provide sons, be they widowed or married, are likely to face heightened social and economic vulnerability as they grow older.

Information on how caste, religion and other factors affect the wellbeing of older people in India is very limited. There are no grounds for believing that the lifetime disadvantages faced by lower-caste groups such as *dalits* disappear when they reach old age. Data for rural India in 2001 show that population ageing was less advanced among scheduled castes and tribes than for the population as a whole, reflecting both higher fertility rates and premature mortality (Alam, 2008). The same survey found that per capita incomes in households containing at least one person aged 60 or over were 17% lower for scheduled castes than for the general rural population (Alam, 2008). These income differentials do not capture the full range of social and economic disadvantages and stigma imposed by the caste system (Mendelsohn, 1998). At the same time, older people from other castes may also face specific disadvantages. For example, higher-caste groups such as Brahmans impose particularly stringent restrictions on widows (Lamb, 2000).

Despite the slow pace of development in most of rural India, there are increasing accounts that traditional structures of support for older people are starting to break down (Dharmalingam, 1994; Bhat and Dhrubarajan, 2001). It has been claimed that migration, changing social mores and economic development are undermining traditional family values of patriarchy and respect for older generations (Rajan et al, 1999; Jamuna, 2003). However, these processes have complex effects and varied impacts on different groups of older people. This can be seen by comparing migration in Kerala and Uttar Pradesh. With a well-educated population but lacking appropriate opportunities, Kerala has seen high levels of out-migration of younger age groups. A high proportion of these migrants have gone overseas to work in the services sector, and it is estimated that they send home income equivalent to nearly double the total state budget (Rajan and Zachariah, 2007). These remittances represent an important source of economic support for many households, including those containing older people. In some cases, however, this advantage may be offset by older people's reduced daily contact with migrant children and increased grandparenting duties

(Department of Health Services, Government of Kerala, 2005).There are also large migratory flows in Uttar Pradesh, but here migrants are more likely to be unskilled workers and mainly remain in India (Dyson andVisaria, 2005). Much of this migration takes the form of poorly paid seasonal agriculture labouring (Yadava, 1997). In this case, remittances are likely to be much less substantial than in Kerala, and the potential benefits from migration more limited.

Similarly, trends in female salaried employment may have complex impacts on older people. For India as a whole, patterns of female employment vary sharply across castes, socioeconomic groups and rural and urban settings, and there are signs that the proportion of working women may have fallen significantly in recent years (Olsen and Mehta, 2006). As with migration, female salaried employment may boost household income, but may also interfere with the supply of care traditionally provided by daughters–in–law. New patterns of employment may also contribute to changing attitudes to consumption among the younger generation. In parts of rural India during the 1990s, targeted marketing strategies promoted demand for shampoo and cosmetics among younger low-caste women. It is claimed that these raised expectations may have reduced the amount of material assistance that younger relatives were prepared to offer older people (Vera–Sanso, 2007).

Taking rural India as a whole, there is a lack of clear evidence about the relative importance of these potentially positive and negative outcomes, and it should not be assumed that these changes are entirely harmful for all older people. Nevertheless, as the numbers of older people living in poor rural communities grow, it is likely there will be an increased need for more formalised old-age support, such as pensions and LTC facilities.

In urban areas, the situation for many older people will be significantly different. Overall, there is more socioeconomic diversity among the older urban population, ranging from retired civil servants with generous pensions to destitute older people living in run-down slums. While it is dangerous to generalise, there is some evidence that socioeconomic changes in the larger cities may be especially rapid, reducing the reliability of family support for older people. For example, a study from Chennai found that shifts in attitudes to children's needs led daughters-in-law to become increasingly assertive towards their husbands' parents (Vera–Sanso, 1999). Despite this, family relations remain the predominant form of economic security for most older people in cities. A survey of people aged 60 and over living in Delhi in 2002 found that more than twice as many reported significant economic support from relatives, as those in receipt of pensions (Alam, 2006).

In sum, for most older people in India, material security depends on access to children (especially sons) and land. Urbanisation, declining fertility and changing social norms are likely to alter these forms of support in future decades. Another key influence on older people's wellbeing is the extent to which they and their households are affected by health problems. Disease and illness are among the main causes of poverty and vulnerability for rural and urban households, particularly when these households contain older people (Ajwad, 2007). We turn to this in the next section.

Health in later life: stroke and dementia

Since independence, India has had little success in extending effective healthcare services to most of its population, especially those living in rural areas. This has contributed to stubbornly high fertility rates in states such as Uttar Pradesh (World Bank, 2002). Even in recent years, India has spent a lower proportion of its economic output on primary healthcare than almost any other developing country (UNDP, 2005). Since the early 1990s, health services have become increasingly marketised and expensive, leading to growing access barriers between rich and poor (Visaria, 2005a). Given the country's youthful age structure, the focus has been understandably on the health of mothers and young children (Banerji, 2004). By contrast, health services dealing with conditions more likely to affect older people are largely neglected. This section argues that India's current health system is increasingly out of kilter with a new epidemiological reality dominated by chronic diseases, and that older people suffer disproportionately as a result.

Research mapping the general epidemiological profile of older populations and comparing it to younger age groups is limited and the data are often unreliable. Most studies rely on self-reported health data, which are as much a reflection of subjects' awareness and expectations of health as their actual physiological status (Kumar, 2003b; Alam, 2008). Table 8.8 shows that older people living in rural districts of Uttar Pradesh reported significantly lower levels of chronic disease than those living in the state of Kerala. However, this is more likely to reflect the relatively limited healthcare infrastructure in rural Uttar Pradesh (and hence reduced *awareness* of disease) than actual variations in health status. Consequently, the data in Table 8.8 are of limited value, and may significantly understate the real extent of chronic conditions.

Table 8.8: Proportion of people aged 60 and over reporting one or more chronic illness, 1995–96 (%)

	Rural areas	Urban areas
Uttar Pradesh	52	55
Kerala	69	61
India	52	54

Source: Alam (2006)

Rather than general age-based studies, more detailed information is available for specific diseases. Consequently, this section focuses on two particular conditions, both of which are especially prevalent among older populations. *Stroke* is taken as broadly representative of a wider set of chronic illnesses, such as heart disease and cancer. Even with the limited available data, it is evident that chronic conditions already account for the bulk of illness and mortality among older Indians, as well as a growing share for those in mid-life (Visaria, 2005a; Joshi et al, 2006). Among other effects, such as changing diet and lifestyle, population ageing is seen as a key factor behind the growing prevalence of these conditions. *Dementia* is taken as very broadly representative of a wide range of mental health problems. Although conditions such as dementia and depression do not directly contribute to a high proportion of deaths, their impact on the quality of life of older people and those around them is usually substantial (Patel and Prince, 2001).

Chapter Four discussed the general increase in chronic disease across the developing world, its relationship to population ageing and its impact on older people. As far as the data allow us to see, India is broadly typical of these trends.[7] That said, specific surveys of stroke prevalence provide very different estimates, and some conclude that it is relatively insignificant. A meta-analysis of seven separate studies estimated that strokes accounted for 1.2% of all deaths in India, rising to 2.4% of deaths for people aged 70 or more (Anand et al, 2001). However, the two largest surveys in recent years provide a strikingly different view. Research from rural Andhra Pradesh found that stroke accounted for 13% of all deaths between 2003 and 2004, rising to 18% for people aged 60 and over (Joshi et al, 2006). Stroke was clearly the leading cause of death for older people, followed by heart disease (14%) and cancer (7%).[8] A separate study comparing slum and non-slum districts in urban Kolkata found that stroke was significantly more prevalent than in the US or Europe (Das et al, 2007). It reported that a much higher proportion of stroke victims did not survive and that 86% of deaths occurred among people aged 50 and over.

To restrict the risk of death and long-term effects from stroke requires immediate treatment with specialist drugs, as well as considerable follow-up care and rehabilitation. However, the provision of health services for stroke victims remains very limited, especially in the public health system (Pandian et al, 2007a). While some private clinics in the larger cities provide effective treatment, the necessary drugs for the standard procedure (thrombolysis) cost on average US$1,217 per person (Pandian et al, 2007b). A study of a private hospital in north-western India found that only 1% of patients received this drug, as the rest could not pay for it (Pandian et al, 2005). Treating hypertension to prevent stroke is a much more affordable option, with effective drugs costing on average US$10 per month (Pandian et al, 2005). Even so, this still represents a substantial financial drain for most households, especially in rural areas. Given these high costs, the focus of policy should be on preventing high blood pressure, by reducing smoking, improving diets and promoting exercise. To date, there is little evidence of health education campaigns, and smoking among the rural poor increased significantly during the 1990s (Visaria, 2005a).

Stroke has a large and growing impact on the lives of all Indians, but especially on older people. This age group is more at risk of stroke, and also faces the risks of stroke-related widowhood or caring for stroke-affected relatives. The burden of care is particularly high for older women, since the incidence of stroke is higher among men than women, and due to the seven-year average age gap between husbands and wives (Wyller, 1999). Government stroke rehabilitation services and other interventions to support carers remain very poorly developed (Pandian et al, 2007a).

Older people in India are also vulnerable to a wide range of mental health problems, with some surveys showing prevalence levels at least double those of the total population (Kumar, 2003b).[9] Dementia refers to a range of physical conditions that lead to the progressive decline of cognitive function, such as memory. Assessing the actual extent of mental illnesses, such as dementia, is more difficult than for diseases such as stroke, since diagnosis involves subjective judgements. Estimates of dementia prevalence for people aged 65 and over vary from 14 to 34 per 1,000 people, with significantly higher rates among the very old (Brijnath, 2008). Interestingly, these rates of prevalence are significantly lower than in Europe or the US. The reasons for this difference are not fully understood and may be genetic or dietary, although misdiagnosis should not be ruled out (Biswas et al, 2005). Rather than a disease, dementia is often viewed as a natural part of the ageing process or as a 'weak' or 'hot' brain (Cohen, 1995; Patel and Prince, 2001). This has implications both for measuring its prevalence and for how it is managed by sufferers and their families.

Around a fifth of dementia cases are reversible and others have viable treatments for slowing their progression and mitigating some symptoms. The great majority of people affected require increasingly intensive care and help with daily activities. However, the barriers to adequate health services and care are just as formidable as for stroke. First, levels of awareness are often very low among healthcare professionals. For example, doctors interviewed in Goa, southern India, failed to recognise dementia as a clinical condition, although most were familiar with the symptoms when described to them and reported that they were widespread in the community (Patel and Prince, 2001). As with stroke, few specific services for dementia are offered by the public healthcare system, and none of the main drugs for treating the condition is currently freely available (McCabe, 2006; Brijnath, 2008). Dementia is often stigmatised and affected people can be denied access to hospitals and residential care homes (Patel and Prince, 2001). The disease imposes a particularly heavy burden on carers, many of whom themselves are older people (Emmatty et al, 2006). The Goa study found that in 75% of families the main caregiver was female and that carers received little outside support and understanding (Prince, 2004). In some cases, dementia is seen by outsiders as a consequence of abuse or neglect, thus further stigmatising family members (Cohen, 1995; Varghese and Patel, 2004).

These case studies of stroke and dementia demonstrate the extent to which specific health conditions limit both the duration and the quality of older people's lives, as well as the lives of other family members, particularly women. Both these illnesses have been generally neglected by the state, which is also true with regard to other conditions associated with later life. Developing more concerted policies to prevent and mitigate their impact could do much to increase older people's wellbeing and reduce the care burden of sickness and disability.

Pension policies and older people

Rather than health policies for older people, the main focus of government policy in recent years has been on pension provision. This is in keeping with a global tendency to emphasise pensions at the expense of other relevant interventions. Current Indian pension schemes are complex and highly fragmented, with important variations across states. Also, there have been a number of important changes and reforms over the past decade. This section provides a brief review of the main elements of the pension system, and focuses on the extent to which provision benefits the largest and most vulnerable section of India's older population: the rural poor.

India roughly conforms to the first pathway of pension development presented in Chapter Four. As part of this, schemes have traditionally been focused on the civil service, with relatively minimal provision for the rest of the population. The first civil service pension funds were set up by the British in 1881, and a recent study observed that the current system 'still operates much as it did prior to independence' (Palacios, 2005: no page number). This reflects the continuity of the established civil service after independence and its subsequent expansion. Retirement conditions and benefits are generous, and members are also entitled to free programmes of health services exclusively for government staff (Kumar, 2003a). These schemes are paid entirely by government, and their cost has grown rapidly in recent years, reaching around 3.7% of GDP in 2003 (Kumar, 2003a; Chou, 2008). Rising expenditure has been driven by a significant increase in the life expectancy of retired civil servants, along with a reluctance to introduce more stringent terms and benefits.

Programmes for the private sector are extremely fragmented and considerably less generous than civil servants' pensions. A number of occupation-specific provident funds were established during the 1950s, the largest being the Employee Provident Fund (EPF) (Kumar, 2003a). By the 1990s, the EPF covered around 200,000 enterprises, but the value of pensions it paid out was notoriously small. In 1995, the EPF was partly converted from a provident fund into a defined benefit scheme, but the impact on pension values has been limited. In part, this is because well-paid private sector workers are permitted to opt out of the EPF and into their own 'excluded funds'. It also results from poor returns on investment, as the EPF is obliged to invest in low-yielding government bonds (indirectly subsidising the costs of civil servant pensions). Taken together, it is estimated that the various schemes in operation, including private life insurance companies, covered around 12% of the non-state workforce in 2005 (Palacios, 2005).[10]

The third component of India's pension system consists of non-contributory schemes, which seek to target the poorest and most vulnerable older people. These were mainly run at the state level, with considerable variation across the country. For example, average monthly pension values paid out by the different state schemes ranged from 60 to 300 rupees (£1 to £5) in 2005 (Pal and Palacios, 2005). Uttar Pradesh's programme is quite typical of schemes in many states, paying out derisory amounts to small numbers of poorly targeted individuals. A survey of assistance pensioners in the state reported that half admitted to paying bribes to obtain the benefit and that most had seen their pensions cut or discontinued for no apparent reason (Srivastava, 2002). In Kerala assistance pensions are worth even less than in Uttar Pradesh, although it is claimed that they are managed less corruptly. Since 1995, the Central Government has developed a new National Old Age Pension Scheme, to supplement state initiatives, as well as a parallel programme offering food aid. There is disagreement about whether these new initiatives have been able to break with the corruption and ineffectiveness of most anti-poverty programmes in India (Kumar, 2003a; Farrington and Saxena, 2004; Palacios, 2005). However, the low value of benefits (less than US$2 per month) and the limited number being offered (seven million for the whole country) mean that the overall impact on the rural poor will be small. Government spending on these initiatives is about a 10th of that devoted to civil servant pensions.

Since 2005, a series of reforms have been implemented, seeking to radically overhaul pension provision for both civil servants and the private sector. Newly appointed civil servants are now obliged to join a considerably less generous defined contribution scheme (ADB, 2007).[11] This new scheme is to be extended to non-state sector workers, replacing the government-managed EPF with privately run asset management companies (PFRDA, 2007). It is also hoped that informal sector workers will be encouraged to join the new scheme on a voluntary basis. In many ways, this reform is in keeping with the pension privatisation agenda that has been promoted by the World Bank and allied organisations since the early 1990s. As seen in Chapter Four, the impact of such reforms in other developing countries has been mixed at best.

Presently, pensions have little effect on the lives of most older people in India and this is unlikely to change in the foreseeable future. In 2007, it was estimated that only around 22% of people aged 60 or over were receiving some form of pension (PFRDA, 2007).[12] Other than for civil servants, most pension benefits represent a fraction of older people's living needs. Despite some optimistic projections, the likelihood that the new privately run scheme will substantially extend coverage to India's rural poor is remote. There are no indications of political support for the further extension of targeted assistance pensions and there are few signs that existing programmes are being improved.[13] It is arguable that the overall impact of pension policy on older people's wellbeing has been negative. Generous provision for relatively wealthy civil servants is highly inequitable and deflects government resources away from other programmes, including basic healthcare, which would benefit all age groups.

Three lives[14]

Albina

Albina is 67 years old and lives in a fishing village about 10 kilometres from Trivandrum, the state capital of Kerala. She has spent her whole life in the same village. Her father was a fisherman, and she was one of 10 brothers and sisters. Albina was only able to attend school for a few months: it was expensive and her parents prioritised the boys' education. She married a local fisherman when she was 22 and they went on to have five children (four girls and a boy). Her husband worked hard as a fisherman, but was unable to buy his own boat. Despite their poor economic situation, Albina is proud that she was able to send all but one of her children to school. She and her husband were obliged to pay a substantial dowry when their eldest daughter married: "My husband wanted to see his eldest daughter married before he died. Suddenly there was a proposal. We gave them 7,000 rupees and seven gold sovereigns, which was all we could afford." Shortly after this marriage, Albina's husband died of cancer. The family used up their remaining savings on hospital treatment for him and were forced to borrow from friends and neighbours. Over the following years, the family's economic situation became increasingly precarious: "It was a struggle for us. My husband's family helped us out as best they could." At the same time, both her two younger daughters became blind. Albina has no idea what led to this, and she herself also became blind when she was 52. She now lives with these two blind daughters. Together, they receive a disability pension worth £2 per month and a food parcel from a local NGO worth around £7 per month. Other than this, they are entirely dependent on the support of their extended family. This has become more difficult in recent years, as the entire community has suffered from sharp falls in fish catches. They blame this on increased levels of activity by large offshore trawlers, and the combined effects of the tsunami and changing sea temperatures. Two years ago Albina fainted and discovered that she has high blood pressure. She now needs to buy anti-hypertensive drugs, which represent a major expense: "God helps me." Despite these problems, she is confident that her children will be able to find the money by some means or other to pay for her future health needs. Albina is still able to enjoy aspects of her life, such as spending time with her young grandchildren, and her strong religious faith helps her face up to her daily hardships: "I go to the prayer hall with some other women every day, and every Sunday I go to church to pray."

Yadev

Yadev is 67 years old and was born in the village of Bijnore, 11 kilometres north of Lucknow, the capital of Uttar Pradesh. He has continued to live there for his entire life, and is one of five brothers and sisters. His parents were smallholders and owned two *bighas* of land (between one and two acres), where they cultivated wheat and rice. Yadev went to school for just two years, as his family was too poor to pay for his school fees, uniform and books. Despite this, he was able to pick up the rudiments of reading and writing at home and considers himself to be literate. He started to work on the land when he was 12, helping on the family farm as well as being a hired labourer. Two *bighas* of land were insufficient to support the whole family and so, as he got older, Yadev took on occasional building work in Lucknow city, three hours away by bullock cart. Yadev had sometimes thought about moving away from the village, but was not convinced that this would have improved his situation: "I would have had to work hard to earn any money wherever I went, so what was the use of moving? And then I still had a bit of land here." When he was 23 his family arranged his marriage and his wife came to live with them. After a series of miscarriages and still births, they had their first child when he was 33, going on to have two boys and two girls. When Yadev was 43 his father died and the two *bighas* of land were split equally between him and his two brothers. As a result, Yadev and his family found it even harder to make ends meet: "It became very difficult for us. Before then, the whole family had been living together, sharing everything." Fortunately, a new road was built, reducing the travel time to Lucknow, and this helped him find more work outside the village. A few years later, his sons were old enough to start work and the family's situation improved. Yadev's wife died of cholera when he was 52: "There was a lot of it around in those days. There were no doctors. You had to go to Lucknow hospital on a cart." In the same year, his daughter married and moved to a different village. Yadev now lives with his two sons, who work as a taxi driver and a school bus driver. He continues to farm the small piece of land remaining to him, but stopped working as a builder and hired labourer about 10 years ago. He eats together with his sons and they buy him homemade '*bidi*' cigarettes. Yadev applied for a pension two years ago and made several visits to the pension office in Lucknow. He claims he was denied the pension because he did not pay a bribe: "I sent off the forms several times, but I'm fed up with all the red tape....They kept telling me the forms were missing ... I'd need to pay a bribe of 800 rupees to get it." Yadev feels that he is in reasonable health, and is confident that his sons will pay for any treatment he may need in future. Overall, Yadev is positive about his life. He is pleased that he no longer needs to work hard and he has a wide range of friends living nearby. He feels that the village has progressed greatly during his lifetime, with improved roads and housing, as well as new schools and a clinic. Yadev feels that he has done well in his life and has been lucky to have two good sons. Nevertheless, he observes that the younger generations are not as respectful to older people as they were in the past, blaming this on too much television and western influence.

Munni

Munni is unsure of her exact age, but guesses that she must be at least 82. She was born in a village about 20 kilometres away from Lucknow. She went to school for four years and claims she can read and write reasonably well: "Education was not so important in those days, especially for girls. Our parents said that learning to read and write in Hindi was more than enough." She helped her family with their smallholding, before an arranged marriage to a man in a nearby village: "I'd been happy in my parents' village. It hurt to move away, but that was the tradition in those days....You had to go along with what your parents said." They had a daughter, but she died when she was just 12 days old. After that they were not able to have any more children. Her husband's family owned about eight *bighas* of land and her husband's share was just one and a half *bighas* (an acre), some of which was infertile. She used to help her husband farm this small plot, as well as helping out other families in the village. Her husband died on 24 May 1992 – Munni is very precise about the date. He had been out of doors drinking alcohol in a bad storm and injured his head in a fall. After his death, their smallholding was inherited by her brother-in-law and she now has no independent means of support. She continues to live on her own, but eats with her in-laws. In exchange for this, she helps them out with various household chores, although she is finding this increasingly difficult as she has developed arthritis. "They care for me, but it's not the same as having children of your own. I wish so much that I had been able to have children of my own." Munni feels that she should be entitled to an assistance pension and is extremely bitter that she has been unfairly denied one: "Those bastards! I filled in all the forms. I went to the village head, but what's the use? You'll never get anything without bribing." Overall, Munni feels that she has had a hard life and is clearly unhappy about her current situation: "I feel like a slave here. As long as I work all the hours I can, they'll give me something to eat." However, she takes considerable pride in a small Hindu temple that she paid to be built close to her house after her husband's death, using all her savings and selling her jewellery. "At least people will remember me after my death, even though I didn't have any children." Her strong religious convictions help her to face up to the uncertainties and loneliness of her old age.

Conclusions

India's 20th-century development was framed by two influential and interrelated features: limited progress in reducing poverty, alongside a slow and incomplete fertility transition. A wide range of effects contributed to these problems, including entrenched traditional attitudes towards gender and caste, a mixed colonial legacy, and ineffective post-independence policies. Together, they gave rise to a vicious cycle of rapid population growth and poverty, which the country is still struggling to escape. The recent economic boom has created relatively few jobs, but has led to a large increase in government revenue. These new resources might be used to develop more effective social policies for older people and others, but there is little sign of that happening. Instead, most parts of the civil service remain highly inefficient, funnelling funds into high-pay, fringe benefits and pensions for their own.

This chapter has focused on poor rural older people in India and has made a number of generalisations about their experiences. The realities of their lives are, of course, far more complex and heterogeneous than this limited analysis suggests, and this is seen in the three personal experiences presented above. Nevertheless, it is evident that the lives of the vast majority of rural older people continue to be framed by poverty and a lack of access to public services. While there has been some improvement in the provision of basic education, this came too late for current cohorts of older people, so that the majority are illiterate. Indeed, among older women in rural areas, fewer than one in ten were literate in 1996 (Table 8.6). Access to effective health services remains minimal, despite the challenges of emerging chronic diseases and mental health conditions. As such, for most Indians, old age brings continued material deprivation, along with worsening health and premature mortality.

How will the lives of future old-age cohorts differ from today's, and are there any grounds for optimism? By 2030, a significantly higher proportion of older people will be literate and living in cities, although the majority may still lack access to a meaningful pension. This means that older people will continue to rely on their own means and their children. However, shifting family dynamics and changing social attitudes mean that continued support from younger relatives should not be taken for granted. For example, one study reports a sharp fall in the proportion of adult children who feel it is their duty to support their parents (Jamuna, 2003). As such, the growing numbers of Indians who reach old age over the coming decades face a far from secure future.

Notes

[1] Some parts of India, known as the 'Princely States', were granted notional autonomy and were absorbed into the main political system after independence.

[2] *Adivasis* comprise of groups who have traditionally been marginal to the rest of Indian society, such as peoples living in very remote regions or practising nomadism.

[3] One reason for this increase may have been that mortality decline reduced the incidence of widowhood, which thus promoted childbearing (Dyson, 2005).

[4] Demographic dependency ratios provide a useful indication of the age structure of a population, but they do not accurately reflect economic dependency, since significant numbers of older people and some children continue to work in India. See Chapter One for a detailed discussion of this indicator.

[5] See Chapter Two for a discussion of these effects.

[6] Despite being a secular state, most aspects of family law, including divorce and inheritance, fall within the particular codes of the different religious groups (Luce, 2006). Although formalised religious codes have been updated to avoid blatant gender discrimination, customary practices still predominate, especially in poorer rural areas (Agnes, 1999). Again, Kerala provides an important exception, and its matrilineal inheritance traditions have played a large role in boosting the status of all women, young and old (Ramachandran, 1997).

[7] Only 14% of deaths in India in 1994 were medically certified, and so general cause of death data are very uncertain (Banerjee and Das, 2006).

[8] This study was on a larger scale and was more methodologically rigorous than previous ones, and is therefore more likely to represent the true scale of the disease, particularly in rural districts. Comparable research has not been conducted in urban settings. However, since the main risk associated with stroke (hypertension, diabetes, smoking and obesity) were less prevalent in the Andhra Pradesh site than in most Indian cities, it is likely that the disease is even more widespread in urban areas (Yusuf et al, 2004).

[9] The causes and effects of dementia are very different from those of other mental health conditions, such as depression or schizophrenia.

[10] Data on private life insurance are limited, but there is evidence that the industry has grown rapidly in recent years and now accounts for a large share of India's general insurance market (Ghosh, 2009).

[11] Predictably, Kerala is one of a handful of Indian states that refuses to bring its state civil service fund into the new privately run scheme.

[12] Gendered patterns of access to non-state pensions would appear to vary across the country. Research from Kerala reports that protection is particularly limited for widows and older women (Arun and Arun, 2001). By contrast, a survey from Uttar Pradesh found that a higher proportion of older women received pensions than older men (Srivastava, 2002).

[13] For example, the government of Uttar Pradesh reported a fiscal deficit equivalent to 5.3% of its GDP in 2009, yet its spending on civil servant pensions continued to grow significantly (Singh Bisht, 2009).

[14] The names of the informants in this section have been changed to preserve their anonymity.

NINE

Conclusions and overview

This final chapter begins with some comparisons across the three country case studies. It then highlights some of the main themes to emerge from this book and identifies key priorities for policy makers.

Comparing the three country case studies

The central theme of this book is the danger of generalisation: be it about processes of development, patterns of population change or the lives of older people. The varied experiences of the three study countries highlight this point. Table 9.1 shows that each country experienced a unique trajectory of fertility transition and population ageing. In the case of Argentina, this had set in well before 1960, and as a result it already has a relatively aged population structure. In South Africa and India, fertility levels were still high in 1960, but fell sharply thereafter. By 2025, their fertility rates will have converged with Argentina's, but they will still be some way behind in terms of population ageing.

Table 9.1: Population trends for the case study countries, 1960–2025

		1960	1990	2005	2025*
South Africa	Total fertility rate	6.3	3.3	2.6	2.1
	Population aged 60+ (% of total)	6.1	5.1	6.5	10.5
Argentina	Total fertility rate**	3.1	2.9	2.3	1.9
	Population aged 60+ (% of total)	9.0	13.2	14.1	17.3
India	Total fertility rate	5.8	3.9	2.8	2.0
	Population aged 60+ (% of total)	5.2	6.1	7.0	11.1

Notes: * Projected.
** Average over the following five years (1960–65; 1990–95; 2005–10; and 2025–30).

Source: United Nations Population Division (2008)

These varied demographic profiles are rooted in socioeconomic differences across the study countries, but this relationship is complex. India was a much poorer country than Argentina in 1960 – their per capita GDPs were US$83 and US$524, respectively. This partly explains the slower pace of population change in India. Yet South

Africa's national wealth in 1960 (US$422 per capita) was not far below Argentina's. In this case, high levels of fertility reflected huge disparities in wealth and human development between different racial groups. This shows that it is important to go beyond national-level analysis to assess variations within countries. While race was a less significant issue in India and Argentina, there were important variations in patterns of development and population change across regions and between rural and urban areas.

The country studies also demonstrate the diversity of individual experiences of old age. This is particularly clear in the personal life histories included at the end of each case study chapter. Patterns and causes of diversity vary across countries. For example, it is unlikely that gender effects in Argentina will be identical to those in India. South Africa's generous social pension programme means that lifetime employment has less effect on personal income in old age there than in India or Argentina.

Despite these varied experiences of development, population change and old age, many economic policies across the three countries were remarkably similar. By the early 20th century, each economy was oriented to the export of basic, unprocessed products. By mid-century, each was starting to implement policies to promote economic diversification, through the promotion of manufacturing and the expansion of state activity. The success of this new development model was mixed, and economic crises in the 1980s and 1990s encouraged each country to reorient policy towards more neoliberal market-led approaches. Since 2008, all three countries have been struggling to deal with sudden global economic slowdown.

Since these economic strategies were implemented in different demographic settings, their effects on population welfare were quite different. In Argentina the labour needs of the export boom outstripped the capacity of the local population, leading to mass immigration from Europe. Although the economy faltered in mid-century, slow rates of population growth meant that the majority were still able to obtain formal sector employment. Labour scarcity increased the power of trades unions to influence the shape of the country's social welfare system. By contrast, India's population growth greatly exceeded the capacity of the formal labour market, even with the rapid extension of public sector employment. Consequently, the great majority of Indians saw little if any benefit from development, remaining on the fringes of the modern economy. The picture in South Africa was more complex, due to the influence of racist apartheid policies. As in Argentina, labour needs initially exceeded local supply, but this led to an authoritarian system of forced migration from rural areas, with access to economic opportunities closely correlated with race.

These varied patterns of economic opportunity and welfare entitlements have had an important effect on how different groups have experienced old age in each country. This demonstrates the importance of combining a lifecourse approach with an understanding of long-run development trends. More recent labour market trends are also important. In both Argentina and South Africa, there have been falls in secure formal sector employment. As a result, many older people have children and grandchildren who are better educated than they are and who have higher material expectations, but who have less access to reliable economic opportunities. This will have important effects on intergenerational relations and household dynamics.

The country case studies also demonstrate strong similarities in many aspects of social policy, particularly those directed towards older people. For example, each country has experienced major problems with the financing, efficiency and sustainability of their contributory pension systems. These contributory systems account for a large share of public spending (either directly or indirectly) and mainly redistribute income towards richer groups. As a result, each has considered implementing reforms broadly inspired by the World Bank's Three Pillar Model. To date, only Argentina has implemented these reforms, although they appear to be imminent in India and are under discussion in South Africa. These similarities reflect the strength of global ideas about pension provision, leading to the same policies being implemented in highly diverse settings. At the same time, healthcare services remain heavily focused on expensive curative care, rather than pursuing lifelong health promotion. In each country, the health sector has become increasingly privatised, increasing exclusion and inequality among older populations. Finally, LTC provision is largely neglected across all three countries, despite a lack of evidence that these needs can be met by families.

Overall, social policies in the three countries have not realised their potential to improve the lives of most older people living there. Large amounts of resources have been devoted to privileged pension funds. Fragmented, unaccountable and increasingly privatised pension and healthcare administrators have proved highly inefficient. Instead, these resources could have been channelled into social pension schemes, basic health services focused on prevention and initiatives to support LTC at home and in the community. South Africa's social pension stands out as the only positive policy lesson from the case studies. While it may have been a historical accident, the social pension has become a key source of political legitimacy for post-apartheid governments.

This shows that effective welfare programmes directed towards older people can come to be seen as beneficial for societies as a whole. More negatively, South Africa's abject failure to cope with the HIV/AIDS pandemic may foreshadow similar failures to deal with chronic disease epidemics across the developing world.

Key messages and policy lessons

Many commentators and policy makers share an apocalyptic view of how ageing will affect future economic performance around the world. According to a former Prime Minister of India:

> The crisis of global aging is entirely new and unprecedented.... As old age dependency ratios steadily worsen over the ensuing decades, the fiscal deficits will swell while private savings tumble, and the labor pool declines.... Developing countries, still free of the aging crisis, will also feel the cold wind from the North. After all, their markets, their main sources of aid and investment and, perhaps most critically, new skills and technologies, are located almost entirely in the industrial world. (Gujral, 2001: 28)

At the same time, there is a tendency to generalise about poverty and economic vulnerability in later life. According to HelpAge International (2004b: '[Older people are] the poorest of the poor, [who] lack the financial and social support and resources to meet their own needs and those of the children under their care'.

Taken at face value, these statements provide a grim vision of the future: it would seem that population ageing will cause a rapid decline in economic performance and growing numbers of people will be destined to have a miserable old age. This book assesses the evidence for these general claims and finds that actual experiences are more complex and less predictable. The impacts of population ageing on economic performance and other aspects of development depend on a wide range of factors. How later life is experienced by individuals will play a critical part in this. If old age is largely characterised by high levels of illness, limited functioning and social and economic withdrawal, then it may be fair to talk about a global ageing 'crisis'. In reality, however, experiences of later life are highly variable and there is evidence that policies can do much more to promote positive and active ageing. At the same time, not all older people are poor, even in developing countries, and most are considerably better off than previous generations were.

Since it is dangerous to generalise about older people, it is equally dangerous to generalise about the effects of population ageing on development. Nevertheless, the evidence presented in this book does support one significant set of generalisations. These refer to the failure of most policies in most countries to promote financially sustainable interventions that maximise wellbeing for all in later life. Pension programmes have been expensive and often fail to meet those most in need. Healthcare is also expensive but is doing little to tackle the underlying causes of new chronic disease epidemics. In many developing countries, the availability of cheap labour creates affordable opportunities for extending government care services, but this has been largely left to the families and the market. There has been a less general but equally important failure of economic policies to generate secure employment opportunities. This directly affects the prospects of future cohorts of older people. It also has many indirect impacts on people already in later life, through their relationships with their children and grandchildren. Rather than worry about the supposedly inevitable effects of population ageing, we should be facing up to these failures of policy across the developing world. Unless they are quickly rectified, many of the worst predictions may be proved right.

References

C. Abel and P. Lloyd-Sherlock (2000) 'Health policy in Latin America: themes, trends and challenges', in P. Lloyd-Sherlock (ed) *Healthcare reform and poverty in Latin America*, Institute of Latin American Studies, London.

B. Abel-Smith (1994) *An introduction to health: Policy, planning and financing*, Longman, London.

I. Aboderin (2004) 'Intergenerational family support and old age economic security in Ghana', in P. Lloyd-Sherlock (ed) *Living longer: Ageing, development and social protection*, Zed, London.

L. Abrams (2006) *Bismarck and the German Empire, 1871-1918*, Routledge, London.

S. Acharya, R. Cassen and K. McNay (2005) 'The economy – past and future', in T. Dyson, R. Cassen and L. Visaria (eds), *Twenty-first century India: Population, economy, human development and the environment*, Oxford University Press, Oxford.

O. Adeyi, O. Smith and S. Robles (2007) *Public policy and the challenge of chronic noncommunicable diseases*, World Bank, Washington, DC.

P. Adinarayana Reddy (2004) *Problems of widows in India*, Sarup & Sons, New Delhi.

B. Agarwal (1998) 'Widows versus daughters or widows as daughters? Property, land and economic security in rural India', in M. Chen (ed) *Widows in India: Social neglect and public action*, Sage Publications, London.

F. Agnes (1999) 'Law and women of age: a short note', *Economic and Political Weekly*, 30 October.

K. Ahenkora (1999) 'The contribution of older people to development: the Ghana study', HelpAge International and HelpAge Ghana (mimeo).

E. Ahmad and A. Hussain (1991) 'Social security in China: a historical perspective', in E. Ahmad, J. Dreze, J. Hills and A. Sen (eds) *Social security in developing countries*, Clarendon Press, Oxford.

M. Ajwad (2007) *Performance of social safety net programs in Uttar Pradesh*, Social Protection Discussion Paper 0714, World Bank, Washington, DC.

M. Alam (2006) *Ageing in India: Socio-economic and health dimensions*, Academic Foundation, New Delhi.

M. Alam (2008) *Ageing, socio-economic disparities and health outcomes: Some evidence from rural India*, Institute of Economic Growth Working Paper E/290/2008, Institute of Economic Growth Working, Delhi.

M. Alter Chen (1998) 'Introduction', in M. Alter Chen (ed) *Widows in India: Social neglect and public action*, Sage Publications, London.

K. Anand, D. Chowdhury, K. Singh, C. Pandav and S. Kapoor (2001) 'Estimation of mortality and morbidity due to strokes in India', *Neuroepidemiology*, 20: 208-211.

K. Anand, S. Kant, G. Kumar and S. Kapoor (2000) '"Development" is not essential to reduce infant mortality rate in India: experience from the Ballabgarh project', *Journal of Epidemiology and Community Health*, 54: 247-253.

E. Ardington and F. Lund (1995) 'Pensions and development: social security as complementary to programmes of reconstruction and development', *Development Southern Africa*, 12 (4): 557-577.

Arizona Department of Health Services (2001) *Arizona health status and vital statistics annual report*, Arizona Department of Health Services, Arizona, AZ, www.azdhs.gov/plan/report/ahs

J. Armstrong (2003) 'Is being a grandmother being old? Cross-ethnic perspective from New Zealand', *Journal of Cross-Cultural Gerontology*, 18 (3): 185-202.

A. Arun and T. Arun (2001) 'Gender issues in social security policy in Kerala, India', *International Social Security Review*, 54 (4): 93-100.

C. Arza (2005) 'Models of pension policy and pension reform: distributional principles, ideas and the three-pillar approach', Paper presented for the ESRC Workshop on Social Policy in Latin America, Institute for the Study of the Americas, London, 3 June.

ADB (Asian Development Bank) (2007) *India: Implementing pension reforms*, ADB Technical Assistance Report, ADB, Manila.

L. Baldwin-Ragaven, J. de Gruchy and L. London (1999) *An ambulance of the wrong colour: Health professionals, human rights and ethics in South Africa*, University of Cape Town Press, Cape Town.

C. Balkir and B. Kirkulak (2007) 'Turkey as a new destination for retirement migration', Meeting on international migration, multi-local livelihoods and human security: perspectives from Europe, Asia and Africa, Institute of Social Studies, The Netherlands, 30 and 31 August.

M. Baltes (1996) *The many faces of dependency in old age*, Cambridge University Press, Cambridge.

A. Banerjee and E. Duflo (2007) *Aging and death under a dollar a day*, NBER Working Paper 13683, National Bureau of Economic Research, Cambridge, MA, www.nber.org/papers/w.13683

T. Banerjee and S. Das (2006) 'Epidemiology of stroke in India', *Neurology Asia*, 11: 1-4.

D. Banerji (2004) 'The people and health service development in India: a brief overview', *International Journal of Health Services*, 34 (1): 123–142.

T. Barnett and A. Whiteside (2002) *AIDS in the twenty-first century: Disease and globalisation*, Palgrave, London.

S. Barreto, A. Kaleche and L. Giatti (2006) 'Does health status explain gender dissimilarity in healthcare use among older adults?', *Cadernos de Saúde Pública*, 22 (2): 347–355.

A. Barrientos (2002) 'Old age, poverty and social investment', *Journal of International Development*, 14 (4): 1133–1141.

A. Barrientos (2003) 'Pensions and development in the South', *Geneva Papers on Risk and Social Insurance*, 28: 696–711.

A. Barrientos (2004a) 'Comparing pension schemes in Chile, Singapore, Brazil and South Africa', in P. Lloyd-Sherlock (ed) *Living longer: Ageing, development and social protection*, Zed Books/United Nations Research Institute for Social Development, London.

A. Barrientos (2004b) 'Latin America: towards a liberal–informal welfare regime', in I. Gough and G. Wood (eds) *Insecurity and welfare regimes in Asia, Africa and Latin America: Social policy in development contexts*, Cambridge University Press, Cambridge.

A. Barrientos and D. Hulme (2007) 'Social protection for the poor and poorest: an introduction', in A. Barrientos and D. Hulme (eds) *Social protection of the poor and poorest*, Palgrave, London.

A. Barrientos, M. Gorman and A. Heslop (2003a) 'Old age poverty in developing countries: contributions and dependence in later life', *World Development*, 31 (3): 555–570.

A. Barrientos, M. Ferreira, M. Gorman, A. Heslop, H. Legido-Quigley, P. Lloyd-Sherlock, V. Møller, J. Saboia and M. Lucia Teixeira Werneck Vianna (2003b) *Non-contributory pensions and poverty prevention: A comparative study of Brazil and South Africa*, HelpAge International/ Institute for Development Policy and Management, London.

M. Barth, W. McNought and P. Rizzi (1993) 'Corporations and the ageing workforce', in P. Mirvis (ed) *Building the competitive workforce: Investing in human capital for corporate success*, Wiley and Sons, London.

BBC News (1999) 'Maxwell pledge to pensioners', 18 November, http://news.bbc.co.uk/1/hi/business/526038.stm

BBC News (2002) 'Pensions scandal costs £11.8 billion', 27 June, http://news.bbc.co.uk/1/hi/business/2070271.stm

BBC News (2003) 'Pensions: Chile's other revolution', 25 September, http://news.bbc.co.uk/1/hi/business/3138126.stm

BBC News (2008) 'Warning on private pension choice', 21 June, http://news.bbc.co.uk/go/pr/fr/-/1/hi/business/7465964.stm

R. Bennett (2006) 'Cost of raising a child hits £180,000', *Times Online*, 10 November.

P. Berman, C. Kendall and K. Bhattacharyya (1994) 'The household production of health: integrating social science perspectives on micro-level health determinants', *Social Science and Medicine*, 38 (2): 205-215.

F. Bertranou (2004) 'Pensions and gender in Latin American social protection systems: where do we stand in the Southern Cone?', http://papers.ssrn.com/sol3/papers.cfm?abstract_id=647422

F. Bertranou and D. Bonari (2005) *Protección social en Argentina: Financiamento, cobertura y desempeño 1990-2003*, International Labour Office, Santiago de Chile.

V. Bezrukov and N. Foigt (2004) 'The impact of transition on older people in Ukraine: looking to the future with hope', in P. Lloyd-Sherlock (ed) *Living longer: Ageing, development and social protection*, Zed, London.

A. Bhat and R. Dhrubarajan (2001) 'Ageing in India: drifting intergenerational relations, challenges and options', *Ageing and Society*, 21: 621-640.

W. Bicknell and C. Parks (1989) 'As children survive: dilemmas of ageing in the developing world', *Social Science and Medicine*, 28 (1): 59-67.

W. Bienart (1994) *Twentieth century South Africa*, Oxford University Press, Oxford.

B. Bilton, K. Bonnet, P. Jones, D. Skinner, M. Stanworth and A. Webster (1996) *Introduction to sociology*, Macmillan, Basingstoke.

R. Binstock (1997) 'The 1996 election: older voters and implications for policies on aging', *The Gerontologist*, 37 (1): 15-19.

R. Binstock and C. Day (1995) 'Aging and politics', in R. Binstock and L. George (eds) *A handbook of aging and the social sciences*, Academic Press, London.

A. Biswas, D. Chakraborty, A. Dutt and T. Roy (2005) 'Dementia in India – a critical appraisal', *Journal of the Indian Medical Association*, 103 (3): 154-161.

A. Blaikie (1999) *Ageing and popular culture*, Cambridge University Press, Cambridge.

E. Blas and M. Limbambala (2001) 'The challenge of hospitals in health sector reform: the case of Zambia', *Health Policy and Planning*, 16 (2): 29-43.

D. Bloom and D. Canning (2000) 'The health and wealth of nations', *Science*, 287 (5456): 1207-1208.

P. Blustein (2005) *And the money kept on rolling in (and) out: Wall Street, the IMF and the bankrupting of Argentina*, Public Affairs, New York.

A. Bonvecchi, H. Charosky, C. Garay and D. Urribari (1998) *Instituto Nacional de Servicios Sociales para Jubilados y Pensionados: Un análisis de sus condiciones de viabilidad organizacional, institucional y política*, Fundacíon Argentina para el Desarrollo con Equidad, Buenos Aires.

A. Borges-Yañez and H. Gómez–Dantés (1998) 'Uso de los servicios de salud por la poblacíon de 60 años y más en México', *Salud Pública de México*, 40, 1: 13-22.

V. Borooah (2005) 'Caste, inequality, and poverty in India', *Review of Development Economics*, 9 (3): 399-414.

A. Bowling (2005) *Ageing well: Quality of life in old age*, Open University Press, Milton Keynes.

Bretton Woods Project (2006) 'The World Bank and ageing', www. brettonwoodsproject.org/art.shtml?x=538507, accessed 10 April 2007.

B. Brijnath (2008) 'The legislative and political contexts surrounding dementia care in India', *Ageing and Society*, 28: 913-934.

J. Brodsky, J. Habib and M. Hirschfeld (2003a) *Key policy issues in long-term care*, World Health Organization, Geneva.

J. Brodsky, J. Habib and M. Hirschfeld (2003b) *Long-term care in developing countries: Ten case studies*, World Health Organization, Geneva.

M. Brogden and P. Nijhar (2000) *Crime, abuse and the elderly*, Willan Publishing, Devon.

E. Brown (1996) 'Deconstructing development: alternative perspectives on the history of an idea', *Journal of Historical Geography*, 22 (3): 333-339.

C. Browne and K. Braun (2008) 'Globalization, women's migration, and the long-term care workforce', *The Gerontologist*, 48 (1): 16-24.

K. Browne, C. Hamilton-Giachritsis, R. Johnson and M. Ostergren (2006) 'Overuse of institutional care for children in Europe', *British Medical Journal*, 332: 485-487.

A. Brumer (2002) 'Gender relations and social security in southern Brazil', in C. Abel and C. Lewis (eds) *Exclusion and engagement: Social policy in Latin America*, Institute of Latin American Studies, London.

A. Bucerius (2003) 'The Argentinean pension system: prior and after reform', *Revista de Economía y Estadística*, 39: 221-254.

A. Bunge (1940) *Una nueva Argentina*, Editorial Kraft, Buenos Aires.

S. Burman (1996) 'Intergenerational family care: legacy of the past, implications for the future', *Journal of Southern African Studies*, 22 (4): 585-598.

M. Busemeyer (2005) 'Pension reform in Germany and Austria: system change vs. quantitative retrenchment', *West European Politics*, 28 (3): 569-591.

G. Caiden and P. Sundaram (2004) 'The specificity of public service reform', *Public Administration and Development*, 24 (5): 373-383.

J. Caldwell (1993) 'Health transition: the cultural, social and behavioural determinants of health in the third world', *Social Science and Medicine*, 36 (2): 125-135.

J. Caldwell (1996) 'Demography and social science', *Population Studies*, 50: 305-333.

A. Camarano (2004) 'Social policy and the well-being of older people at a time of economic slowdown: the case of Brazil', in P. Lloyd-Sherlock (ed) *Living longer: Ageing, development and social protection*, Zed Books/United Nations Research Institute for Social Development, London.

A. Case (2001) 'Does money protect health status? Evidence from South African pensions', NBER Working Paper 8495, National Bureau of Economic Research, Cambridge, MA.

R. Cassen and K. McNay (2005) 'The condition of the people', in T. Dyson, R. Cassen and L. Visaria (eds) *Twenty-first century India: Population, economy, human development and the environment*, Oxford University Press, Oxford.

A. Castañeda Sabido (2006) 'Reforma eléctrica en México, los incentivos que están detrás del proceso político', *Foro Internacional*, 183 (1): 5-20.

D. Castro (1991) *To govern is to populate: Development and politics of Argentine immigration policy, 1852-1914*, Edwin Mellen Press, London.

Castro, V., Gómez-Dantés, H., Negrete-Sánchez, J. and Tapia-Conyer, R., 1998. "Chronic diseases among people 60-69 years old" *Salud Pública de México* 38(6): 348-447.

Census of India (2001) www.censusindia.net/

R. Chambers (1995) 'Poverty and livelihoods: whose reality counts', *Environment and Urbanization*, 7 (1): 173-204.

S. Chant (2007) *Gender, generation and poverty: Exploring the 'feminisation' of poverty in Africa, Asia and Latin America*, Edward Elgar, Cheltenham.

R. Charlton and R. McKinnon (2001) *Pensions in development*, Ashgate, Aldershot.

N. Chayovan and J. Knodel (1997) 'A report on the survey of the welfare of the elderly in Thailand', Unpublished paper, Institute of Population Studies, Chulalongkorn University, Bangkok.

M. Chen (ed) (1998) 'Introduction', in M. Chen (ed) *Widows in India: Social neglect and public action*, Sage Publications, London.

M. Chen (2000) *Perpetual mourning: Widowhood in rural India*, Oxford University Press, Oxford.

J. Chesnais (1999) 'Determinants of below-replacement fertility', *Population Bulletin of the United Nations*, 40/41: 126–136.

O. Chimere-Dan (1993) 'Population policy in South Africa', *Studies in Family Planning*, 24 (1): 31–39.

J. Chisholm (1999) 'The sandwich generation', *Journal of Social Distress and the Homeless*, 8 (3): 177–191.

S. Choi (2000) 'Ageing in Korea: issues and policies', in D. Phillips (ed) *Ageing in the Asia-Pacific region: Issues, policies and future trends*, Routledge, London.

H. Chou (2008) 'Building a pensions powerhouse', Global Pensions, London, http://globalpensions.com

Z. Chowdhury (1995) *Essential drugs for the poor: The makings of a successful health strategy: Lessons from Bangladesh*, Zed Books, London.

R. Clark and N. Ogawa (1996) 'Public attitudes and concerns about population aging in Japan', *Ageing and Society*, 16: 443–465.

L. Clarke and C. Roberts (2004) 'The meaning of grandparenthood and its contribution to the quality of life of older people', in A. Walker and C. Hagan (eds) *Growing older: Quality of life in old age*, McGraw Hill, Maidenhead.

D. Clay and J. van den Haar (1993) 'Patterns of intergenerational support and childbearing in the Third World', *Population Studies*, 47 (1): 67–84.

R. Clough (1996) 'The abuse of older people in residential and nursing homes', *Nursing Times Research*, 1 (6): 419–428.

W. Cockerham, K. Sharp and J. Wilcox (1983) 'Aging and perceived health status', *Journal of Gerontology*, 38 (3): 349–355.

L. Cohen (1995) 'Towards an anthropology of senility: anger, weakness and Alzheimer's in Banaras, India', *Medical Anthropology Quarterly*, 9 (3): 314–334.

L. Cohen (1998) *No aging in India: Alzheimer's, the bad family and other modern things*, University of California Press, Berkeley, CA.

CEPAL (Comisión Económica para America Latina) (1959) *Analisis y proyecciones del desarrollo económico*, CEPAL, Santiago de Chile.

Committee for the Enquiry into a Comprehensive System of Social Security for South Africa (2002) *Transforming the present – protecting the future*, Committee for the Enquiry into a Comprehensive System of Social Security for South Africa, Pretoria.

R. Clough (1996) *The abuse of care in institutions*, Whiting and Birch, London.

D. Cowgill (1976) 'Aging and modernization: a revision of the theory', in J. Gubrum (ed) *Late life: Communities and environmental policy*, Charles, C. Thomas, Springfield, Ill.

A. Cronenbold (2007) 'Calculan que hay 400 geriátricos ilegales', *La Nación*, Buenos Aires, 22 August.

D. Cufré (2008) 'Salud, dinero y control', *Página 12*, Buenos Aires, 28 August.

L. Daichman (2005) 'Elder abuse in developing nations', in M. Johnson, V. Bengtson, P. Coleman and T. Kirkwood (eds) *The Cambridge Handbook of Age and Ageing*, Cambridge University Press, Cambridge.

Daily Graphic (2008) 'Pension draft bill ready', 6 May, www.graphicghana.com/

Daily Trust (2007) 'Nigeria: when the aged came under focus', *Daily Trust*, Abuja, 16 November, http://allafrica.com/stories/200711160175.html

K. Dandekar (1996) *The elderly in India*, Sage Publications, London.

T. Dang, P. Antolin and H. Oxley (2001) 'Fiscal implications of ageing: projections of age-related spending', OECD Economics Department Working Papers, Number 305, OECD, Paris.

N. Daniels (1988) *Am I my parents' keeper?*, Oxford University Press, Oxford.

S. Das, T. Banerjee, A. Biswas, T. Roy, D. Raut, C. Mukherjee, C. Chaudhuri, A. Hazra and J. Roy (2007) 'A prospective community-based study of stroke in Kolkata, India', *Stroke*, 38: 906-910.

J. DaVanzo and A. Chan (1994) 'Living arrangements of older Malaysians: who coresides with their adult children?', *Demography* 31 (1): 95-113.

C. De Beer (1984) *The South African disease: Apartheid, health and health services*, Africa World Press, Trenton.

I. De Carvalho Filho (2000) 'Household income as a determinant of child labour and school enrolment in Brazil: evidence from a social security reform', Mimeo, M.I.T.

A. de Gray (2007) 'The natural biogerontology portfolio: defeating ageing as a multi-stage ultra-grand challenge' *Biogerontology: Mechanisms and Interventions*, 1100: 409-423.

C. Degnen (2006) 'Minding the gap: the construction of old age and oldness amongst peers', *Journal of Aging Studies*, 21 (1): 69-80.

H. Dei (2001) 'Pension fund management in Ghana', www1.worldbank.org/finance/assets/images/Henry_Dei_Paper_-_Ghana.pdf

G. Della Paolera and M. Taylor (2003) 'Introduction', in G. Della Paolera and M. Taylor (eds) *A new economic history of Argentina*, Cambridge University Press, Cambridge.

P. Demeny (2002) 'On policy responses to population ageing', *Population Bulletin of the United Nations*, 45: 450–458.

J. De Parle (2007) 'A good provider is one who leaves', *New York Times Magazine*, 22 April.

Department of Health Services, Government of Kerala (2005) *Needs assessment study of older population in Kerala*, Government of Kerala, Thiruvananthapuram.

R. Desjarlais, L. Eisenberg, B. Good and A. Kleinman (1995) *World mental health: Problems and priorities in low-income countries*, Oxford University Press, Oxford.

DFID (Department for International Development) (2006) *Using social transfers to improve human development*, Social Protection Briefing Note Series, Number 3, February, DFID, London.

S. D'Haeseleer and J. Berghman (2004) 'The Latin American pension reform experience: evidence that contradicts discourse', *Policy & Politics*, 32 (4): 521–534.

A. Dharmalingam (1994) 'Old age support: expectations and experiences in a South Indian village', *Population Studies*, 48: 5–19.

C. Diaz-Alejandro (1970) *Essays on the economic history of the Argentine Republic*, Yale University Press, New Haven, CT.

R. Disney (1996) *Can we afford to grow old?*, MIT Press, London.

R. Disney (2000) 'Crises in public pension programmes in OECD: what are the reform options?', *The Economic Journal*, 1110: 1–23.

R. Disney and E. Whitehouse (2003) *Poverty in old age: An international perspective*, Oxford Briefing Paper Number 3, Oxford Institute of Ageing, Oxford, www.ageing.ox.ac.uk/publications/oxbrief3.pdf

R. Disney, C. Emmerson and S. Smith (2003) 'Pension reform and economic performance in Britain in the 1980s and 1990s', NBER Working Paper 9556, National Bureau of Economic Research, Cambridge, MA.

A. Dobronogov and M. Murthi (2005) 'Administrative fees and costs of private pensions in transition economies', *Journal of Pension Economics and Finance*, 4: 31–55.

M. Donoghue (1999) 'People who don't use eye services:"making the invisible visible"', *Journal of Community Eye Health*, 12: 36–38.

W. Dowdle (1998) 'The principles of disease elimination and eradication', *WHO Bulletin*, 76: 22–25.

J. Dreze and H. Gazdar (1997) 'Uttar Pradesh: the burden of inertia', in J. Dreze and A. Sen (eds) *Indian development: Selected regional perspectives*, Oxford University Press, Oxford.

E. Duflo (2000) *Grandmothers and granddaughters: Old age pensions and intra-household allocation in South Africa*, National Bureau of Economic Research, Cambridge, MA.

R. Dugger (2003) 'Why Japan is trapped?', *The Globalist*, 23 May, www. theglobalist.com

T. Dyson (2002) 'India's population – the future', Paper presented at Seminar on the Future of India's Population, India International Centre, New Delhi.

T. Dyson (2005) 'India's population – the past' in T. Dyson, R. Cassen and L. Visaria (eds) *Twenty-first century India: Population, economy, human development and the environment*, Oxford University Press, Oxford.

T. Dyson and P. Visaria (2005) 'Migration and urbanization: retrospect and prospects', in T. Dyson, R. Cassen and L. Visaria (eds) *Twenty-first century India: Population, economy, human development and the environment*, Oxford University Press, Oxford.

Economy Ministry, Republic of Argentina (2003) 'Medicina prepaga: la importancia de la edad en la determinacíon de las cuotas', *Temas del Consumidor*, (61), Economy Ministry, Buenos Aires, www.mecon. gov.ar/secdef/revista/ediciones_2003.htm

G. Elder Jr (1998) 'The life course as developmental theory', *Child Development*, 69 (1): 1-12.

A. El Ghannan (2001) 'Modernisation in Arab societies: the theoretical and analytical view', *International Journal of Sociology and Social Policy*, 21 (11): 99-131.

L. Emmatty, R. Bhatti and M. Mukalel (2006) 'The experience of burden in India: a study of dementia caregivers', *Dementia*, 5 (2): 223-232.

A. Escobar (1995) 'Development planning', in S. Corbridge (ed) *Development studies: A reader*, Arnold, London.

J. Escudero (2003) 'The health crisis in Argentina', *International Journal of Health Services*, 33 (1): 129-136.

V. Esquivel (2008) *The political and social economy of care: Argentina research report 2*, UNRISD, Geneva, www.unrisd.org/unrisd/website/ document.nsf/(httpPublications)/A8ECFF5EFCA90B1FC1257417 002E39BB?OpenDocument

ESRC (Economic and Social Research Council) (2007) *ESRC Today: Adding quality to quantity: Older people's views on their quality of life and its enhancement*, Reading: Economic and Social Research Council, www.esrcsocietytoday.ac.uk/ESRCInfoCentre/Plain_English_Summaries/LLH/index140.aspx?ComponentId=9577&SourcePageId=11772

European Commission (2006) *The impact of ageing on public expenditure: Projections for the EU25 member states on pensions, health care, long-term care, education and unemployment transfers (2004-2050)*, Economic Policy Committee of the European Commission, Brussels, http://ec.europa.eu/economy_finance/epc/documents/2006/ageingreport_en.pdf

U. Ewelukwa (2002) 'Post-colonialism, gender, customary injustice: widows in African societies', *Human Rights Quarterly*, 24 (2): 424-486.

D. Ewing (1999) 'Gender and ageing', in J. Randel, T. German and D. Ewing (eds) *The ageing and development report: Poverty, independence and the world's older people*, Earthscan, London.

F. Eyetsemitan and J. Gire (2003) *Aging and adult development in the developing world: Applying western theories and concepts*, Praeger, London.

J. Farrington and N. Saxena (2004) *Protecting and promoting livelihoods in rural India: What role for pensions?*, Overseas Development Institute, London, www.odi.org.uk/opinions

V. Feigin (2007) 'Stroke in developing countries: can the epidemic be stopped and outcomes improved?', *The Lancet Neurology*, 6 (2): 94-97.

C. Feinstein (2005) *An economic history of South Africa: Conquest, discrimination and development*, Cambridge University Press, Cambridge.

J. Feldman, L. Golbert and E. Isuani (1988) *Maduración y crisis del sistema provisional argentino*, Centro Editor de América Latina, Buenos Aires.

J. Fiedler (1993) 'Increasing reliance on user fees as a response to public health financing crises: a case study of El Salvador', *Social Science and Medicine*, 36 (6): 735-747.

D. Fischer (1977) *Growing old in America*, Oxford University Press, New York.

M. Fisher-French (2007) 'Nest-egg for all', *Mail and Guardian*, South Africa, 16 February.

A. Fiszbein, P. Giovagnoli, I. Adúriz, J. Uribe and N. Schwab (2002) 'The Argentine health sector in the context of the crisis', World Bank Working Paper Number 2/02, World Bank, Washington, DC.

O. Fon Sim (2002) 'Malaysia: national policies on ageing', in D. Phillips and C. Chan (eds) *Ageing and long-term care: National policies in the Asia-Pacific*, IDRC/Institute of Southeast Asian Studies, Ottawa/ Singapore.

C. Fonchingong Che (2008) 'Gender dynamics of elderly welfare and semi-formal social protection in Cameroon (NW and SW provinces)', PhD thesis, School of Social Policy, Sociology and Social Research, University of Kent.

A. Frank (1967) *Capitalism and underdevelopment in Latin America*, Monthly Review Press, New York.

J. Frenk, J. Bobadilla, C. Stern, T. Frejka and R. Lozano (1991) 'Elements for a theory of the health transition', *Health Transition Review*, 1: 21–38.

E. Freysselinard, M. Oddone, J. Paola and N. Passadore (2000) 'Hogares de ancianos: una aproximación al studio de sus características institucionales', in Secretaría de la Tercera Edad y Acción Social *Informe sobre tercera edad en Argentina, año 2000*, Secretaría de la Tercera Edad y Acción Social, Buenos Aires.

V. Fuchs (1984) 'Though much is taken – reflections on aging, health and medical care', *Milbank Memorial Fund Quarterly*, 62 (2): 143–165.

J. Fulcher and J. Scott (2007) *Sociology*, Oxford University Press, Oxford.

R. Garfield (1989) *Health and revolution: The Nicaraguan experience*, Oxford University Press, Oxford.

G. Germani (1955) *La estructura social de la Argentina*, Editorial Raigal, Buenos Aires.

D. Ghosh (2009) 'Pension plans rise in portfolios of insurance companies', *Times of India*, 11 February.

A. Giddens (2005) *Sociology*, Polity, Cambridge.

R. Gillingham and D. Kanda (2001) 'Pension reform in India', IMF Working Paper WP 01/125, IMF, Washington, DC.

L. Gilson and D. McIntyre (2007) *Are South Africa's new health policies making a difference?*, Health Economics Unit/Centre for Health Policy Equity Briefing, Johannesburg/Cape Town.

T. Goergen (2001) 'Stress, conflict, elder abuse and neglect in German nursing homes: a pilot study among professional caregivers', *Journal of Elder Abuse and Neglect*, 13 (1): 1–26.

C. Gomes da Conceição and V. Montes de Oca Zavala (2004) 'Ageing in Mexico: families, informal care and reciprocity', in P. Lloyd-Sherlock (ed) *Living longer: Ageing, development and social protection*, Zed Books/United Nations Research Institute for Social Development, London.

O. Gómez-Dantés (2000) 'Health reform and policies for the poor in Mexico', in P. Lloyd-Sherlock (ed) *Healthcare reform and poverty in Latin America*, Institute of Latin American Studies, London.

P. Gorelick (2004) 'Risk factors for vascular dementia and Alzheimer's disease', *Stroke*, 35 (11), Supplement 1: 2620-2622.

I. Gough, A. McGregor and L. Camfield (2006) *Wellbeing in developing countries: Conceptual foundations of the WeD Programme*, WeD Working Paper Number 19, University of Bath, Bath.

W. Graebner (1980) *A history of retirement: The meaning and function of an American institution, 1885-1978*, Yale University Press, New Haven, CT.

A. Gray (2009) 'The social capital of older people', *Ageing and Society*, 29: 5-31.

E. Greenfield and N. Marks (2004) 'Formal volunteering as a protective factor for older adults' psychological well-being', *Journal of Gerontology: Social Sciences*, 58b: S258-S264.

H. Greenhalgh (2005) 'Poland's newly reformed system of retirement provision stays on course, although consolidation remains in the slow lane', *European Pensions and Investment News*, 4 July.

Groningen Growth and Development Centre (2009) 'Total economy database', www.conference-board.org/economics/database.cfm

R. Guha (2007) *India after Gandhi: The history of the world's largest democracy*, Macmillan, Basingstoke.

C. Guilmoto (2007) *Characteristics of sex-ratio imbalances in India, and future scenarios*, United Nations Population Fund, New York.

I. Gujral (2001) 'Global ageing, depopulation and virtual work', *New Perspectives Quarterly*, 28 (2): 28-32.

E. Gunnarsson (2002) 'The vulnerable life course: poverty and social assistance among middle aged and older women', *Ageing and Society*, 22 (3): 709-728.

Z. Guo (2000) 'Family patterns', in X. Peng and Z. Guo (eds) *The changing population of China*, Blackwell, Oxford.

D. Gwatkin (1979) 'Political will and family planning: the implications of India's emergency experience', *Population and Development Review*, 5 (1): 29-59.

G. Hagestad (2003) 'Interdependent lives and relationships in changing times: a life-course view of families and aging', in R. Settersten Jr (ed) *Invitation to the life course: Towards new understandings of later life*, Baywood Publishing Company, New York.

J. Hall and R. Taylor (2003) 'Health for all beyond 2000: the demise of the Alma Ata declaration and primary health care in developing countries', *Medical Journal of Australia*, 6 January.

R. Ham-Chande (1996) 'Envejecimiento: una nueva dimensión de la salud en México', *Salud Pública de México*, 38 (6): 409-18.

C. Hamlin (1994) 'State medicine in Great Britain', in D. Porter (ed) *The history of public health and the modern state*, Wellcome Trust, London.

K. Hanson, K. Ranson, V. Oliveira-Cruz and A. Mills (2003) 'Expanding access to priority health interventions: a framework for understanding the constraints to scaling up', *Journal of International Development*, 15 (1): 1-14.

R. Harding (2006) 'Palliative care: a basic human right', ID21 Insights, www.id21.org/insights/insights-h08/art00.html

C. Harper and R. Marcus (2003) 'Enduring poverty and the conditions of childhood: lifecourse and intergenerational poverty transmissions', *World Development*, 31 (3): 535-554.

B. Harriss-White (2003) *India working: Essays on society and economy*, Cambridge University Press, Cambridge.

W. He and J. Schachter (2003) 'Internal migration of the older population: 1995 to 2000', US Census Bureau, Washington, DC.

W. Heinz and H. Krüger (2001) 'Life course: innovations and challenges for social research', *Current Sociology*, 49 (2): 29-55.

HelpAge International (1999) 'Ageing and development: the message', in HelpAge International (ed) *The ageing and development report: Poverty, independence and the world's older people*, Earthscan, London.

HelpAge International (2001) *Equal treatment, equal rights: Ten actions to end age discrimination*, HelpAge International, London.

HelpAge International (2003) *Forgotten families: Older people as carers of orphans and vulnerable children*, HelpAge International, London, www.helpage.org/Worldwide/Africa/Resources?autocreate_RelatedHelpagePublicationList_start=21

HelpAge International (2004) *Age and security: How social pensions can deliver effective aid to poor older people and their families*, HelpAge International, London, www.helpage.org/Resources/Policyreports

HelpAge International (2005) *A better deal for older carers in South Africa*, HelpAge International, London, www.helpage.org/Researchandpolicy/HIVAIDS/Resources

HelpAge International (2006) *Why social pensions are needed now?*, HelpAge International, London, www.helpage.org/Researchandpolicy/ Socialprotection/Resources?lfdY_start=11

HelpAge International (2007) *Stronger together: Supporting the vital role played by older people in the fight against the HIV and AIDS pandemic*, HelpAge International Briefing Paper, Helpage International, London, www.helpage.org/Resources/Briefings

HelpAge International (2008) *Social protection: Facts and figures*, Helpage International, London, www.helpage.org/Researchandpolicy/ Socialprotection/Factsandfigures

HelpAge International (2009) 'randparents play pivotal role in migration, Helpage International, London, www.helpage.org/News/ Latestnews/eIIY

Help the Aged (2009) 'NHS accused of ageism in mental health services', Help the Aged, London, http://press.helptheaged.org. uk/_press/Releases/_items/_NHS+accused+of+ageism+in+ment al+health+services.htm

F. Hendricks (2009) *The private affairs of public pensions in South Africa: Debt, development and corporatisation*, UNRISD Social Policy Working Paper Number 38, UNRISD, Geneva.

J. Herbst (2005) 'Mbeki's South Africa', *Foreign Affairs* November/ December.

T. Hesketh and Z. Xing (2005) 'The effect of China's one child family policy after 25 years', *New England Journal of Medicine*, 353: 1171-1176.

B. Hettne (2002) 'Current trends and future options in development studies', in V. Desai and R. Potter (eds) *The companion to development studies*, Arnold, London.

R. Holzmann and R. Hinz (2005) *Old age income-support in the 21st century: An international perspective on pension systems and reform*, World Bank, Washington, DC.

V. Hosegood, A. Vanneste and I. Timaeus (2004) 'Levels and causes of adult mortality in rural South Africa', *AIDS*, 18: 1-19.

V. Hosegood and I. Timaeus (2006) 'HIV/AIDS and older people in South Africa', in B. Cohen and J. Menken (eds) *Aging in sub-Saharan Africa: Recommendations for furthering research*, National Research Council, Washington, DC.

K. Howse (2007) 'Long-term care policy: the difficulties of taking a global view', *Ageing Horizons*, 6: 3-11.

HSBC (2007) The future of retirement: the new old age –global report. Available at: https://www.ageingforum.org/files/8/uk_reports_2007/ entry398.aspx

G. Huff (1995) 'The developmental state, government and Singapore's economic development since 1960', *World Development*, 23 (8): 1421–1438.

G. Hugo (1988) 'The changing urban situation in South East Asia and Australia: some implications for the elderly', Paper presented at the UN Conference on Ageing Populations in the Context of Urbanisation, Sendei, Japan, 12–16 September 1988.

D. Hulme and M. Edwards (eds) (1992) *Making a difference: NGOs and development in a changing world*, Earthscan, London.

Human Sciences Research Council (2002) 'Nelson Mandela HSRD study of HIV/AIDS: full report', HSRC Council Press, Pretoria.

IBGE (Instituto Brasiliero de Geografía y Estadística) (2004) 'Coordenação de população e indicadores sociais', www.ibge.gov.br

IBGE (2008) 'Indicators', www.ibge.gov.br/english/#sub_indicadores

A. Iglesias and R. Palacios (2000) 'Managing public pension reserves. Part 1: evidence from international experience', in World Bank (ed) *Pension primer*, World Bank, Washington, DC.

O. Iheduru (2004) 'Black economic power and nation building in post-apartheid South Africa', *Journal of Modern African Studies*, 42 (1): 1–30.

I. Illich (1976) *Limits to medicine: Medical nemesis: The expropriation of health*, Penguin, London.

J. Ilmarinen (2001) 'Aging workers', *Occupational and Environmental Medicine*, 58: 546–552.

ILO (International Labour Office) (2007) *Global employment trends for women*, Brief, March, ILO, Geneva, www.ilo.org/public/english/employment/strat/download/getw07.pdf

ILO (2008) Setting social security standards in a global society, Social Security Policy Briefings, Paper 2, ILO, Geneva, www.ilo.org/public/english/protection/secsoc/downloads/policy/policy2e.pdf

IMF (International Monetary Fund) (2004) *The IMF and Argentina, 1991-2001*, IMF Independent Evaluation Office, Washington, DC.

INDEC (Instituto Nacional de Estadística y Censo) (2008) 'INDEC-Web', www.indec.gov.ar

International IDEA (International Institute for Democracy and Electoral Assistance) (2002) *Voter turnout since 1945: A global report*, IDEA, Stockholm, www.idea.int

IOM (International Organisation for Migration) (2008) *World migration report 2008: Managing labour mobility in the evolving global economy*, IOM, Geneva.

ISSA (International Social Security Association) (2009) *Survey on social security in times of crisis: Summary of findings and conclusions*, ISSA Survey Report, 23 April, ISSA, Geneva.

W. Jackson (1998) *The political economy of population ageing*, Edward Elgar, Cheltenham.

D. James (1988) *Resistance and integration: Peronism and the Argentine working class, 1946-1976*, Cambridge University Press, Cambridge.

D. Jamuna (2003) 'Issues of elder care and elder abuse in the Indian context', in P. Liebig and S. Irudaya Rajan (eds) *An aging India: Perspectives, prospects and policies*, Haworth Press, London.

J. Jarallah and S. Al-Shammari (1999) 'Factors associated with health perception of Saudi elderly', *Journal of Cross-Cultural Gerontology*, 14: 323-334.

S. Jayasinghe (2006) 'Where next for China? User fees increase China's health challenges', *British Medical Journal*, 333: 499-500.

R. Jewkes and N. Abrahams (2002) 'The epidemiology of rape and sexual coercion in South Africa: an overview', *Social Science and Medicine*, 55 (7): 1231-1244.

R. Jewkes, L. Penn-Kekana, J. Levin, M. Ratsaka and M. Schrieber (1999) *He must give me money, he mustn't beat me: Violence against women in three South African provinces*, Medical Research Council, Pretoria.

P. Jha and F. Chaloupka (2000) 'Overview', in P. Jha and F. Chaloupka (eds) *Tobacco control in developing countries*, Oxford University Press, Oxford.

S. Jitapunkul and S. Bunnag (1998) *Ageing in Thailand 1997*, Thai Society of Gerontology and Geriatric Medicine, Bangkok.

P. Johnson (2004) 'Long-term historical changes in the status of elders: the United Kingdom as an exemplar of advanced industrial economies', in P. Lloyd-Sherlock (ed), *Living longer: Ageing, development and social protection*, Zed, London.

S. Jones and J. Inggs (1999) 'An overview of the South African economy in the 1970s', *South African Journal of Economic History*, 14 (1): 1-10.

R. Joshi, M. Cardona, S. Iyengar, A. Sukumar, C. Ravi Raju, K. Rama Raju, K. Raju, K. Srinath Reddy, A. Lopez and B. Neal (2006) 'Chronic diseases now a leading cause of death in rural India – mortality data from the Andhra Pradesh Rural Health Initiative', *International Journal of Epidemiology*, 35: 1522-1529.

K. Kahn, S. Tollman, M. Thorogood, M. Connor, M. Garenne, M. Collinson and G. Hundt (2006) 'Older adults and the health transition in Agincourt, rural South Africa: new understanding, growing complexity', in B. Cohen and J. Menken (eds) *Aging in sub-Saharan Africa: Recommendations for furthering research*, National Research Council, Washington, DC.

R. Kalaria, G. Maestre, R. Artzaga, R. Friedland, D. Galasko, K. Hall, J. Luchsinger, A. Ogunniyi, E. Perry, F. Potocnik, M. Prince, R. Stewart, A. Wimo, Z. Zhang and P. Antuono (2008) 'Alzheimer's disease and vascular dementia in developing countries: prevalence, management and risk factors', *The Lancet Neurology*, 7 (9): 812–826.

E. Karagiannaki (2005) 'Changes in the living arrangements of elderly people in Greece: 1974–1999', Centre for Analysis of Social Exclusion, London, http://sticerd.lse.ac.uk/dps/case/cp/CASEpaper104.pdf

S. Katz (1996) *Disciplining old age*, University Press of Virginia, Charlottseville, VA.

K. Kawabata, K. Xu and G. Carrin (2002) 'Preventing impoverishment through protection against catastrophic health expenditure', *Bulletin of the World Health Organization*, 80: 612.

L. Kelley (2005) 'Growing old in St. Lucia: expectations and experiences in a Caribbean village', *Journal of Cross-Cultural Gerontology*, 20 (1): 67–78.

D. Kertzer and P. Laslett (eds) (1995) *Ageing in the past: Demography, society and old age*, University of California Press, Berkeley, CA.

J. Kespichayawattana and M. VanLandingham (2003) 'Effects of coresidence and caregiving on health of Thai patents of adult children with AIDS', *Journal of Nursing Scholarship*, 35 (3): 217–224.

R. Khanna, A. Kumar, D. Vaghela, V. Sreenivas and J. Puliyel (2003) 'Community based retrospective study of sex in infant mortality in India', *British Medical Journal*, 327: 126–129.

N. Khe, N. Toan, L. Xuan, B. Eriksson, B. Hojer and V. Diwan (2002) 'Primary health concept revisited: where do people seek health care in rural areas of Vietnam?', *Health Policy*, 61 (1): 95–109.

J. Kim and P. Moen (2002) 'Retirement transitions, gender and psychological well-being: a life-course, ecological model', *The Journal of Gerontology: Psychological Sciences*, 57 (3): 212–222.

J. Kim, J. Kang, M. Lee and Y. Lee (2007) 'Volunteering among older people in Korea', *Journal of Gerontology: Social Sciences*, 62B (1): S69–S73.

R. King, T. Warnes and A. Williams (2000) *Sunset lives: British retirement migration to the Mediterranean*, Macmillan, Basingstoke.

G. Kingdon, R. Cassen, K. McNay and L.Visaria (2005) 'Education and literacy', in T. Dyson, R. Cassen and L.Visaria (eds) *Twenty-first century India: Population, economy, human development and the environment*, Oxford University Press, Oxford.

K. Kinsella and M. Ferreira (1997) 'Aging trends; South Africa', US Bureau of the Census, Center for International Research, Washington, DC.

P. Kirk (2001) 'State adviser linked to loans for elderly', *Mail and Guardian*, 31 August.

J. Knodel and N. Chayovan (2008) 'Gender and ageing in Thailand: a situation analysis of older women and men', Population Studies Center Research Report Number 08-664, University of Michigan, Michigan, MI.

J. Knodel and C. Saengtienchai (2004) 'AIDS and older persons: the view from Thailand', in P. Lloyd-Sherlock (ed) *Living longer: Ageing, development and social protection*, Zed Books/United Nations Research Institute for Social Development, London.

J. Knodel, N. Chayovan, S. Graisurapong and C. Suraratdecha (2000) 'Ageing in Thailand: an overview of formal and informal support', in D. Phillips (ed) *Ageing in the Asia-Pacific region: Issues, policies and future trends*, Routledge, London.

J. Knodel, J. Kespichayawattana, S. Wiwatwanich and C. Saengtienchai (2007) *Migration and intergenerational solidarity: Evidence from rural Thailand*, Papers in Population Ageing Number 2, UNFPA Thailand, Bangkok.

J. Knodel, S. Watkins and M. VanLandingham (2003) 'AIDS and older persons: an international perspective', *Journal of Acquired Immune Deficiency Syndrome*, 33 (Supplement 2): 153-165.

A. Kochar (2008) 'The effectiveness of India's anti-poverty programmes', *Journal of Development Studies*, 44 (9): 1289-1308.

A. Kokayi Khalfani and T. Zuberi (2003) 'Racial classification and the modern census in South Africa, 1911-1996', *Race and Society*, 4 (2): 161-176.

V. Kumar (2003a) 'Economic security for the elderly in India: an overview', in P. Liebig and S. Irudaya Rajan (eds) *An aging India: Perspectives, prospects and policies*, Haworth Press, London.

V. Kumar (2003b) 'Health status and health care services among older persons in India', in P. Liebig and S. Irudaya Rajan (eds) *An aging India: Perspectives, prospects and policies*, Haworth Press, London.

D. Lam, M. Leibbrandt and V. Ranchhod (2006) 'Labor force withdrawal of the elderly in South Africa', in B. Cohen and J. Menken (eds) *Aging in sub-Saharan Africa: Recommendations for furthering research*, National Research Council, Washington, DC.

S. Lamb (1999) 'Aging, gender and widowhood: perspectives from rural West Bengal', *Contributions to Indian Sociology*, 33 (3): 541-570.

S. Lamb (2000) *White saris and sweet mangoes: Aging, gender, and body in north India*, University of California Press, London.

P. Laslett (1992) 'Is there a generational contract?', in P. Laslett and J. Fishki (eds) *Justice between age groups and generations*, Yale University Press, New Haven, CT.

T. Laslett and R. Wall (1972) *Household and family in past time*, Cambridge University Press, Cambridge.

A. Lattes (1974) 'Los cambios en la composición de la población', in Z. Recchini de Lattes and A. Lattes (eds) *La población de Argentina*, CICRED, Buenos Aires.

P. Leary and J. Lewis (1965) 'Some observations on the state of nutrition of infants and toddlers in the Sekhukhuniland', *South African Medical Journal*, 39: 1156-1158.

K. Lerman (2004) *Bismarck: Profiles in power*, Longman, London.

B. Leven (1998) 'Changes in Poland's transfer payments in the 1990s: the fate of pensioners', The William Davidson Institute Working Paper Number 148, University of Michigan, MI.

C. Lewis (1993) 'Social insurance: ideology and policy in the Argentine, c.1920-1966', in C. Abel and C. Lewis (eds) *Welfare, poverty and development in Latin America*, Macmillan, London.

C. Lewis (2002) *Argentina: A short history*, Oneworld, Oxford.

C. Lewis and P. Lloyd-Sherlock (2008) 'Social policy and economic development in South America: an historical approach to social insurance', *Economy and Society*, 38 (1): 109-131.

O. Lewis (1951) *Life in a Mexican village: Tepoztlán restudied*, University of Illinois Press, Urbana, IL.

M. Lima-Costa, H. Guerra, J. Firmo, P. Vidigal, E. Uchoa and S. Barreto (2002) 'The Banbui health and aging study (BHAS): private health plans and medical care utilization by older adults', *Cadernos de Saúde Pública*, 18 (1): 177-186.

M. Lipton and R. Longhurst (1989) *New seeds and poor people*, John Hopkins University Press, Baltimore, MD.

P. Lloyd-Sherlock (1997a) 'Policy, distribution and poverty in Argentina since redemocratization', *Latin American Perspectives*, 24 (6): 22-55.

P. Lloyd-Sherlock (1997b) *Old age and urban poverty in the developing world: The shanty towns of Buenos Aires*, Macmillan, London.

P. Lloyd-Sherlock (1998) 'Old age, migration and poverty in the shanty towns of São Paulo, Brazil', *Journal of Developing Areas*, 32 (4): 491-514.

P. Lloyd-Sherlock (2001a) *Old age, poverty and economic survival: rural and urban case studies from Thailand*, Department for International Development, London.

P. Lloyd-Sherlock (2001b) 'Evaluando el impacto en el bienestar del Programa de Atencíon Médica Integral (PAMI)', Mimeo, School of Development Studies, www.ciepp.org.ar/trabajo.htm

P. Lloyd-Sherlock (2002a) 'Nussbaum, capabilities and older people', *Journal of International Development*, 14 (3): 1163-1173.

P. Lloyd-Sherlock (2002b) 'Formal social protection and older people in developing countries: three different approaches', *Journal of Social Policy*, 31 (4): 695-713.

P. Lloyd-Sherlock (2003) 'Financing health services for pensioners in Argentina: a salutary tale', *International Journal of Social Welfare*, 12: 24-30.

P. Lloyd-Sherlock (2004) 'Primary health care and older people in the South – a forgotten issue', *European Journal for Development Research*, 16 (2): 283-290.

P. Lloyd-Sherlock (2005) 'Health sector reform in Argentina: a cautionary tale', *Social Science and Medicine*, 60: 1893-1903.

P. Lloyd-Sherlock (2006) 'Vulnerability, poverty and older people in developing countries: insights from Thailand', *Ageing and Society*, 26 (1): 81-103.

P. Lloyd-Sherlock (2007) 'Simple transfers, complex outcomes: the impacts of pensions on poor households in Brazil', *Development and Change*, 37 (5): 969-95.

P. Lloyd-Sherlock (2009) 'The situation of older people in Cape Town: preliminary findings from the in–depth interviews', www.sed. manchester.ac.uk/research/ageingandwellbeing/index.htm

P. Lloyd-Sherlock and C. Locke (2008) 'Vulnerable relations: lifecourse, wellbeing and social exclusion in a neighbourhood of Buenos Aires, Argentina', *Ageing and Society*,28 (6): 779-803.

P. Longman (2004) *The empty cradle: How falling birthrates threaten our prosperity and what to do about it*, Basic Books, New York.

E. Luce (2006) *In spite of the gods: The strange rise of modern India*, Little, Brown, London.

W. Lutz, W. Sanderson and B. O'Niell (2004) 'Conceptualizing population in sustainable development: from "population stabilization" to "population balance"', in W. Lutz, W. Sanderson and S. Scherbov (eds) *The end of world population growth in the 21st century: New challenges for human capital formation and sustainable development*, Earthscan, London.

W. Lutz, V. Skirbekk and M. Testa (2006) 'The low fertility trap hypothesis: forces that may lead to further postponement and fewer births in Europe', *Vienna yearbook of population research 2006*, Austrian Academy of Sciences, Vienna, pp 213-234.

M. Lyons (1994) 'Public health in colonial Africa: the Belgian Congo', in D. Porter (ed) *The history of public health and the modern state*, Wellcome Trust, London.

Maeda, D. and Ishikawa, H. (2000) 'Ageing in Japan: daily lives, pensions and social security', in D. Phillips (ed) *Ageing in the Asia-Pacific region: Issues, policies and future trends*, Routledge: London.

A. Maddison (2001) *The world economy: A millennial perspective*, OECD, Paris.

J. Malloy (1979) *The politics of social security in Brazil*, University of Pittsburgh Press, Pittsburgh, PA.

P. Mari Bhat (1998) 'Widowhood and mortality in India', in M. Chen (ed) *Widows in India: Social neglect and public action*, Sage Publications, London.

G. Martine (1996) 'Brazil's fertility decline, 1965-95: a fresh look at the key factors', *Population and Development Review*, 22 (1): 47-75.

C. Martínez and G. Leal (2003) 'Epidemiological transition: model or illusion? A look at the problem of health in Mexico', *Social Science and Medicine*, 57 (4): 539-550.

A. Mason and R. Lee (2006) 'Reform and support systems of the elderly in developing countries: capturing the "second demographic dividend"', *Genus*, 57 (2): 11-35.

C. Mathers and D. Loncar (2006) 'Projections of global mortality and burden of disease from 2002 to 2030', *PLoS Medicine*, 3 (11): 2011-2030.

C. Mathers, K. Moesgaard Iburg, J. Saloman, A. Tandon, S. Chatterji, B. Ustün and C. Murray (2004) 'Global patterns of healthy life expectancy in the year 2002', *BMC Public Health*, 4 (66): 1-12.

J. May (2003) 'Chronic poverty and older people in South Africa', Chronic Poverty Research Centre, University of Manchester, Manchester.

R. Mazur (1998) 'Migration dynamics and development in rural South Africa: demographic and socioeconomic perspectives', *Research in Rural Sociology and Development*, 7: 197-225.

C. Mba (2005) 'Racial differences in marital status and living arrangements of older persons in South Africa', *Generations Review*, 15 (2): 23-31.

L. McCabe (2006) 'The cultural and political context of the lives of people with dementia in Kerala, India', *Dementia*, 5 (1): 117-136.

J. McCulloch (2002) *Asbestos blues: Labour, capital, physicians and the state in South Africa*, James Currey, Oxford.

K. McGrail, B. Green, M. Barer, R. Evans, C. Hertzman and C. Normand (2000) 'Age, costs of acute and long term care and proximity to death: evidence for 1987/88 and 1994/95 in British Columbia', *Age and Ageing*, 29: 249-253.

J. McGregor and L. Gray (2002) 'Stereotypes and older workers: the New Zealand experience', *Social Policy Journal of New Zealand*, 18: 163-177.

J. McIntosh (2009) 'Elders and "frauds": commodified expertise and politicized authenticity among Mijikenda', *Africa*, 79 (1): 35-52.

D. McIntyre (2004) 'Health policy and older people in Africa', in P. Lloyd-Sherlock (ed) *Living longer: Ageing, development and social protection*, Zed Books, London.

A. McMichael, M. McKee, V. Shkolnikov and T. Valkonen (2004) 'Mortality trends and setbacks: global convergence or divergence', *The Lancet*, 363: 1155-1159.

O. Mendelsohn (1998) *The untouchables: Subordination, poverty and the state in modern India*, Oxford University Press, Oxford.

S. Mendis, D. Abegunde, S. Yusuf, S. Ebrahim, G. Shaper, H. Ghannem and B. Shengelia (2005) 'WHO study on recurrence of myocardial infarction and stroke (WHO-PREMISEE)', *Bulletin of the World Health Organization*, 83 (11): 820-828.

M. Meredith (2005) *The state of Africa: A history of fifty years of independence*, Free Press, London.

M. Merli and A. Palloni (2006) 'The HIV/AIDS epidemic, kin relations, living arrangements, and the African elderly in South Africa', in B. Cohen and J. Menken (eds) *Aging in sub-Saharan Africa: Recommendations for furthering research*, National Research Council, Washington, DC.

C. Mesa-Lago (1978) *Social security in Latin America: Pressure groups, stratification and inequality*, University of Pittsburgh Press, Pittsburgh, PA.

C. Mesa-Lago (1989) *Ascent to bankruptcy: Financing social security in Latin America*, University of Pittsburgh Press, Pittsburgh, PA.

C. Mesa-Lago and K. Muller (2002) 'The politics of pension reform in Latin America', *Journal of Latin American Studies*, 34: 687-715.

MIDEPLAN (2006) *Serie de análisis de resultados de la Encuesta de Caracterización Socioeconómica Nacional (CASEN) 2006. N 1. La situación de la Pobreza en Chile 2006*, MIDEPLAN, Santiago de Chile.

J. Midgley (1984) *Social security, inequality and the Third World*, Wiley, Chichester.

Ministry of Health, Labour and Welfare, Japan (2004) 'Abridged life table for 2004', www.mhlw.go.jp/english

A. Minujin (1992) 'En la rodada', in A. Minujin (ed) *Cuesta abajo: Los nuevos pobres: Los efectos de la crisis en la sociedad Argentina*, Unicef/Losada, Buenos Aires.

O. Mitchell, J. Piggott and S. Shimizutani (2008) 'Developments in long-term care insurance in Japan', Research Paper Number 2008 Econ 01, Australian School of Business, Sydney.

T. Mohatle and R. de Graft Agyarko (1999) *Contributions of older people to development: The South Africa study*, HelpAge International, London.

K. Moli (2004) 'Ageism in Kerala', *Kerala Calling*, August.

V. Moller and M. Ferreira (2003) *Getting by: Benefits of non-contributory pension income for older South African households*, Institute of Social and Economic Research, Rhodes University and the Albertina and Walter Sisulu Institute of Ageing in Africa, University of Cape Town, Grahamstown and Cape Town.

C. Montenegro and C. Pagés (2003) 'Who benefits from labor market regulations? Chile 1960-1998', Working Paper Number 494, Inter-American Development Bank, Washington, DC.

M. Monteverde, K. Noronha, A. Palloni and K. Angeletti (2008) 'Costos individuales esperados de cuidados de larga duración en Buenos Aires, México y Puerto Rico', Paper presented at 3rd Conference of the Latin American Population Association, Córdoba, Argentina, 24-26 September.

R. Montgomery, L. Holley, J. Diechert and K. Kosloski (2005) 'A profile of home care workers from the 2000 Census: how it changed and what we know', *The Gerontologist*, 45: 593-600.

H. Moody (1993) *Ethics in an aging society*, Johns Hopkins University Press, Baltimore, MD.

O. Moon (2002) 'Alternative systems of health and welfare service delivery for older persons in developed and developing countries', in WHO (ed) *Development of health and welfare systems – adjusting to ageing*, WHO Kobe Centre, Kobe.

Morgan Stanley Global Economic Forum (2005) "Waking up to a nightmare", 25 October, Morgan Stanley, New York, Available at www.morganstanley.com/GEFdata/digests/20051025-tue.html#anchor1

K. Müller (1999) 'Pension reform paths in comparison: the case of Central-Eastern Europe', *Czech Sociological Review*, 7 (1): 51-66.

K. Müller (2003) *Privatising old-age security: Latin America and Eastern Europe compared*, Edward Elgar, London.

M. Murphy (2008) 'Variations in kinship networks across geographic and social space', *Population and Development Review*, 34 (1): 19-49.

C. Murray (1994) 'Quantifying the burden of disease: the technical basis for disability-adjusted life years', *Bulletin of the World Health Organization*, 72: 429-455.

M. Murthi, A. Guio and J. Dreze (1997) 'Mortality, fertility and gender bias in India: a district-level analysis', in J. Dreze and A. Sen (eds) *Indian development: Selected regional perspectives*, Oxford University Press, Oxford.

G. Naegele (1999) 'The politics of old age in Germany', in A. Walker and G. Naegele (eds) *The politics of old age in Europe*, Open University Press, Buckingham.

M. Nari (1996) 'Las prácticas anticonceptivas, la disminución de la natalidad y el debate médico, 1890-1940', in M. Zaida Lobato (ed) *Política, médicos y enfermedades: Lecturas de historia de la salud en Argentina*, Editorial Biblios, Buenos Aires.

National Population Stabilisation Fund (2007) 'India's population', http://jsk.gov.in/indias_population.asp

National Research Council (2000) *Beyond six billion: Forecasting the world's population*, National Academy Press, Washington, DC.

N. Nattrass (2006) 'Disability and welfare in South Africa's era of unemployment and AIDS', Research Working Paper Number 147, Centre for Social Science, University of Cape Town, Cape Town.

NHS (National Health Service) (2001) *National service framework for older people: Short summary*, Department of Health, London.

J. Nilsson, A. Masud Rana and Z. Kabir (2006) 'Social capital and quality of life in old age', *Journal of Aging and Health*, 18 (3): 419-434.

M. Noble, H. Barnes, G. Wright and S. Noble (2006) *The old age grant: A sub-provincial analysis of eligibility and take-up in January 2004*, Department of Social Development, Republic of South Africa Pretoria.

H. Nogami (2005) 'Gender perspectives in family planning: the development of family planning in postwar Japan and policy implications from the Japanese experience', in M. Murayama (ed) *Gender and development: The Japanese experience in comparative perspective*, Palgrave, Basingstoke.

M. Noriuchi, Y. Kikuchi and A. Senoo (2008) 'The functional neuroanatomy of maternal love: mother's response to infant's attachment behaviors', *Biological Psychiatry*, 63 (4): 415-423.

A. Noumbissi and T. Zuberi (2001) 'Household structure and aging in South Africa: a research note', www.pop.upenn.edu/africahh/NoubissiZuberi.pdf

M. Oahn (2002) 'Reported illness patterns and health seeking behaviour of the elderly in a district of Vietnam: the differences between men and women', Masters of Public Health Thesis, Department of Public Health Sciences, Karolinska Institutet, Stockholm.

OECD (Organisation for Economic Cooperation and Development) (1998) *Maintaining prosperity in an ageing society*, OECD, Paris.

OECD (2005) *Ensuring quality long-term care for older people*, OECD Observer Policy Brief, March, OECD, Paris.

M. Oftsedal and J. Natavidad (2003) 'Patterns of health care utilisation', in A. Hermalin (ed) *The well-being of the elderly in Asia*, University of Michigan Press, Ann Arbor, MI.

M. Ofstedal, E. Reidy and J. Knodel (2004) 'Gender differences in economic support and well-being of older Asians', *Journal of Cross-Cultural Gerontology*, 19: 165-201.

T. Ogawa (2004) 'Ageing in Japan: an issue of social contract in welfare transfer or generational conflict?', in P. Lloyd-Sherlock (ed) *Living longer: Ageing, development and social protection*, Zed Books, London.

Y. Ohenaba-Sakyi and B. Tayki (2006) 'Introduction to the study of African families: a framework for analysis', in Y. Ohenaba-Sakyi and B. Tayki (eds) *African families at the turn of the 21st century*, Praeger, London.

M. Olivarria-Gambi (2003) 'Poverty reduction in Chile: has economic growth been enough?', *Journal of Human Development*, 4 (1): 112-124.

W. Olsen and S. Mehta (2006) *A pluralist account of labour participation in India*, ESRC Global Poverty Research Group, Oxford/Manchester, www.gprg.org/pubs/workingpapers/pdfs/gprg-wps-042.pdf

S. Olshansky, D. Passaro, R. Hershow, J. Layden, B. Carnes, J. Brody, L. Hayflick, R. Butler, D. Allison and D. Ludwig (2005) 'A potential decline in life expectancy in the United States in the 21st century', *New England Journal of Medicine*, 352 (11): 1138-1145.

A. Omran (2005) 'The epidemiologic transition: a theory of the epidemiology of population change', *Millbank Quarterly*, 83 (4): 731-757.

ONS (Office for National Statistics) (2004) *Focus on social inequalities*, ONS, London, www.statistics.gov.uk/STATBASE/Product.asp?vlnk=13488

ONS (2008) *General household survey 2006*, ONS, London, www.statistics.gov.uk/Statbase/Product.asp?vlnk=5756

P. Orszag and J. Stiglitz (2001) 'Rethinking pension reform: ten myths about social security systems', in R. Holzman and J. Stiglitz (eds) *New ideas about old age security: Towards sustainable pension systems in the 21st century*, World Bank, Washington, DC.

J. Pagan and A. Puig (2005) 'Differences in access to health care services between insured and uninsured adults with diabetes in Mexico', *Diabetes Care*, 28 (2): 425-426.

S. Pal and R. Palacios (2006) 'Old age poverty in the Indian status: what do the household data tell us?', Department of Economics and Finance, Brunel University, Uxbridge, www.brunel.ac.uk/329/efwps/0616.pdf

E. Palacios and E. Whitehouse (2006) *Civil-service pension schemes around the world*, Social Protection Discussion Paper Number 0602, World Bank, Washington, DC.

R. Palacios (2005) 'The challenges for India: do new initiatives go far enough?', *ID21 Insights*, 2, www.id21.org/insights

A. Palloni (2001) 'Living arrangements of older persons', *Population Bulletin of the United Nations*, 42/43 (special issue): 54-110.

A. Palloni and M. McEniry (2007) 'Aging and health status of elderly in Latin America and the Caribbean: preliminary findings', *Journal of Cross-Cultural Gerontology*, 22: 263-285.

J. Pandian, V. Padma, P. Vijaya, P. Sylaja and J. Murthy (2007b) 'Stroke and thrombylosis in developing countries', *International Journal of Stroke*, 2: 17-26.

J. Pandian, V. Sethi, R. Dhillon, R. Kaur, S. Padala, R. Chakravorty and Y. Singh (2005) 'Is intravenous thrombolysis feasible in a developing country?', *Cerebrovascular Disease*, 20: 134-136.

J. Pandian, V. Srikanth, S. Read and A. Thrift (2007a) 'Poverty and stroke in India: time to act', *Stroke*, 38: 3063-3069.

E. Pantelides (2006) *La transición de la fecundidad en la Argentina 1869-1947*, Centro de Estudios de Poblacíon, Buenos Aires.

G. Parayil (2000) 'Introduction: is Kerala's development experience a "model"', in G. Parayil (ed) *Kerala: The development experience: Reflections on sustainability*, Macmillan, London.

M. Parker and G. Wilson (2000) 'Diseases of poverty', in T. Allen and A. Thomas (eds) *Poverty and development: Into the 21st century*, Oxford University Press, Oxford.

C. Parry (1998) *Substance abuse in South Africa: Country report focussing on young persons*, Medical Research Council, Tygerberg, South Africa, www.sahealthinfo.org/admodule/countryreport.pdf

V. Patel and M. Prince (2001) 'Ageing and mental health in a developing country: who cares? Qualitative studies from Goa, India', *Psychological Medicine*, 32 (1): 29-38.

D. Peng and G. Zhi-Gang (2000) 'Population ageing in China', in D. Phillips (ed) *Ageing in the Asia-Pacific region: Issues, policies and future trends*, Routledge, London.

P. Petersen (1999) 'Gray dawn: the global aging crisis', *Foreign Affairs*, 78 (1): 42-55.

PFRDA (Pension Fund Regulatory and Development Authority) (2007) *India's pension reform initiative*, PFDRA, New Delhi, www.pfrda.org.in/writereaddata/linkimages/IPAI9695458514.pdf

D. Phillips (1990) *Health and health care in the Third World*, Longman, London.

D. Phillips and A. Chan (2002) 'National policies on ageing and long-term care in the Asia-Pacific: issues and challenges', in D. Phillips and A. Chan (eds) *Ageing and long-term care: National policies in the Asia-Pacific*, IDRC/Institute of Southeast Asian Studies, Ottawa/Singapore.

D. Platt and G. Di Tella (eds) (1985) *Argentina, Australia and Canada: Studies in comparative development, 1870-1965*, St Martin's Press, New York.

D. Posel (2001) 'How do households work? Migration, the household and remittance behaviour in South Africa', *Social Dynamics*, 27 (1): 167-192.

C. Power, K. Atherton and O. Manor (2008) 'Co-occurrence of risk factors for cardiovascular disease by social class: the 1958 British birth cohort', Journal *of Epidemiology and Community Health*, 62: 1030-1035.

E. Preston-Whyte (1988) 'Women-headed households and development: the relevance of cross-cultural models for research on black women in Southern Africa', *Africanus*, 18: 58-76.

M. Prince (2004) 'Care arrangements for people with dementia in developing countries', *International Journal of Geriatric Psychiatry*, 19 (2): 170-177.

N. Protasia and K. Torkington (2000) *Community health needs in South Africa*, Ashgate, Aldershot.

S. Quah (2003) *Major trends affecting families in East and Southeast Asia*, United Nations – Department of Economic and Social Affairs (UN-DESA), New York.

S. Rajan and K. Zachariah (2007) 'Remittances and its impact on the Kerala economy and society', Paper presented at the Institute of Social Studies Conference 'International migration, multi-local livelihoods and human security: perspectives from Europe, Asia and Africa', 30-31 August.

S. Rajan, U. Mishra and P. Sarma (1999) *India's elderly: Burden or challenge*, Sage Publications, London.

V. Ramachandran (1997) 'On Kerala's development achievements', in J. Dreze and A. Sen (eds) *Indian development: Selected regional perspectives*, Oxford University Press, Oxford.

L. Ramos (1992) 'Family support for the elderly in Latin America: the role of the multigenerational household', in H. Kendig, A. Hashimoto and L. Coppard (eds) *Family support to elderly people: The international experience*, Oxford University Press, Oxford.

S. Razavi (2007) *The political and social economy of care in a development context: Conceptual issues, research questions and policy options*, United Nations Research Institute for Social Development, Geneva.

H. Recalde (1991) *Beneficencia, asistencialismo estatal y prevision social/1*, Centro Editor de América Latina, Buenos Aires.

D. Redfoot and A. Houser (2005) *We travel on: Quality of care, economic development and the international migration of long-term care workers*, American Association of Retired Persons, Washington, DC.

N. Redondo (2004) 'Social health insurance for older people: a comparison of Argentina and the United States', in P. Lloyd-Sherlock (ed) *Living longer: Ageing, development and social protection*, Zed Books, London.

N. Redondo and P. Lloyd-Sherlock (2009) *Institutional care for older people in developing countries: Repressing rights or promoting autonomy? The case of Buenos Aires, Argentina*, School of International Development Working Paper Number 13, University of East Anglia, Norwich.

N. Redondo and M. Salzman (2000) *Encuesta de satisfacción a los usuarios del INSSJP: Alcances e inferencias*, INAP, Buenos Aires.

A. Reil-Held (2006) 'Crowding out or crowding in? Public and private transfers in Germany', *European Journal of Population*, 22 (3): 263-280.

J. Remenyi (2004) 'What is development?', in D. Kingsbury (ed) *Key issues in development*, Palgrave, Basingstoke.

M. Rendall and R. Bahchieva (1998) 'An old-age security motive for fertility in the United States?', *Population and Development Review*, 24 (2):293-307.

R. Retherford, N. Ogawa and S. Sakamoto (1996) 'Values and fertility change in Japan', *Population Studies*, 50: 5-25.

J. Reynolds (2007) 'China's elderly care conundrum', *BBC News Online*, 23 August.

A. Ribeiro (1990) *Previdênica: Terror e mortes no reino das fraudes*, Melhoramentos, São Paulo.

B. Rickayzen (2003) 'A review of the state pension scheme in Ghana', MSc Dissertation, City University, London.

M. Riesco (2005) *25 years reveal myths of privatized federal pensions in Chile*, Global Action on Aging, New York, www.globalaging.org/pension/us/socialsec/2005/federal.htm

S. Rifkin and G. Walt (1986) 'Why health improves: defining the issues concerning "comprehensive primary health care" and "selective primary health care"', *Social Science and Medicine*, 23 (6): 559-566.

J. Riley (2001) *Rising life expectancy: A global history*, Cambridge University Press, Cambridge.

P. Robinson, S. Coberly and C. Paul (1985) 'Work and retirement', in R. Binstock and E. Shanas (eds) *Handbook of aging and the social sciences*, Van Nostrand Reinhold, New York.

W. Robinson (1992) 'Kenya enters the fertility transition', *Population Studies*, 46: 445-457.

E. Roca and M. Bourquin (2007) 'Las modificaciones al sistema previsional argentino: indicios de universalización?', *Estudios de la Seguridad Social*, 100: 91-132.

D. Rock (1991) 'Argentina, 1930-1946', in L. Bethell (ed) *The Cambridge history of Latin America: Volume VIII*, Cambridge University Press, Cambridge.

J. Rodgríguez (1999) *In praise and criticism of Mexico's pension reform*, Policy Analysis Paper Number 340, Cato Institute, Washington, DC.

A. Rofman (2004) *The economic crisis in Argentina and its impacts on the pension system*, Working Paper, Inter-American Development Bank, Washington, DC.

R. Rofman and C. Grushka (2003) 'Protección social, jublicaiones, pensiones y género en Argentina', in F. Bertranou and A. Arenas de Mesa (eds) *Protección social, pensiones y género*, International Labour Office, Santiago de Chile.

R. Rofman and L. Lucchetti (2006) Pension systems in Latin America: concepts and measurements of coverage, World Bank, Washington, DC, http://siteresources.worldbank.org/EXTGDLNREGIONLAC/Resources/PensionCoverage_LAC-Rofman-Lucchetti_Final.pdf

P. Rosenblatt and C. Nkosi (2007) 'South African Zulu widows in a time of poverty and social change', *Death Studies*, 31 (1): 67-85.

P. Ross (1989) 'Policy formation and implementation of social welfare in Peronist Argentina', PhD dissertation, University of New South Wales.

J. Roth (2001) *Informal micro-finance schemes:The case of funeral insurance in South Africa*, International Labour Office Employment SectorWorking Paper 22, International Labour Office, Geneva.

J. Rowe and H. Kahn (1998) *Successful aging*, Pantheon Books, New York.

I. Roxborough (1993) 'Urban wages and welfare', in C. Lewis and C. Abel (eds) *Welfare, poverty and development in Latin America*, Macmillan, London.

T. Roy (2000) *The economic history of India*, Oxford University Press, Oxford.

S. Ruggles (1994) 'The transformation of American family structure', *American Historical Review*, 99 (1): 103-128.

S. Ruggles (2001) 'Living arrangements and well-being of older persons in the past', *Population Bulletin of the United Nations: Living arrangements of older persons*, Special Issue, Number 42/43, United Nations Population Division, New York.

R. Rusconi (2004) 'Costs of saving for retirement, options for South Africa', Paper presented at the Actuarial Society of South Africa, 2004 Convention, 13-14 October, Cape Town.

S. Russell and L. Gilson (1997) 'User fee policies to promote health service access for the poor: a wolf in sheep's clothing?', *International Journal of Health Services*, 27 (2): 359-79.

R. Sadana, A. Tandon, C. Murray, I. Serdobova, Y. Cao, W. Xie, B. Ustun and S. Chatterji (2001) *Describing population health in six domains: Comparable results from 66 household surveys*, Research Paper 01.16, The Harvard Global Burden of Disease Unit, Boston M.A.

A. Sagner (2000) 'Ageing and social policy in South Africa: historical perspectives with particular reference to the Eastern Cape', *Journal of Southern African Studies*, 26 (3): 523-553.

A. Sagner and R. Mtati (1999) 'The politics of pension sharing in urban South Africa', *Ageing and Society*, 19 (4): 393-416.

N. Sánchez Albornoz (1974) *The population of Argentina*, University of California Press, Berkeley, CA.

S. Sarkar (2005) 'Women as paid domestic workers', *Journal of Social Science*, 11 (1): 35–41.

L. Sawers (1996) *The other Argentina: The interior and national development*, Westview Press, Oxford.

J. Schatan (1998) *Distribución del ingreso y pobreza en Chile*, Centro de Estudios Nacionales de Desarrollo Alternativo, Santiago de Chile.

N. Scheepers (2006) 'Stokvels in South Africa: exploring data discrepancies in the estimates of stokvel membership', www.finmark. org.za/documents/2007/SEPTEMBER/Stokvels_SA.pdf

H. Schneider (2002) 'On the fault-line: the politics of AIDS in contemporary South Africa', *African Studies*, 61 (1): 145–167.

B. Schramm (2001) 'Explaining social policy: the development of social security in Thailand', Paper presented at the International Workshop 'Asian welfare policy responses to the crash of 1997', Bergen, Norway, 16–18 August.

E. Schröder-Butterfill (2004) 'Intergenerational support provided by older people in Indonesia', *Ageing and Society*, 24 (4): 497–530.

E. Schröder-Butterfill and P. Kreager (2005) 'Actual and de facto childlessness in old age: evidence and implications from East Java, Indonesia', *Population and Development Review*, 31 (1): 19–55.

E. Schröder-Butterfill and P. Kreager (2007) 'Gaps in the family networks of older people in three Indonesian communities', *Journal of Cross-Cultural Gerontology*, 22 (1): 1–25.

E. Schröder-Butterfill and P. Lloyd-Sherlock (2008) *Social security pension 'reforms' in Thailand and Indonesia: Unsustainable and unjust*, Working Paper Number 3, School of Development Studies, University of East Anglia, Norwich.

E. Schröder-Butterfill and R. Marianti (2006) 'A framework for understanding old-age vulnerabilities', *Ageing and Society*, 26 (1): 9–35.

H. Schwartzer and A. Querino (2002) *Non-contributory pensions in Brazil: The impact on poverty reduction*, ESS Paper Number 11, ILO Social Security Policy and Development Branch Geneva.

J. Scott (2008) 'Social security and inequality in Mexico: from polarization to universality', *Well-Being and Social Policy*, 1 (1): 55–76.

C. Seale (2000) 'Changing patterns of death and dying', *Social Science and Medicine*, 51 (6): 917–930.

E. Sebrie, J. Barnoya, E. Perez-Stable and S. Glantz (2005) 'Tobacco industry dominating national tobacco policy making in Argentina, 1966-2005', Centre for Tobacco Control Research and Education, San Fransisco, CA, http://repositories.cdlib.org/cgi/viewcontent.cgi?article=1051&context=ctcre

SEDESOL (2008) 'Programa de Atención a los Adultos Mayores de 70 años y más en Zonas Rurales', www.sedesol.gob.mx/index/index.php?sec=3003&len=1

A. Seedat (1984) *Crippling a nation: Health in apartheid South Africa*, International Defence and Aid Fund for Southern Africa, London.

J. Seeley, B. Wolff, E. Kabunga, G. Tumwekwase and H. Grosskurth (2009) 'And this is where we buried our sons: people of advanced old age coping with the impact of the AIDS epidemic in a resource-poor setting in rural Uganda', *Ageing and Society*, 29: 115-134.

N. Sekhri and W. Savedoff (2005) 'Private health insurance – implications for developing countries', *Bulletin of the World Health Organization*, 83 (2): 127-138.

A. Sen (1999) *Development as freedom*, Oxford University Press, Oxford.

G. Sen and P. Östlin (2007) *Unequal, unfair, ineffective and inefficient: Gender inequity in health: Why it exists and how we can change it*, WHO Commission of Social Determinants of Health, Geneva.

M. Shaw (1995) *Partners in crime? Crime, political transition and changing forms of policing control*, Centre for Policy Studies, Johannesburg.

O. Shisana, T. Rehle, L. Simbayi, W. Parker, K. Zuma, A. Bhana, C. Connolly, S. Jooste, and V. Pillay (eds) (2005) *South African national HIV prevalence, HIV incidence, behaviour and communication survey 2005*, HSRC Press, Pretoria.

C. Simkins (1999) 'The political economy of South Africa in the 1970s', *South African Journal of Economic History*, 14 (1): 11-36.

G. Singh (2003) 'Corruption, transparency and the good governance agenda in India', Paper presented at the 'EU-India: beyond the New Delhi summit', Brussels, 4 December, http://unpan1.un.org/intradoc/groups/public/documents/APCITY/UNPAN019874.pdf

I. Singh, A. Ayyar and S. Bhat (2005) 'Tackling ageism and promoting equality in health care', *British Journal of Hospital Medicine*, 66 (10): 510-511.

K. Singh (2007) *Women issues: Empowerment and gender discrimination*, Vista International, Delhi.

A. Singh Bisht (2009) 'Fiscal imbalance looms over UP', *Times of India*, 15 February.

D. Sjoblom and J. Farrington (2008) *The Indian National Rural Employment: Guarantee Act: Will it reduce poverty and boost the economy?*, Social Protection Project Briefing, Number 7, Overseas Development Institute, London, www.odi.org.uk/resources/odi-publications/project-briefings/7-indian-national-rural-employment-guarantee-act.pdf

K. Smith and H. Joshi (2002) 'The Millennium Cohort Study', *Population Trends*, 107: 30-34.

Social Trends (2006) *Social trends: 2006*, www.statistics.co.uk

J. Sokolovsky (2001) 'Living arrangements of older persons and family support in less developed countries', *Population Bulletin of the United Nations*, 42/43: 162-192.

B. Spillman and K. Black (2005) *The size of the long-term care population in residential care: A review of estimates and methodology*, US Department of Health and Human Services, Washington, DC.

R. Srivastava (2002) *Anti-poverty programmes in Uttar Pradesh: An evaluation*, Institute of Human Development, New Delhi.

G. Standing (1999) 'Global feminization: through flexible labor: a theme revisited', *World Development*, 27 (3): 583-602.

Statistics South Africa (2001) *Population Census 2001*, www.statssa.gov.za/publications/populationstats.asp

Statistics South Africa (2004) *Labour force survey*, September, www.statssa.gov.za

Statistics South Africa (2007) *Mortality and causes of death in South Africa, 1997-2003: Findings from death notification*, www.statssa.gov.za/publications/P03093/P03093.pdf

B. Stein (1998) *A history of India*, Blackwell. Oxford.

M. Steinberg, S. Johnson and G. Schierhout (2002) *Hitting home: How households cope with the impact of the HIV/AIDS epidemic: A survey of households affected by HIV/AIDS in South Africa*, The Henry J. Kaiser Family Foundation, Menlo Park, CA.

L. Stloukal (2001) 'Rural population ageing in poorer countries: possible implications for rural development', *SD Dimensions*, Food and Agriculture Organisation, Rome.

E. Stone (1999) 'Disability and development in the majority world', in E. Stone (ed) *Disability and development: Learning from action and research on disability in the majority world*, The Disability Press, Leeds.

D. Strang and P. Chang (1993) 'The International Labour Organisation and the welfare state: institutional effects on national welfare spending', *International Organization*, 47 (2): 235-262.

L. Swartz (2002) 'Fertility transition in South Africa and its implications on the four major population groups', in United Nations Population Division *Fertility levels and trends in countries with intermediate levels of fertility*, United Nations Secretariat, New York, NY, www.un.org/esa/population/publications/completingfertility/FFPSPOPDIVpaper. PDF.

A. Taylor (1992) 'External dependence, demographic burdens, and Argentine economic decline after the Belle Époque', *Journal of Economic History*, 52 (4): 907-936.

P. Thane (2000) *Old age in English history: Past experiences, present issues*, Oxford University Press, Oxford.

The Times of India (2008) 'One-third of the world's poor in India: survey', 27 August, http://timesofindia.indiatimes.com/India/One-third_of_worlds_poor_in_India/articleshow/3409374.cms

B. Thylefors, A.-D. Négrel, R. Pararajasegaram and K. Dadzie (1995) 'Global data on blindness', *Bulletin of the World Health Organization*, 73 (1): 115-121.

Tiempo Pyme (2008) 'El gasto en salud superará los $65 mil millones este año', *Tiempo Pyme*, Buenos Aires, 18 September, www.tiempopyme.com/despachos.asp?cod_des=60654&ID_Seccion=136

S. Torrado (1994) *Estructura social de la Argentina: 1945-1983*, Ediciones de la Flor, Buenos Aires.

C. Tung (2000) 'Cost of caring: the social reproductive labor of Filipina live-in home health caregivers', *Frontiers: A Journal of Women's Studies*, 21 (1-2): 61-82.

UK Department of Health (2001) *National service framework for older people*, Department of Health, London.

UK House of Lords Select Committee on Economic Affairs (2003) *Aspects of the economics of an ageing population: Volume 1 – Report*, The Stationery Office, London, www.publications.parliament.uk/pa/ld200203/ldselect/ldeconaf/179/179.pdf

UNAIDS (2006) *Report on the global AIDS epidemic*, UNAIDS, New York, NY.

UN-DESA (2002) *Gender dimensions of ageing*, UN-DESA, New York, www.un.org/womenwatch/daw/public/ageing-final.pdf

UN-DESA (2003a) *Major trends affecting families: A background document*, UN-DESA, New York.

UN-DESA (2003b) *Trends in total migrant stock: The 2003 revision*, UN-DESA, New York.

UN-DESA (2008) *Guide to the implementation of the Madrid International Plan of Action on Ageing*, UN-DESA, New York.

UNDP (United Nations Development Programme) (1994) *Human development report 1994: New dimensions of human security*, UNDP, New York.

UNDP (2005) *Human development report 2005: International cooperation at a crossroads: Aid, trade and security in an unequal world*, UNDP, New York.

UNDP (2006) *Human development report 2006: Beyond scarcity: Power, poverty and the global water crisis*, UNDP, New York.

United Nations Population Division (2001) *World population prospects: The 2000 revision*, United Nations, New York.

United Nations Population Division (2002) *World population ageing 1950-2050*, United Nations, New York.

United Nations Population Division (2005) *Living arrangements of older persons around the world*, United Nations, New York.

United Nations Population Division (2008) *World population prospects: The 2008 revision*, United Nations, New York.

US Census Bureau (2008) *International Data Base*, US Census Bureau, Washington, DC, www.census.gov/ipc/www/idb/

US Social Security Administration (2008) 'International update: recent developments in foreign public and private pensions', www.ssa.gov/policy/docs/progdesc/intl_update/2006-08/2006-08.html

S. Valdés-Prieto (2007) *Pension reform and the development of pension systems: An evaluation of World Bank assistance*, Independent Evaluation Group, World Bank, Washington, DC.

A. van den Heever (2007) 'Pension reform and old age grants in South Africa', Mimeo, University of Pretoria, South Africa.

S. van der Berg (1997) 'South African social security under apartheid and beyond', *Development Southern Africa*, 14: 481-503.

J. van der Gaag and A. Precker (1997) 'Health care for an aging population: issues and options', Mimeo, World Bank, Washington, DC.

S. van der Geest (2004a) 'Grandparents and grandchildren in Kwahu, Ghana: the performance of respect', *Africa*, 74 (1): 47-61.

S. van der Geest (2004b) '"They don't come to listen": the experience of loneliness among older people in Kwahu, Ghana', *Journal of Cross-Cultural Gerontology*, 19 (2): 77-96.

S. van der Geest (2004c) 'Linkages between migration and the care of frail older people: observations from Greece, Ghana and the Netherlands', *Ageing and Society*, 24: 431-450.

E. van Dongen (2005) 'Remembering in times of misery: can older people in South Africa "get through"?', *Ageing and Society*, 25: 525-541.

M. Varghese and V. Patel (2004) 'The greying of India: mental health perspective', in S. Agarwal (ed) *Mental health: An Indian perspective 1946-2003*, Ministry of Health and Family Services, New Delhi.

A. Varley and M. Blasco (2003) 'Older women's living arrangements and family relationships in urban Mexico', *Women's Studies International Forum*, 26 (6): 525-539.

C. Vassallo and M. Sellanes (2000) 'Salud en la tercera edad', in Secretaría de la Tercera Edad y Acción Social *Informe sobre tercera edad en Argentina, año 2000*, Secretaría de la Tercera Edad y Acción Social, Buenos Aires.

P. Vera-Sanso (1999) 'Dominant daughters-in-law and submissive mothers-in-law? Cooperation and conflict in southern India', *Journal of the Royal Anthropological Institute*, 5 (4): 577-593.

P. Vera-Sanso (2006) 'Experiences in old age: a South Indian example of how functional age is socially constructed', *Oxford Development Studies*, 34 (4): 457-472.

P. Vera-Sanso (2007) 'Increasing consumption, decreasing support: a multi-generational study of family relations among South Indian Chakkliyars', *Contributions to Indian Sociology*, 41 (2): 225-248.

L. Visaria (2005a) 'Mortality trends and the health transition', in T. Dyson, R. Cassen and L. Visaria (eds) *Twenty-first century India: Population, economy, human development and the environment*, Oxford University Press, Oxford.

L. Visaria (2005b) 'The continuing fertility transition', in T. Dyson, R. Cassen and L. Visaria (eds) *Twenty-first century India: Population, economy, human development and the environment*, Oxford University Press, Oxford.

D. Vittas and A. Iglesias (1992) *The rationale and performance of personal pension plans in Chile*, Policy Research Working Paper Number 867, World Bank, Washington, DC.

J. Vullnetari and R. King (2008) '"Does your granny eat grass?" On mass migration, care drain and the fate of older people in rural Albania', *Global Networks: A Journal of Transnational Affairs*, 8 (2): 139-171.

A. Walker (1990) 'The social construction of dependency in old age', in M. Loney, J. Clarke, A. Cochrane, P. Graham and M. Wilson (eds) *The state or the market: Politics and welfare in contemporary Britain*, Sage Publications, London.

R. Walker, D. McLarty, H. Kitange, D. Whiting, G. Masuki, D. Mtasiwa, H. Machibya, N. Unwin and K. Alberti (2000) 'Stroke mortality in urban and rural Tanzania: adult morbidity and mortality project', *The Lancet*, 355 (9216): 1684-1687.

C. Wenger, R. Davies, S. Shahtahmasebi and A. Scott (1996) 'Social isolation and loneliness in old age', *Ageing and Society*, 16 (3): 333-358.

C. Westoff and A. Cross (2006) *The stall in fertility transition in Kenya*, DHS Analytical Studies Number 9, ORC Macro, Calverton, Maryland, MD, www.measuredhs.com/pubs/pdf/AS9/AS9.pdf

P. Whiteford and E. Whitehouse (2006) 'Pension challenges and pension reforms in OECD countries', *Oxford Review of Economic Policy*, 22 (1): 78-94.

A. Whitehead and N. Kabeer (2001) *Living with uncertainty: Gender, livelihood and pro-poor growth in rural sub-Saharan Africa*, Working Paper 134, Institute of Development Studies, Brighton.

WHO (World Health Organization) (2000) *Women, ageing and health*, WHO Factsheet Number 252, WHO, Geneva.

WHO (2002a) *Active ageing: A policy framework*, WHO, Geneva

WHO (2002b) *World report on violence and health*, WHO, Geneva.

WHO (2003) *WHO definition of health*, WHO, Geneva, www.who. int/about/definition/en/print.html

WHO (2004a) *World health report, 2004*, WHO, Geneva.

WHO (2004b) *Why are chronic conditions increasing?*, WHO, Geneva, www.who.int.

WHO (2005a) *Preventing chronic diseases: A vital investment*, WHO, Geneva.

WHO (2005b) *WHO multi-country study on women's health and domestic violence against women: Initial results on prevalence, health outcomes and women's responses*, WHO, Geneva.

WHO (2007) *Global burden of disease and risk factors*, WHO, Geneva.

J. Williamson and F. Pampel (1993) *Old-age security in comparative perspective*, Oxford University Press, Oxford.

L. Willmore (2007) *Universal age pensions: Strategies for the extension of social protection*, ILO International Training Centre, Turin.

G. Wilson (2000) *Understanding old age: Critical and global perspectives*, Sage Publications, London.

W. Winkvist and H. Akhtar (2000) 'God should give daughters to rich families only: attitudes towards childbearing among low-income women in Punjab, Pakistan', *Social Science and Medicine*, 51 (1): 73-81.

R. Wong, A. Palloni and B. Soldo (2007) 'Wealth in middle and old age in Mexico: the role of international migration', *International Migration Review*, 41 (1): 127-151.

P. Woodrow (2002a) 'Theories of biological ageing', in P. Woodrow (ed) *Ageing: Issues for physical, psychological and social health*, Whurr, London.

P. Woodrow (2002b) 'Conclusion', in P. Woodrow (ed) *Ageing: Issues for physical, psychological and social health*, Whurr, London.

World Bank (1993a) *Poland: Income support and the social safety net during the transition*, World Bank, Washington, DC.

World Bank (1993b) *World development report: Investing in health*, Oxford: Oxford University Press.

World Bank (1994a) *Averting the old age crisis: Policies to protect the old and promote growth*, Oxford University Press, Oxford.

World Bank (1997) *Argentina: Facing the challenge of health insurance reform*, World Bank, Washington, DC.

World Bank (2000) *Pension systems in East Asia and the Pacific: Annex B11: Country profile for Thailand*, World Bank, Washington, DC.

World Bank (2001) *Vietnam growing health: A review of the health sector*, World Bank, Washington, DC, Available at www.worldbank.org. vn/data_pub/reports/Bank1/rep25/Viet_Health.pdf

World Bank (2002) *Poverty in India: The challenge of Uttar Pradesh*, World Bank, Washington, DC.

World Bank (2004) *World development report 2004: Making services work for poor people*, Oxford University Press, Oxford.

World Bank (2006a) *Disease and mortality in sub-Saharan Africa*, World Bank, Washington, DC.

World Bank (2006b) *Social safety nets*, World Bank, Washington, DC, www.worldbank.org/safetynets

World Bank (2009) *The financial crisis and mandatory pension systems in developing countries*, World Bank Human Development Network, Washington, DC.

World Commission on Environment and Development (1987) *Our common future*, Oxford University Press, Oxford.

World Public Opinion.org (2009) Poll: across the world many see discrimination against widows and divorced women, World Public Opinion.org, Washington, DC, www.worldpublicopinion.org/pipa/articles/btjusticehuman_rightsra/494.php

T. Wyller (1999) 'Stroke and gender', *Journal of Gender Specific Medicine*, 2 (3): 41–45.

K. Xu, D. Evans, P. Kadama, J. Nabyonga, P. Ogwang Ogwal and A. Aguilar (2005) *The elimination of user fees in Uganda: Impact on utilization and catastrophic health expenditures*, Discussion Paper Number 4/05, World Health Organization, Geneva.

D. Yach, C. Hawkes, L. Gould and K. Hofman (2004) 'The global burden of chronic diseases: overcoming impediments to prevention and control', *Journal of the American Medical Association*, 291 (21): 2616-2622.

K. Yadava (1997) 'Rural out-migration in Uttar Pradesh and its economic implications for migrant households', in K. Gupta and A. Pandey (eds) *Population and development in Uttar Pradesh*, B.R. Publishing Corporation, New Delhi.

K. Yount, E. Agree and C. Rebellion (2004) 'Gender and use of health care among older women and men in Egypt and Tunisia', *Social Science and Medicine*, 59: 2479-2497.

O. Yujnovsky (1984) *Claves políticas del problema habitacional argentino, 1955/1981*, Grupo Editor Latinoamericano, Buenos Aires.

S. Yusuf, S. Hawken, S. Ounpuu, T. Dans, A. Avezum, F. Lanas, M. McQueen, A. Budaj, P. Pais, J. Varigos and L. Lisheng (2004) 'Effects of potentially modifiable risk factors associated with myocardial infarction in 52 countries (the INTERHEART study): case-control study', *Lancet*, 364: 937-952.

T. Zhang and Y. Chen (2006) 'Meeting the needs of elderly people in China', *British Medical Journal*, 333 (7564): 363.

Z. Zimmer, J. Natavidad, M. Ofstedal and H. Lin (2003) 'Physical and mental health of the elderly', in A. Hermalin (ed) *The well-being of the elderly in Asia*, University of Michigan Press, Ann Arbor, MI.

A. Zwi, R. Brugha and E. Smith (2001) 'Private health care in developing countries', *British Medical Journal*, 323: 463-464.

Index